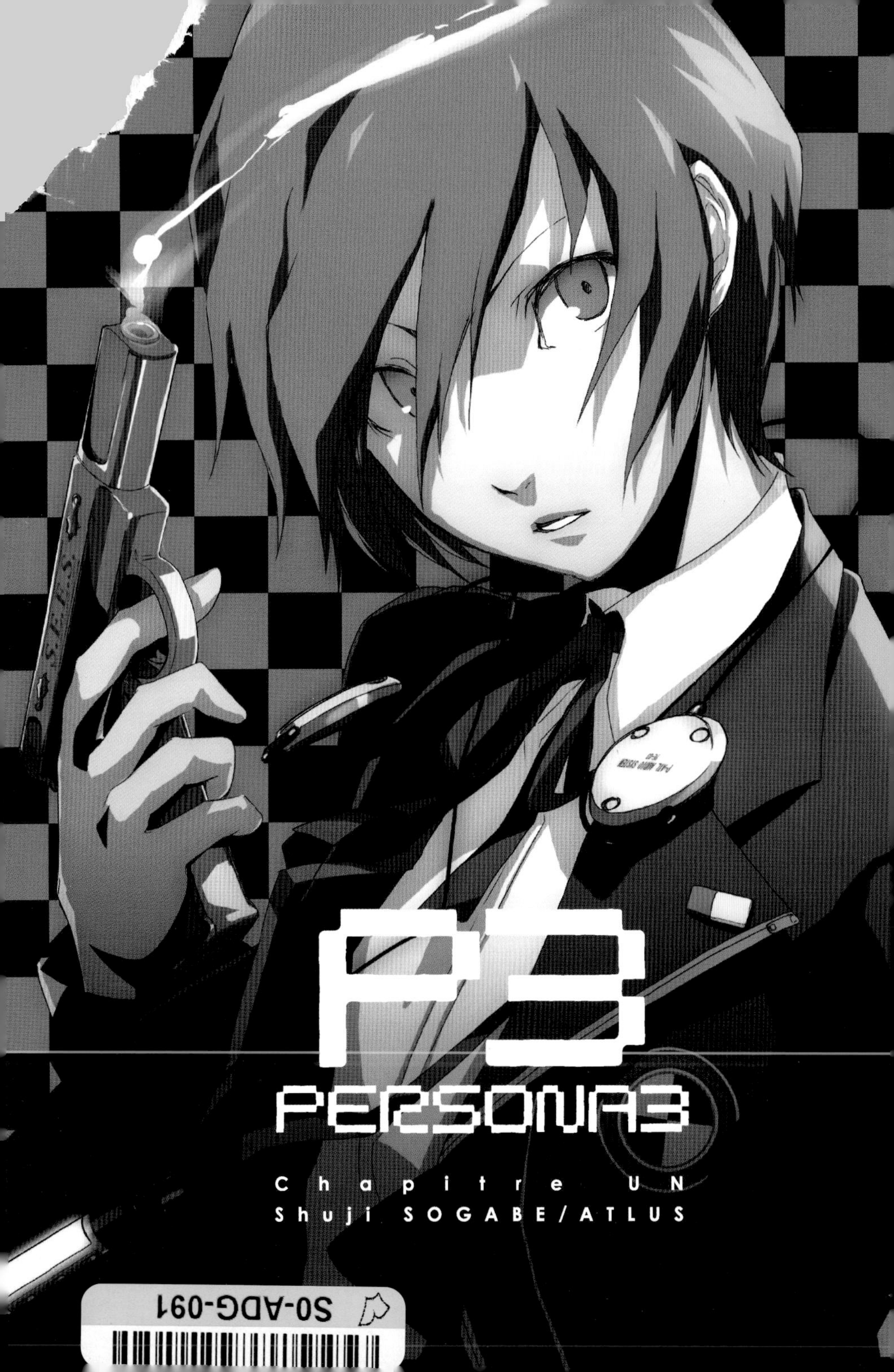
P3
PERSONA3
Chapitre UN
Shuji SOGABE/ATLUS

story

In November of 2009, a group of young men and women found themselves in the middle of a war. Not a single one of them could have known that the battles they were struggling through held much more significance than they ever would have dreamed.

This story began in April of 2009, when Minato Arisato moved back to Port Island as a student transferring into Gekkoukan High School. As Minato explored the unfamiliar scenery of the school and its dorm, the people he met there would change his life forever.

In-between each day, inserting itself into reality at midnight, comes what is known as the Dark Hour. This special time separates humans from Shadows, as well as those with powers from those without. These eternal borders are fluid yet absolute, and it is upon this stage that our story unfolds.

When Minato encountered a Shadow for the first time, he found himself facing certain death. It was in this moment that his instincts pulled the trigger on his dormant abilities.

Prologue

#01

003

THE BEGINNING OF THE END
Le commencement de la fin

Piece01

#02

047

TRANSFER STUDENT
L'arrivée

Piece02

#03

081

THE DIVIDING LINE
La première pleine lune

Piece03

#04

119

TRIGGER OF INSTINCT
L'éveil

2007 04~07

COMIC
152/162p
93.8%

monochrome
B6

P3 PERSONA3
Prologue
#01 終わりの始まり
曽我部修司　原作／アトラス
Design&Finished : Studio Shortcake Screamer

P3 PERSONA3
#02 転校生
曽我部修司　原作／アトラス
Design&Finished:StudioShortcakeScreamer

P3 Piece01 PERSONA3
#03
線の在り様
Piece:01 せんのありよう
曽我部修司　原作／アトラス
Design&Finished : Studio Shortcake Screamer
subtitle logo
#04 none

GEKKOUKAN PRIVATE HIGH SCHOOL
Since 1982

GEKKOUKAN PrivateHighSchool logo

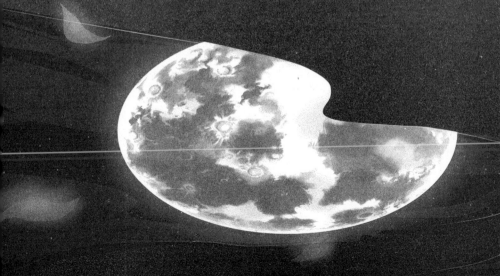

Time does not wait. It carries all equally toward the inevitable end. Those who seek to preserve the potential of the finite future should heed these words.

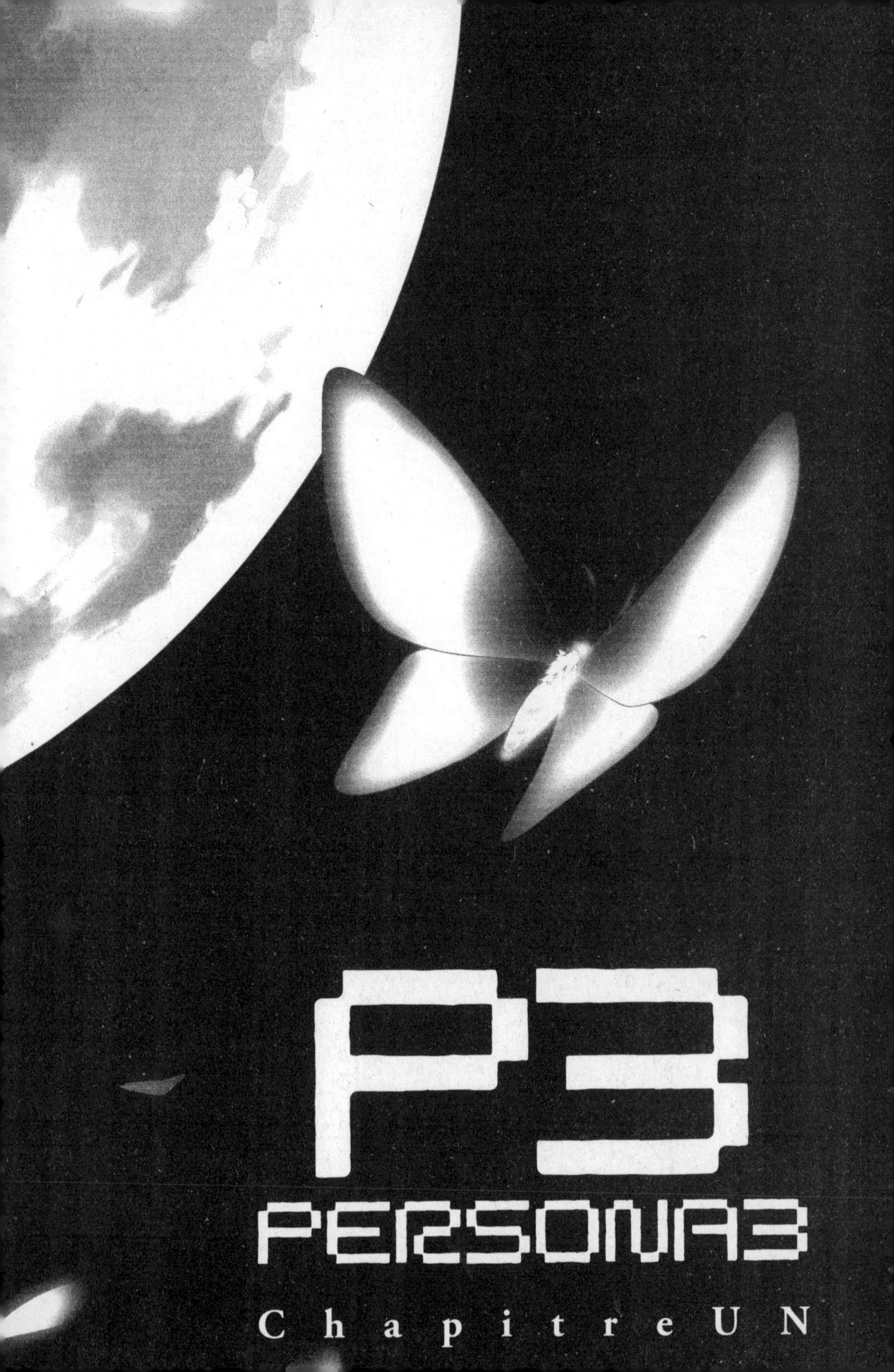
P3
PERSONA3
ChapitreUN

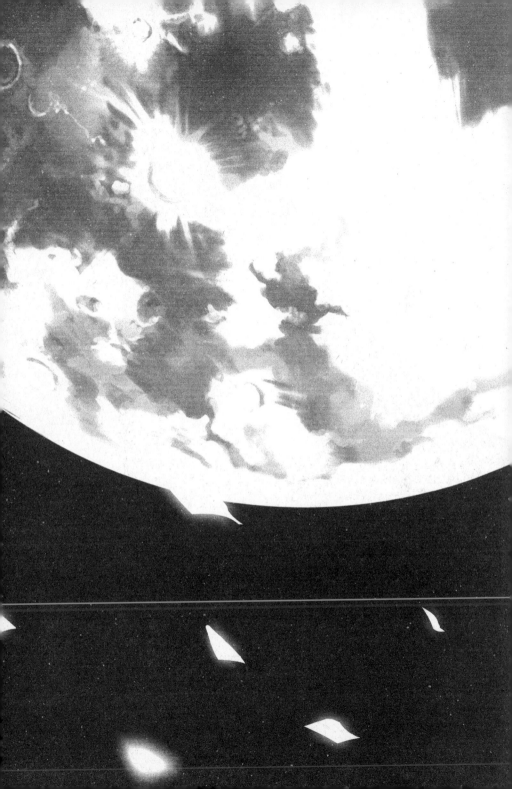

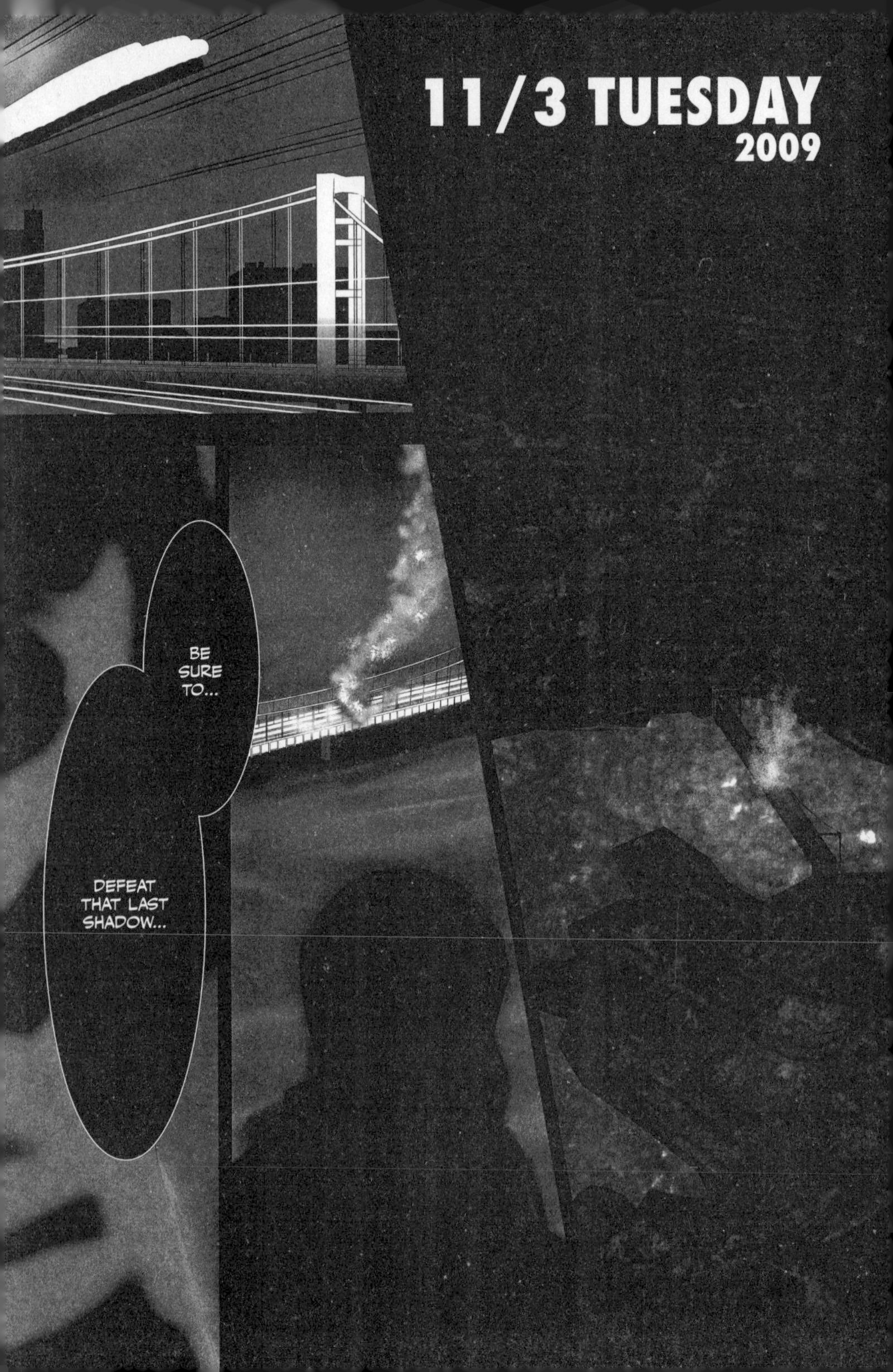
11/3 TUESDAY
2009
BE SURE TO...
DEFEAT THAT LAST SHADOW...

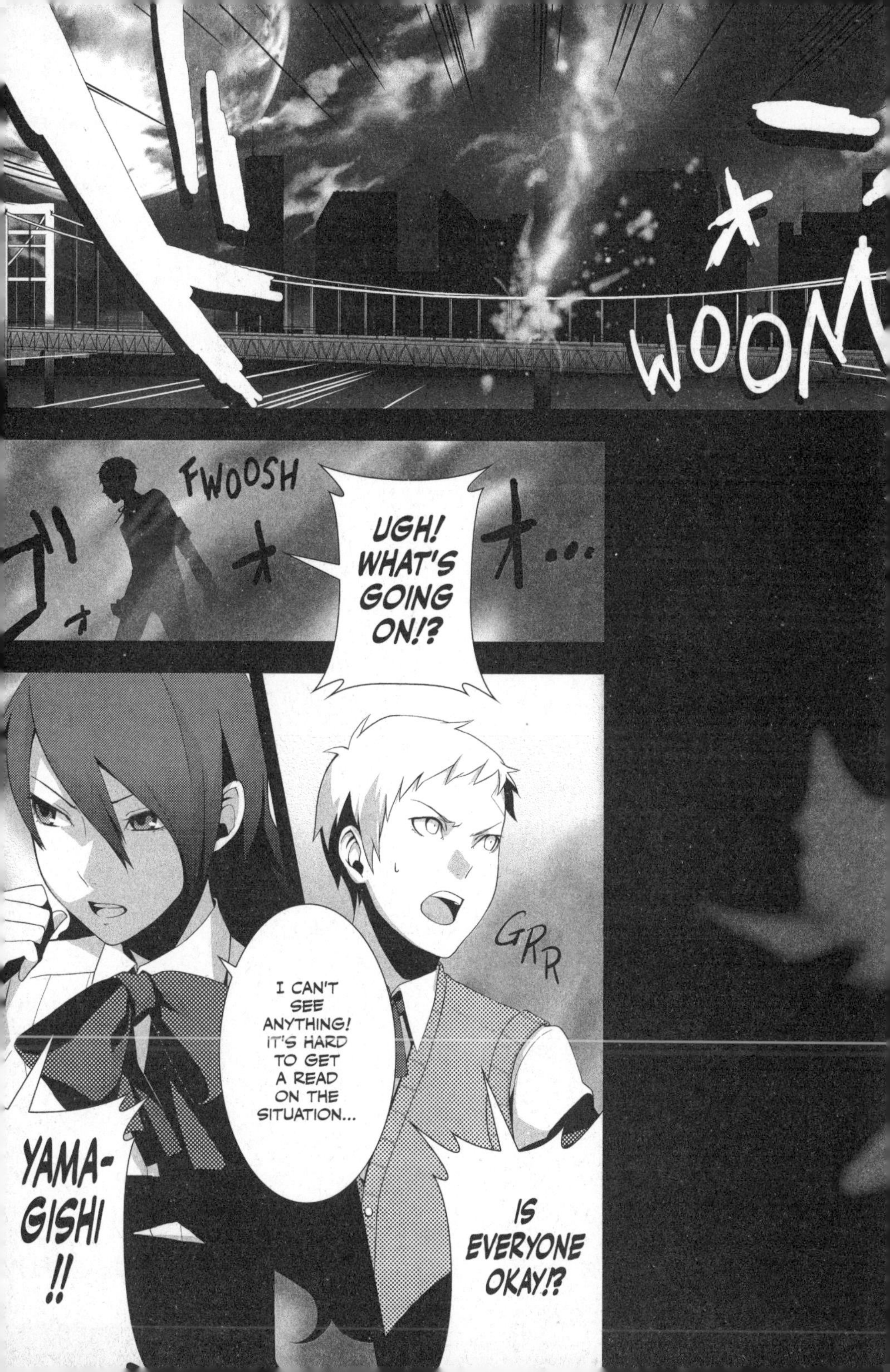
WOOM
UGH! WHAT'S GOING ON!?
FWOOSH
GRR
I CAN'T SEE ANYTHING! IT'S HARD TO GET A READ ON THE SITUATION...
IS EVERYONE OKAY!?
YAMA-GISHI !!

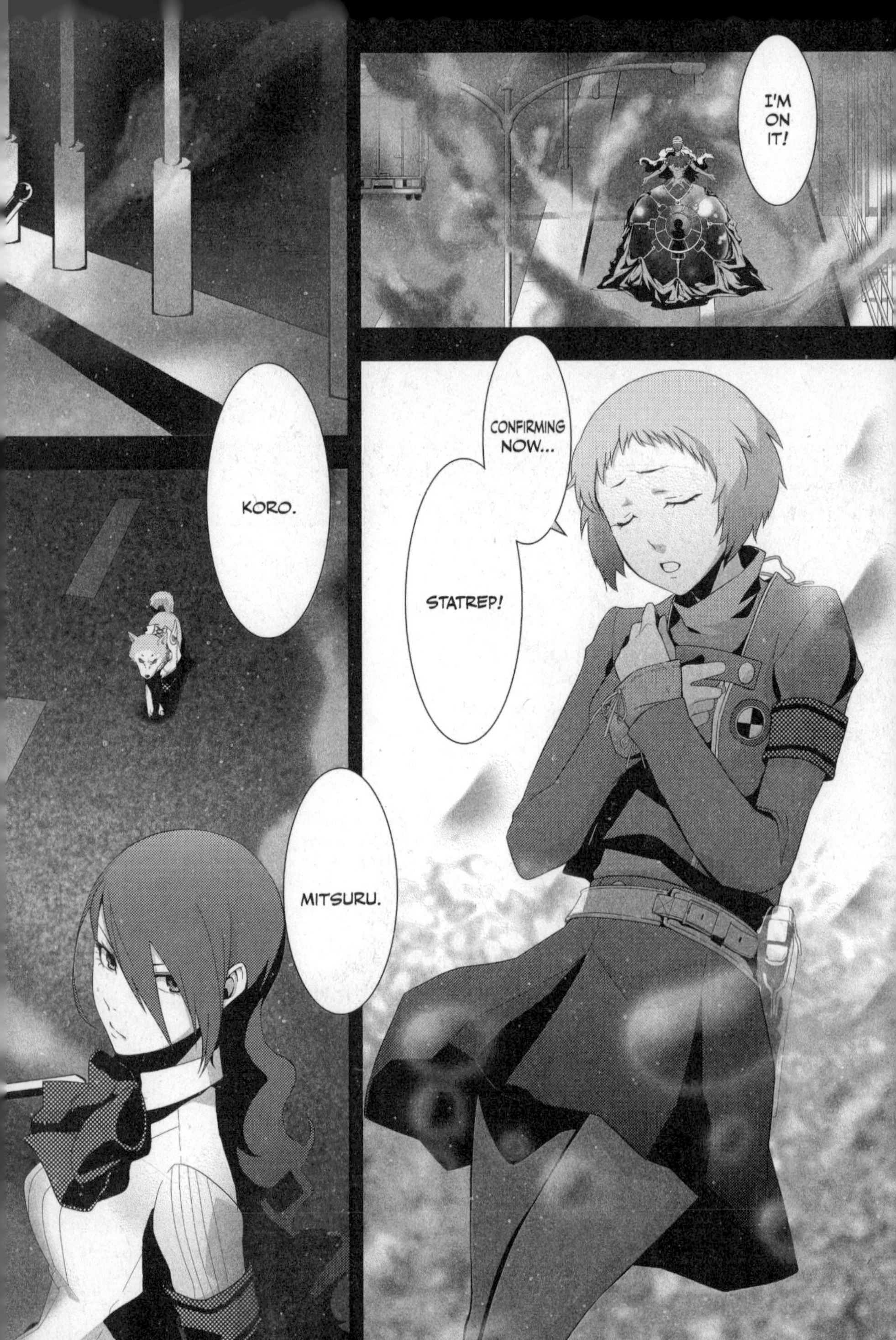
I'M ON IT!
CONFIRMING NOW...
STATREP!
KORO.
MITSURU.

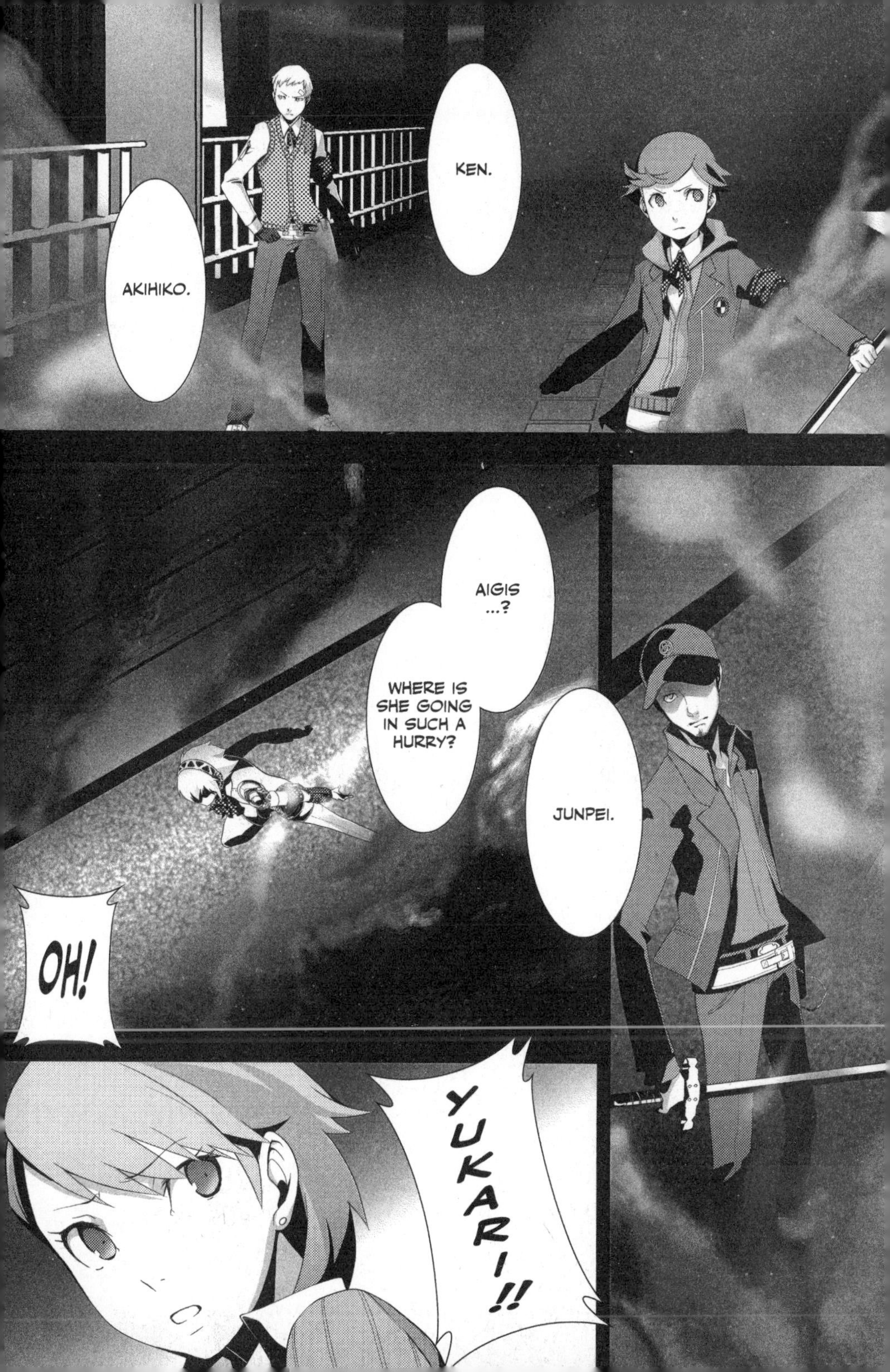
KEN.
AKIHIKO.
JUNPEI.
AIGIS ...?
WHERE IS SHE GOING IN SUCH A HURRY?
OH!
YUKARI!!

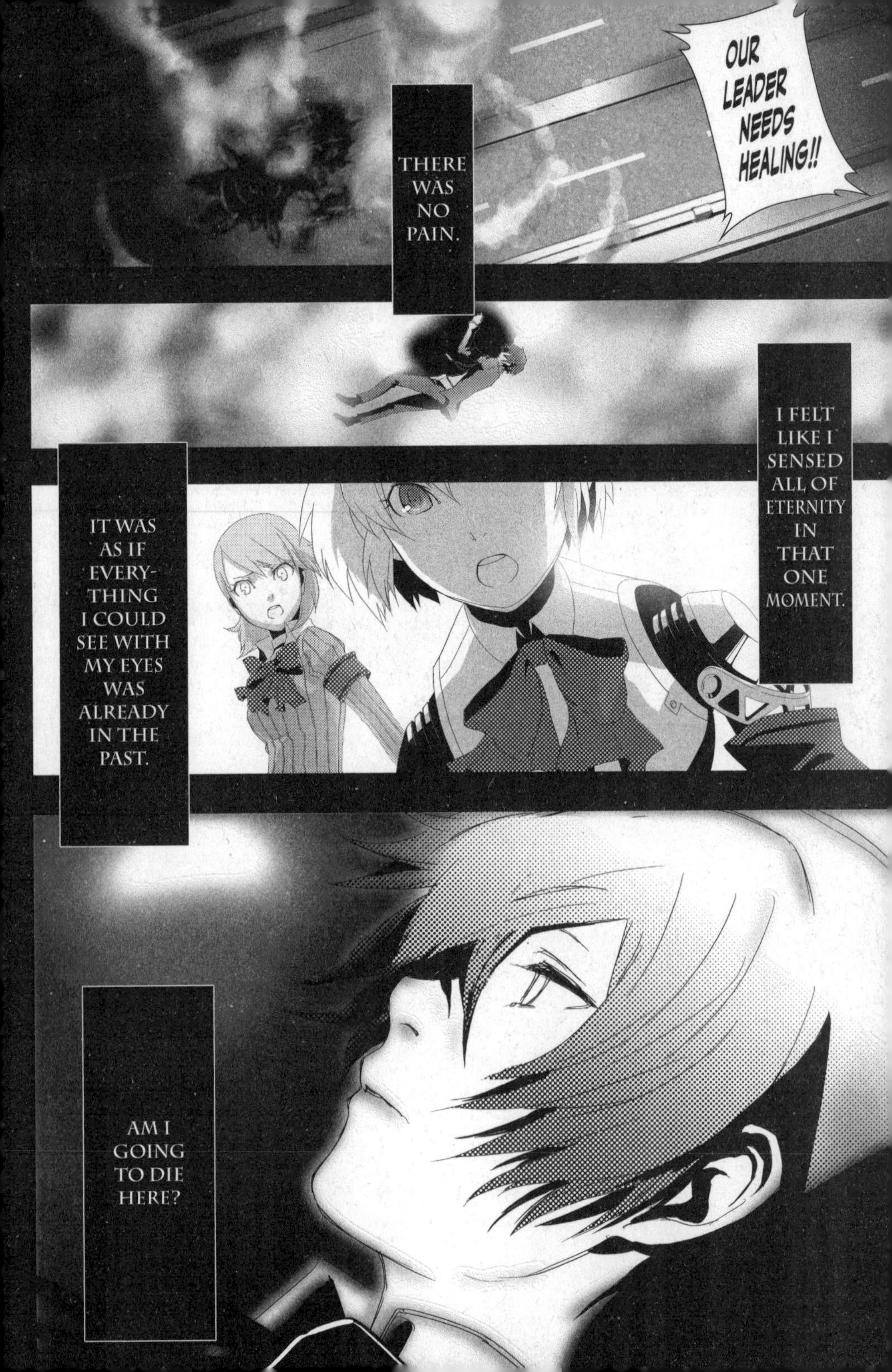
OUR LEADER NEEDS HEALING!!
THERE WAS NO PAIN.
I FELT LIKE I SENSED ALL OF ETERNITY IN THAT ONE MOMENT.
IT WAS AS IF EVERY-THING I COULD SEE WITH MY EYES WAS ALREADY IN THE PAST.
AM I GOING TO DIE HERE?

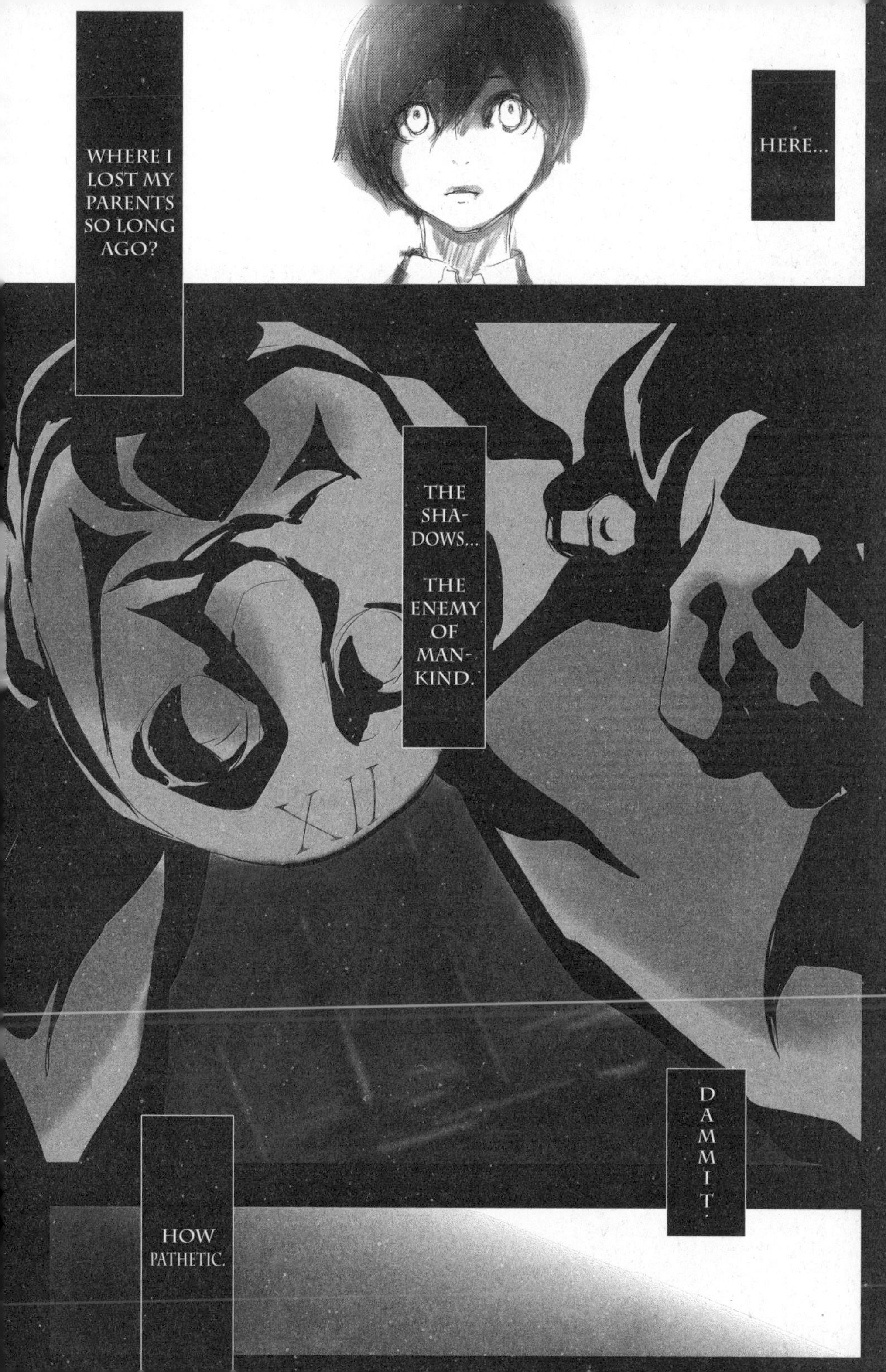
HERE...
WHERE I LOST MY PARENTS SO LONG AGO?
THE SHADOWS...
THE ENEMY OF MANKIND.
DAMMIT.
HOW PATHETIC.

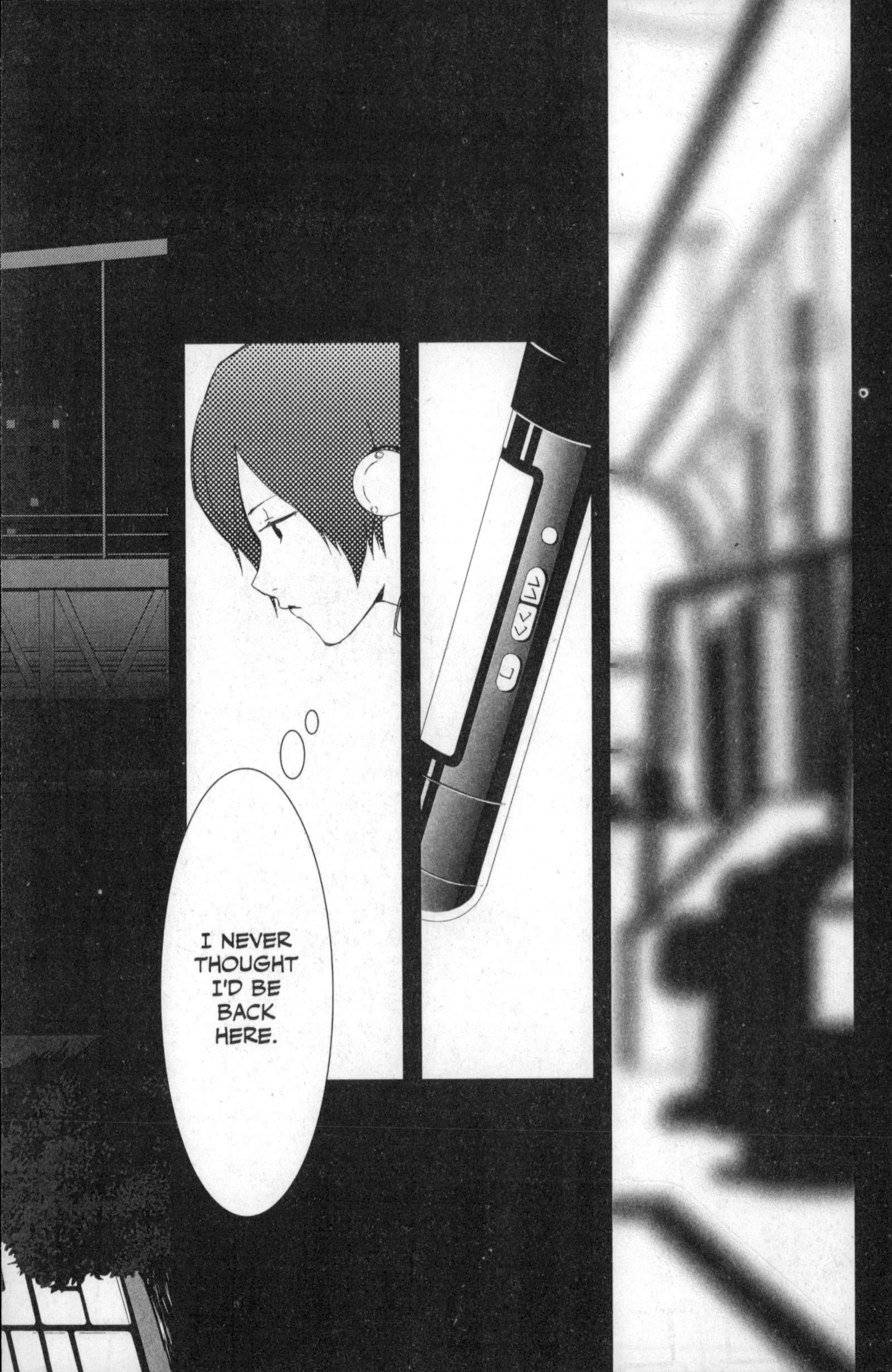
I NEVER THOUGHT I'D BE BACK HERE.

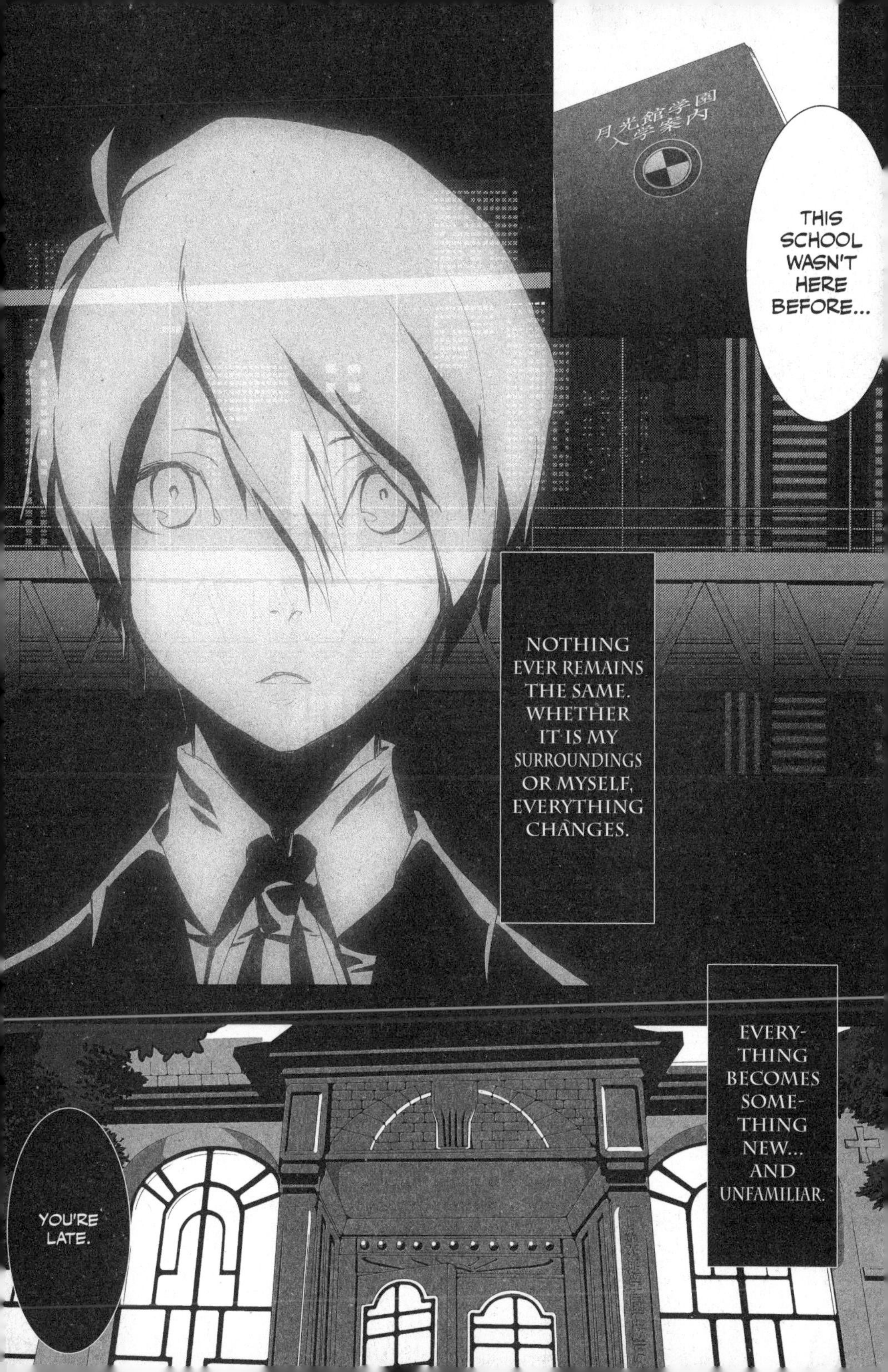
月光館学園
入学案内
THIS SCHOOL WASN'T HERE BEFORE...
NOTHING EVER REMAINS THE SAME. WHETHER IT IS MY SURROUNDINGS OR MYSELF, EVERYTHING CHANGES.
EVERY-THING BECOMES SOME-THING NEW... AND UNFAMILIAR.
YOU'RE LATE.

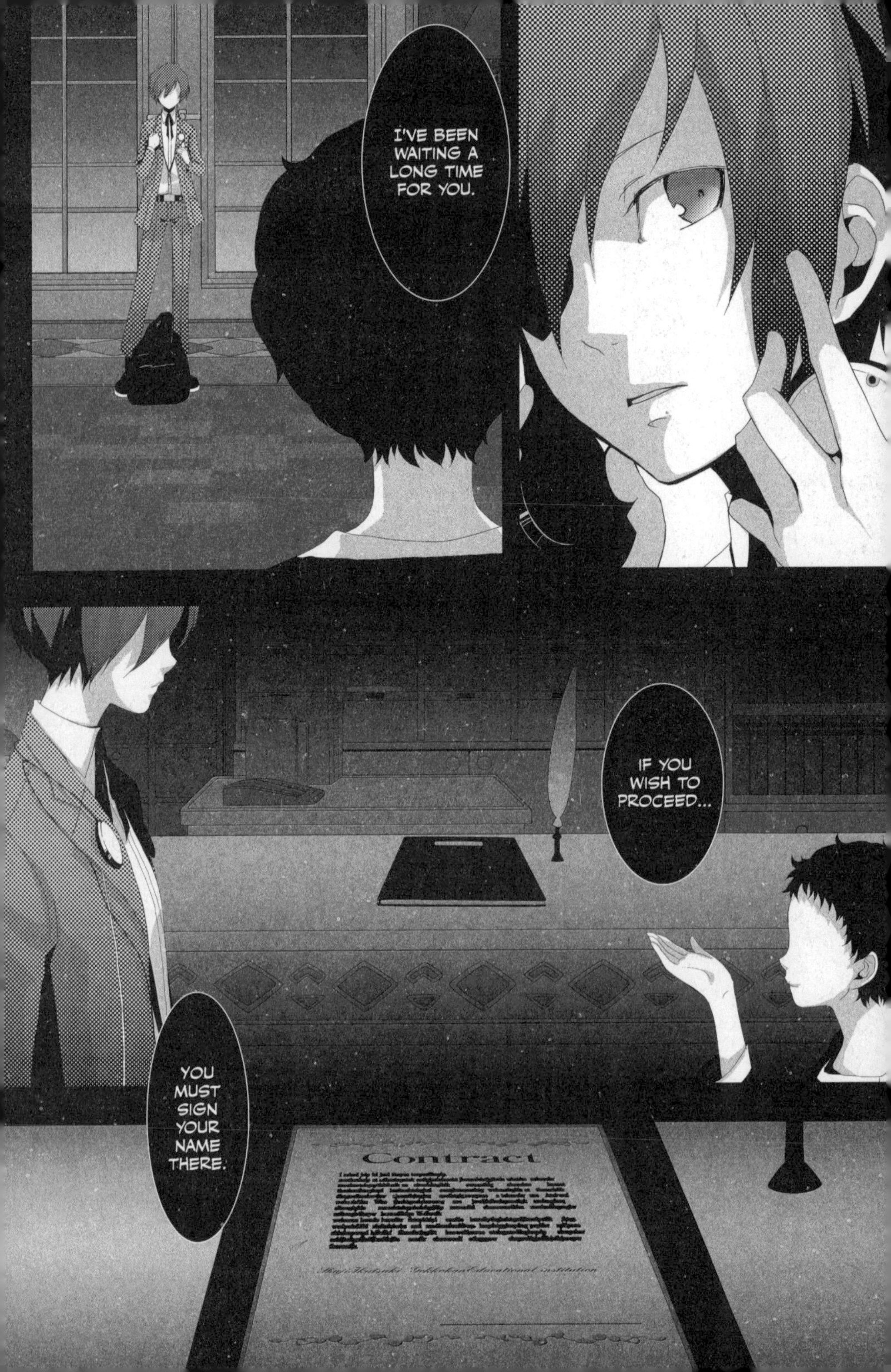
I'VE BEEN WAITING A LONG TIME FOR YOU.
IF YOU WISH TO PROCEED...
YOU MUST SIGN YOUR NAME THERE.
Contract

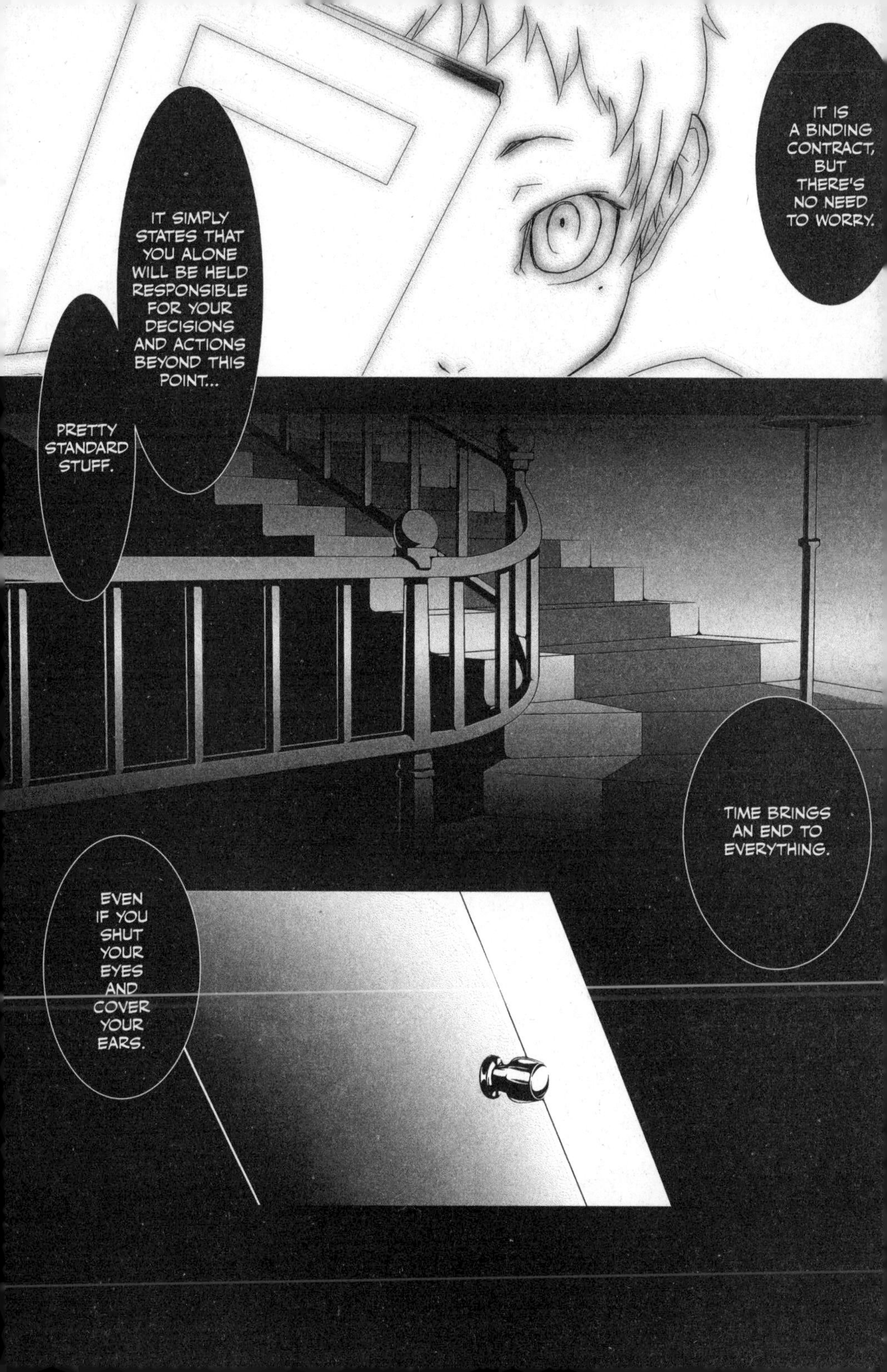
IT IS A BINDING CONTRACT, BUT THERE'S NO NEED TO WORRY.
IT SIMPLY STATES THAT YOU ALONE WILL BE HELD RESPONSIBLE FOR YOUR DECISIONS AND ACTIONS BEYOND THIS POINT...
PRETTY STANDARD STUFF.
TIME BRINGS AN END TO EVERYTHING.
EVEN IF YOU SHUT YOUR EYES AND COVER YOUR EARS.

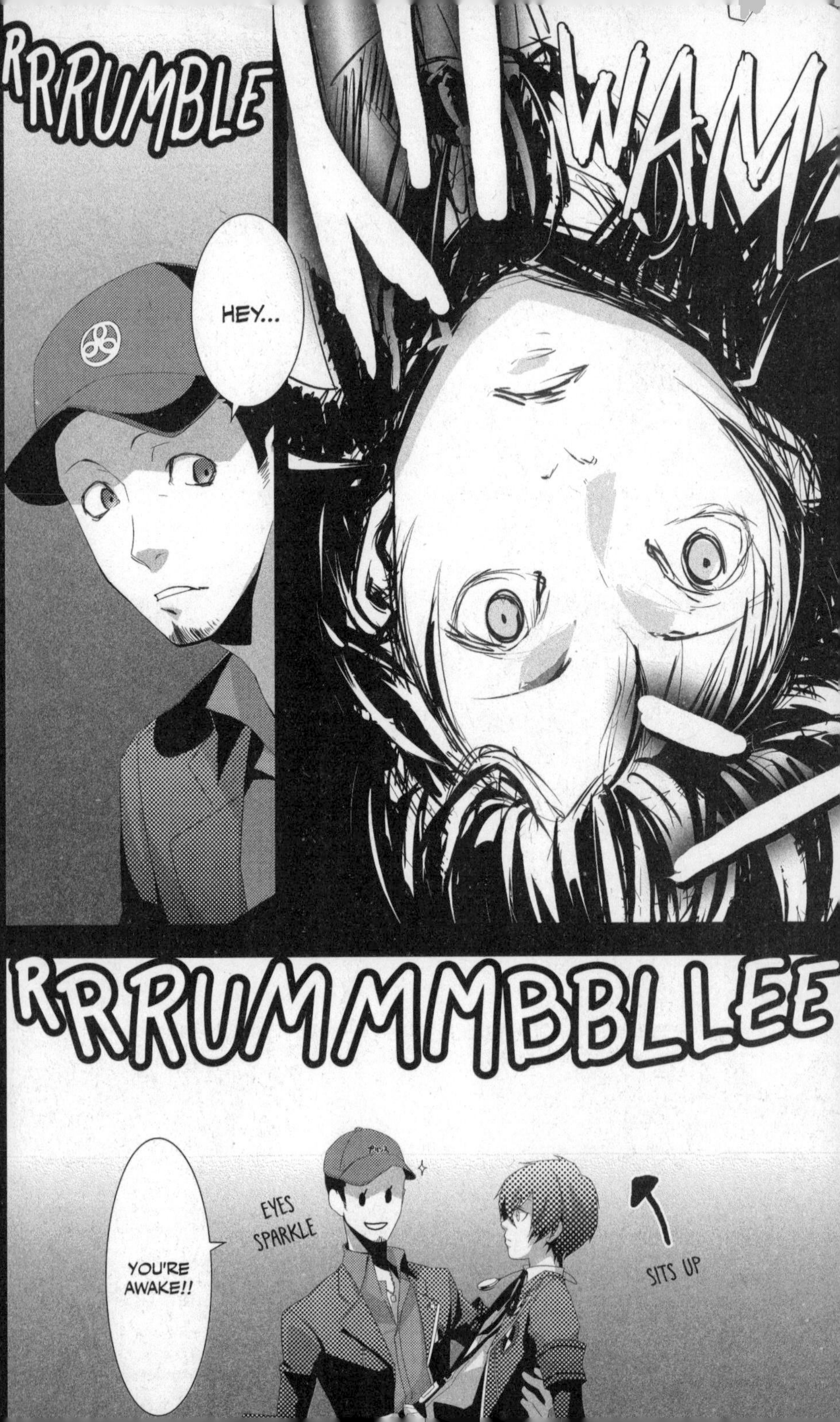
WAM
RRRUMBLE
HEY...
RRRUMMMBBLLEE
SITS UP
EYES SPARKLE
YOU'RE AWAKE!!

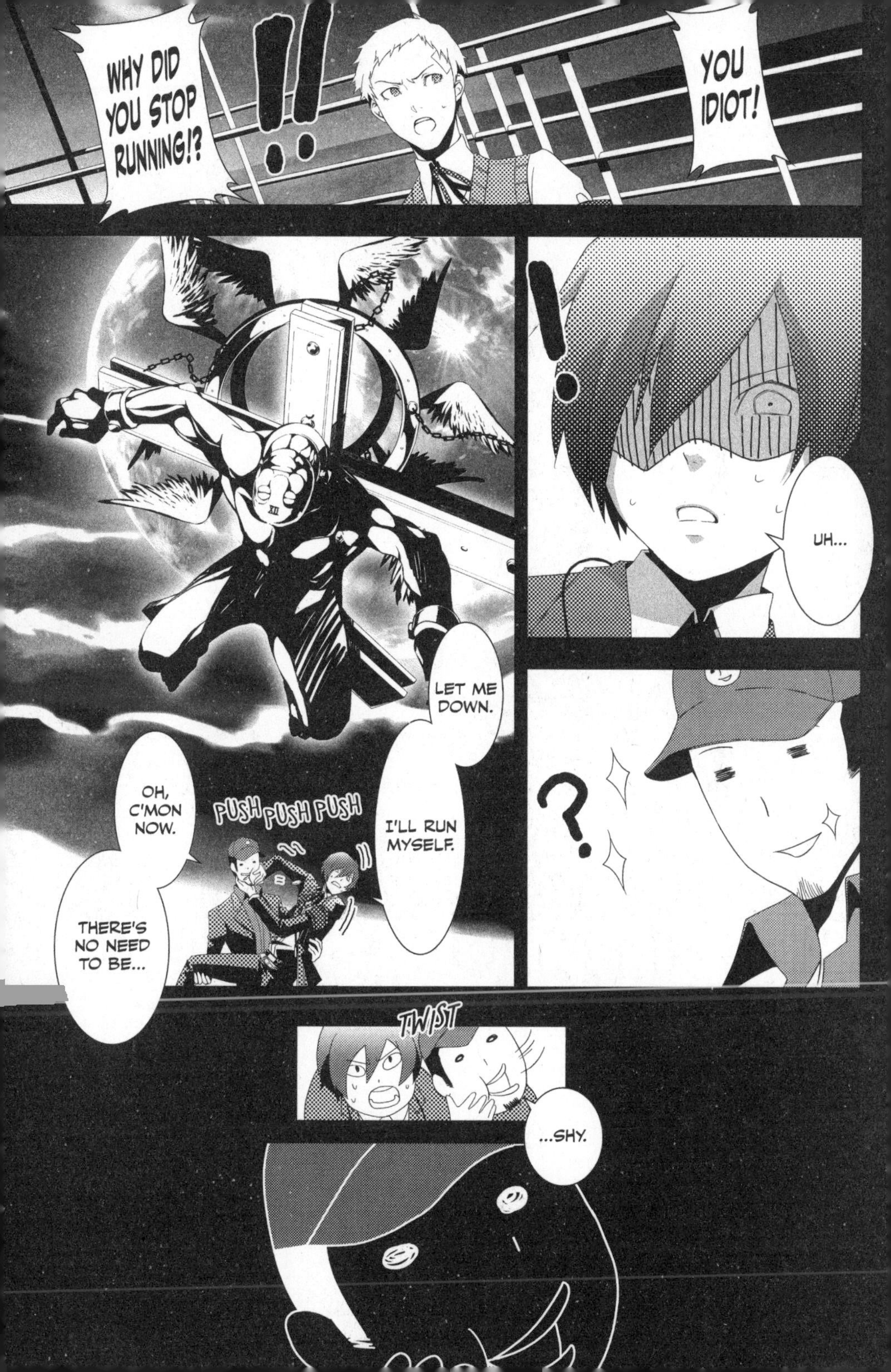
YOU IDIOT!
WHY DID YOU STOP RUNNING!?
UH...
?
LET ME DOWN.
I'LL RUN MYSELF.
PUSH PUSH PUSH
OH, C'MON NOW.
THERE'S NO NEED TO BE...
TWIST
...SHY.

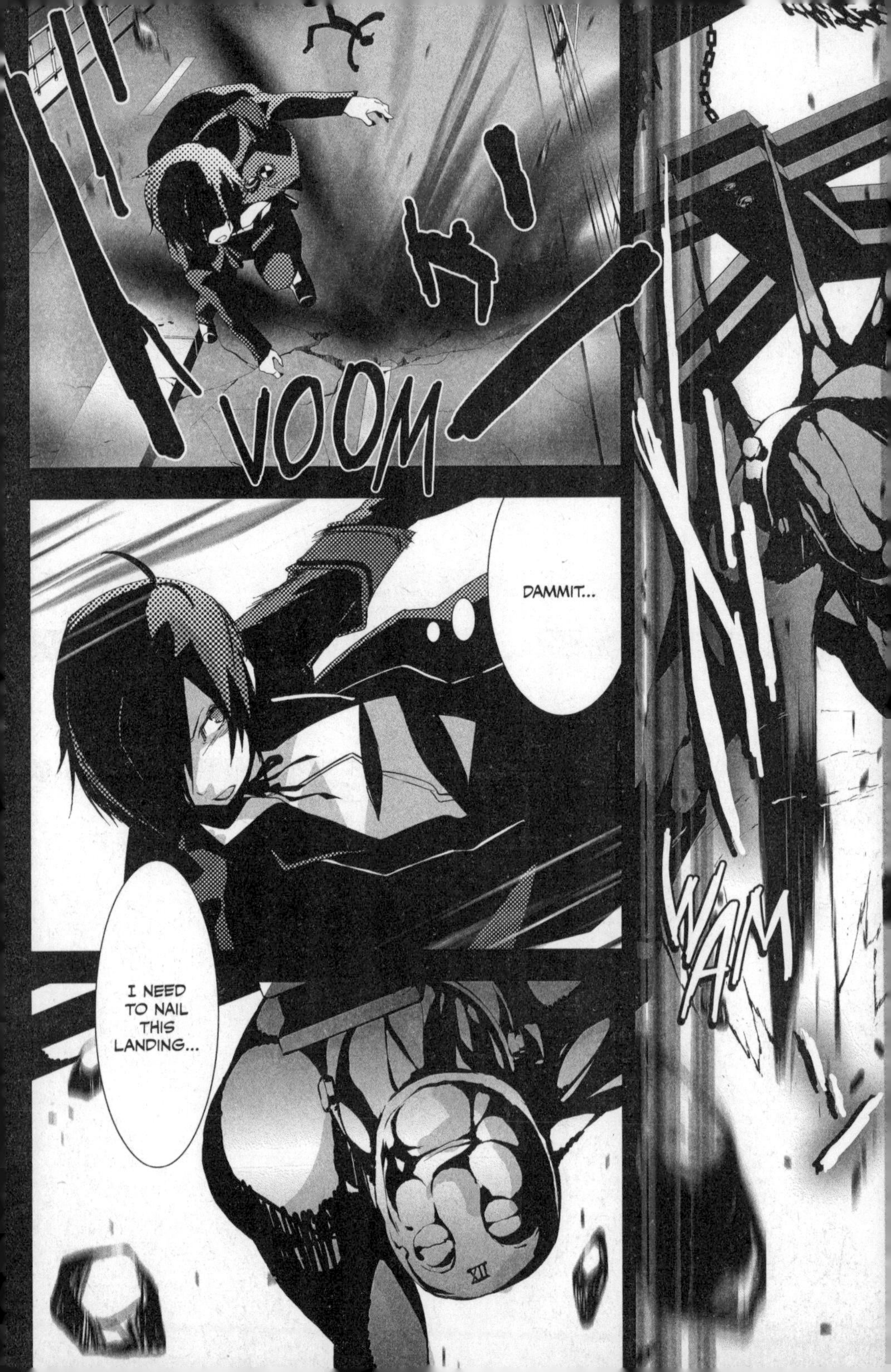
WAM
VOOM
DAMMIT...
I NEED TO NAIL THIS LANDING...

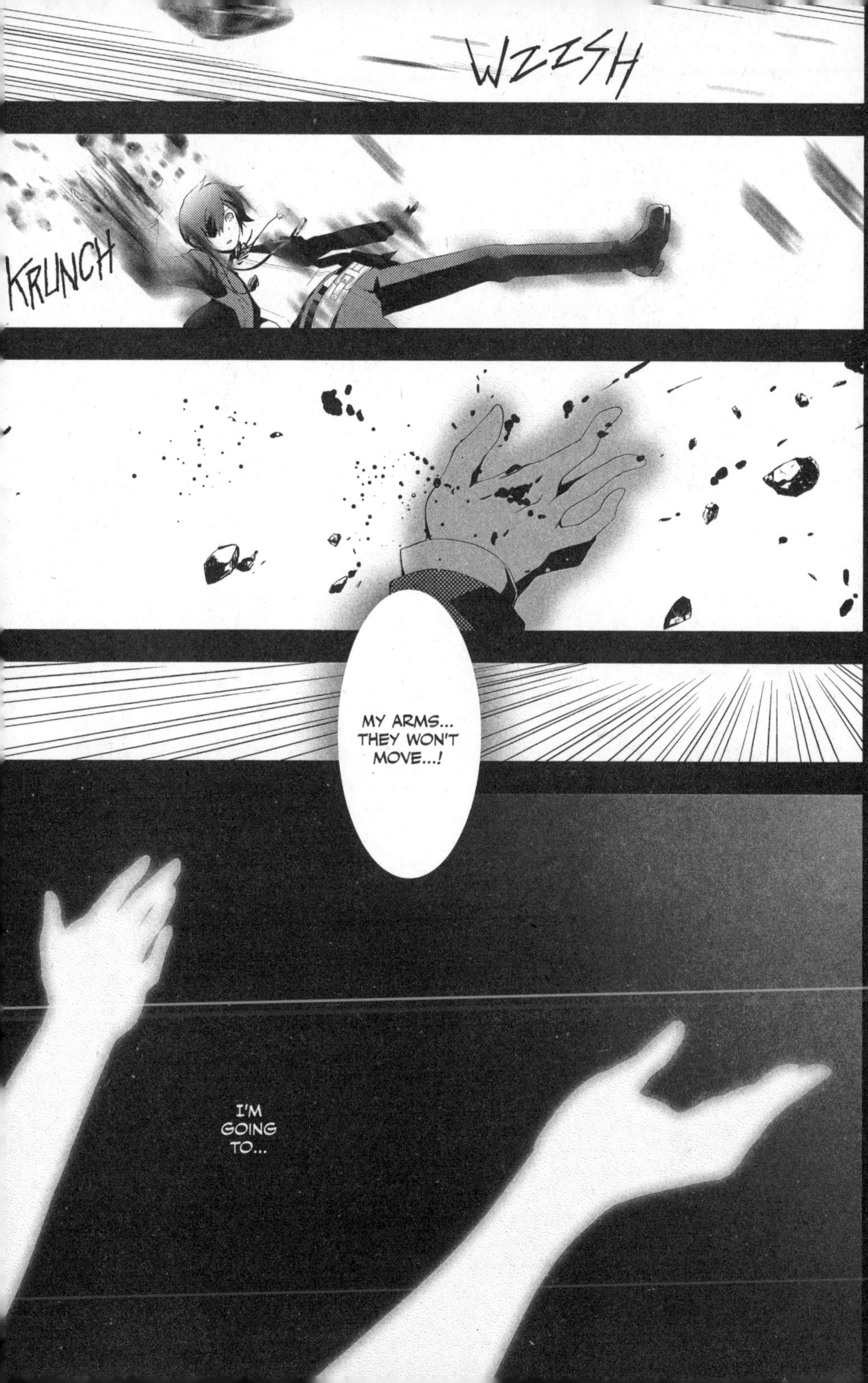
WZZSH
KRUNCH
MY ARMS... THEY WON'T MOVE...!
I'M GOING TO...

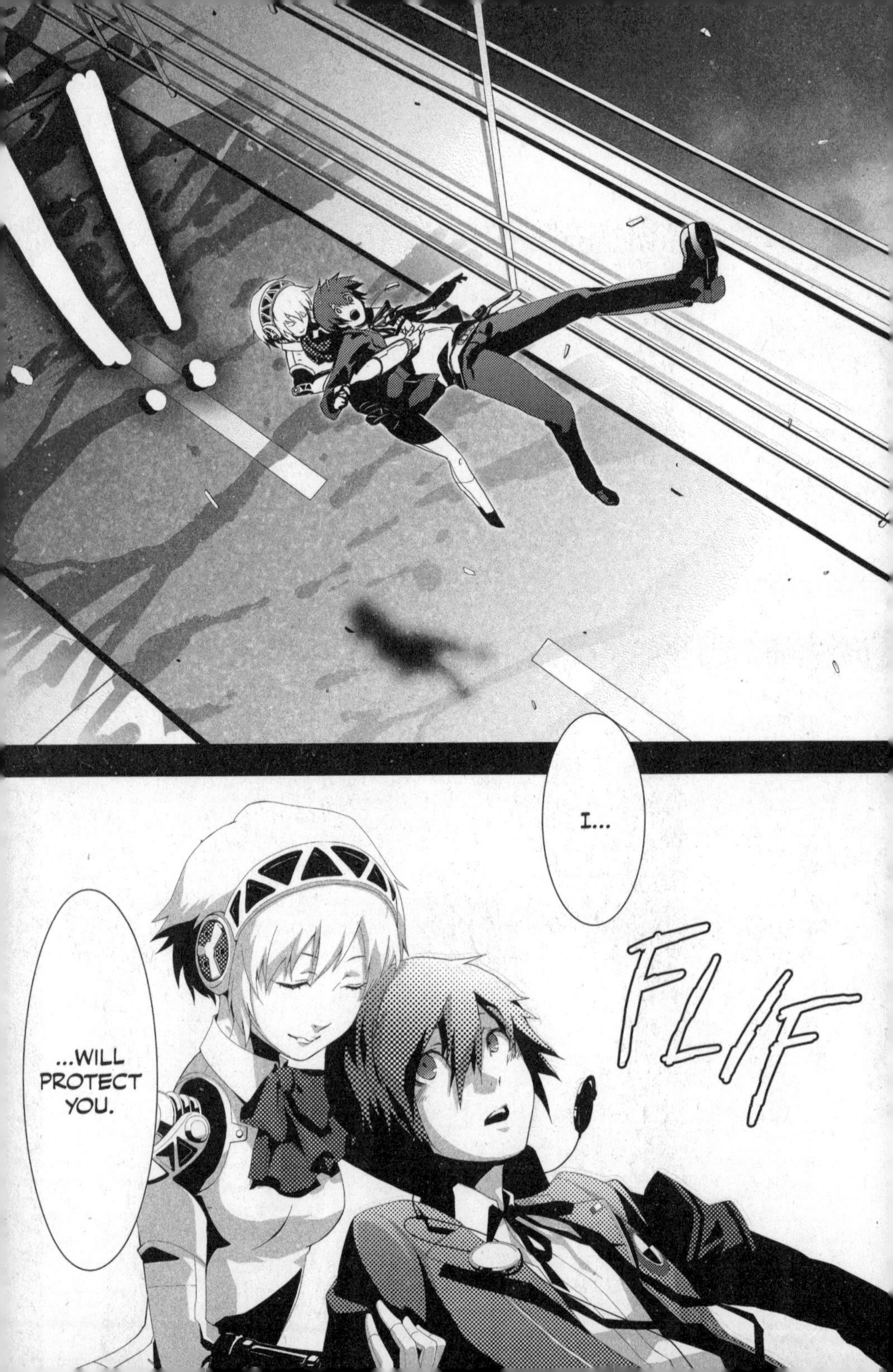
I...
FLIF
...WILL PROTECT YOU.

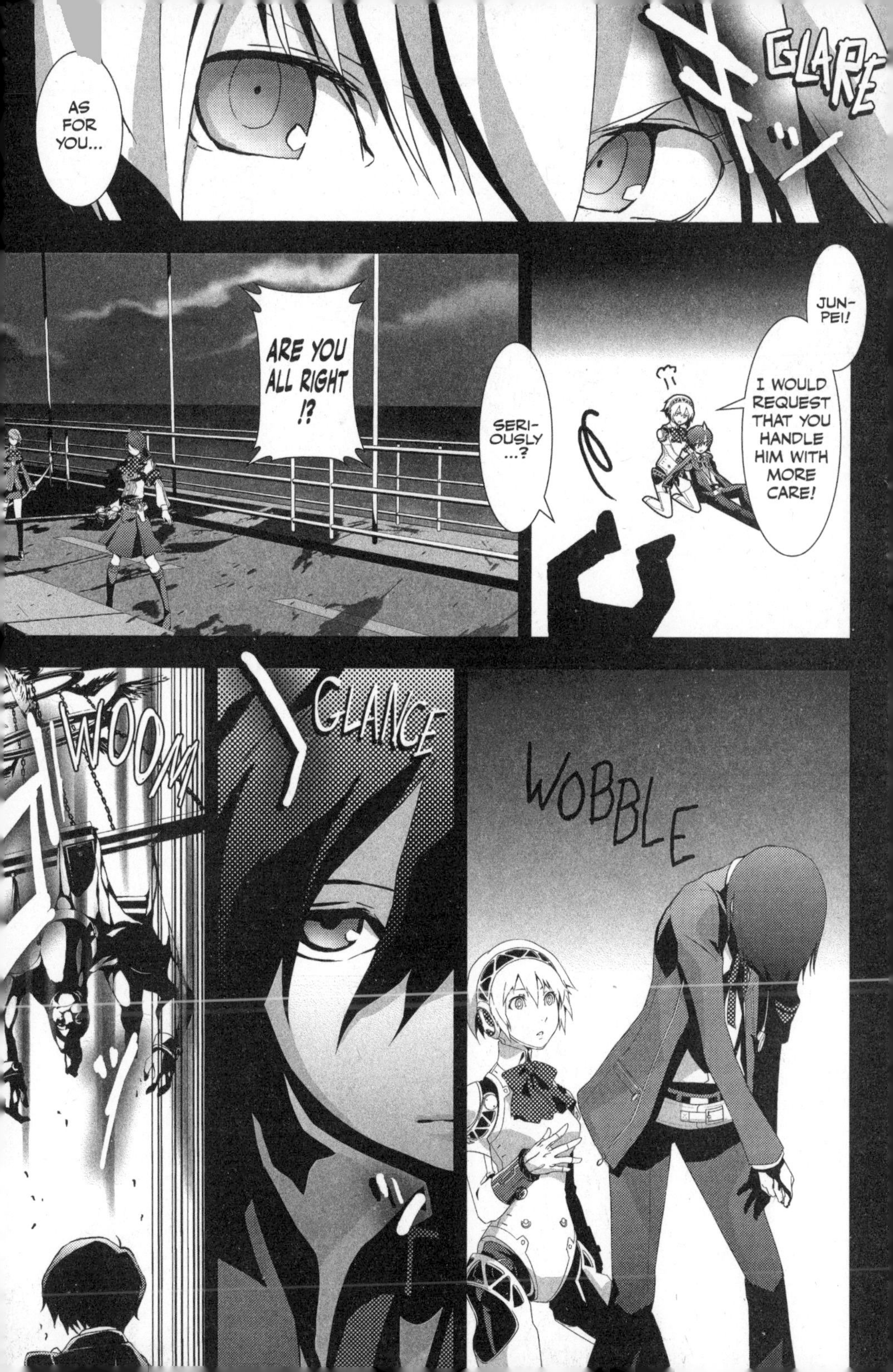
GLARE
AS FOR YOU...
JUN-PEI!
I WOULD REQUEST THAT YOU HANDLE HIM WITH MORE CARE!
SERI-OUSLY ...?
ARE YOU ALL RIGHT !?
WOBBLE
GLANCE
WOOM

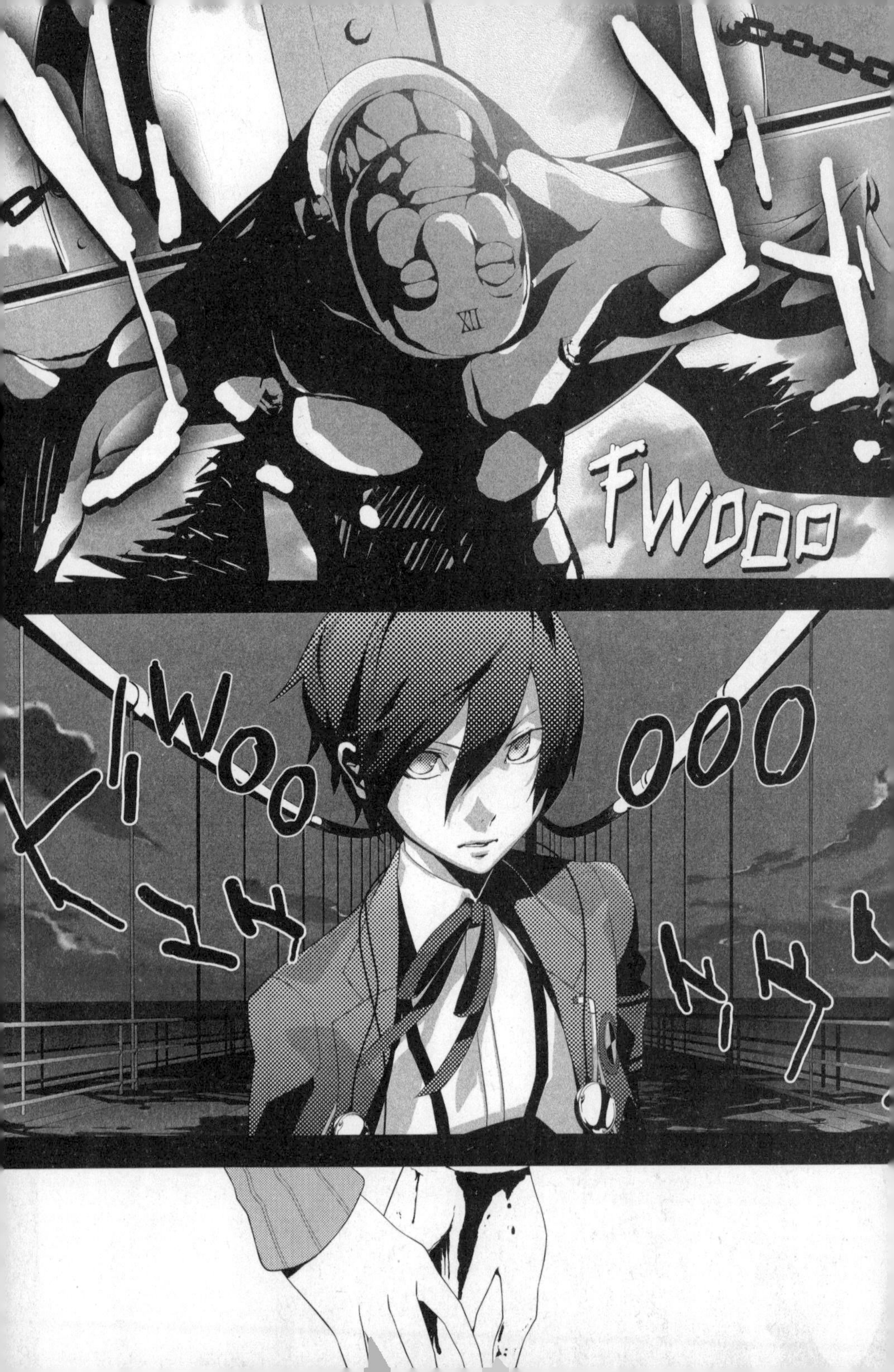
FWOOO
WOO
OOO

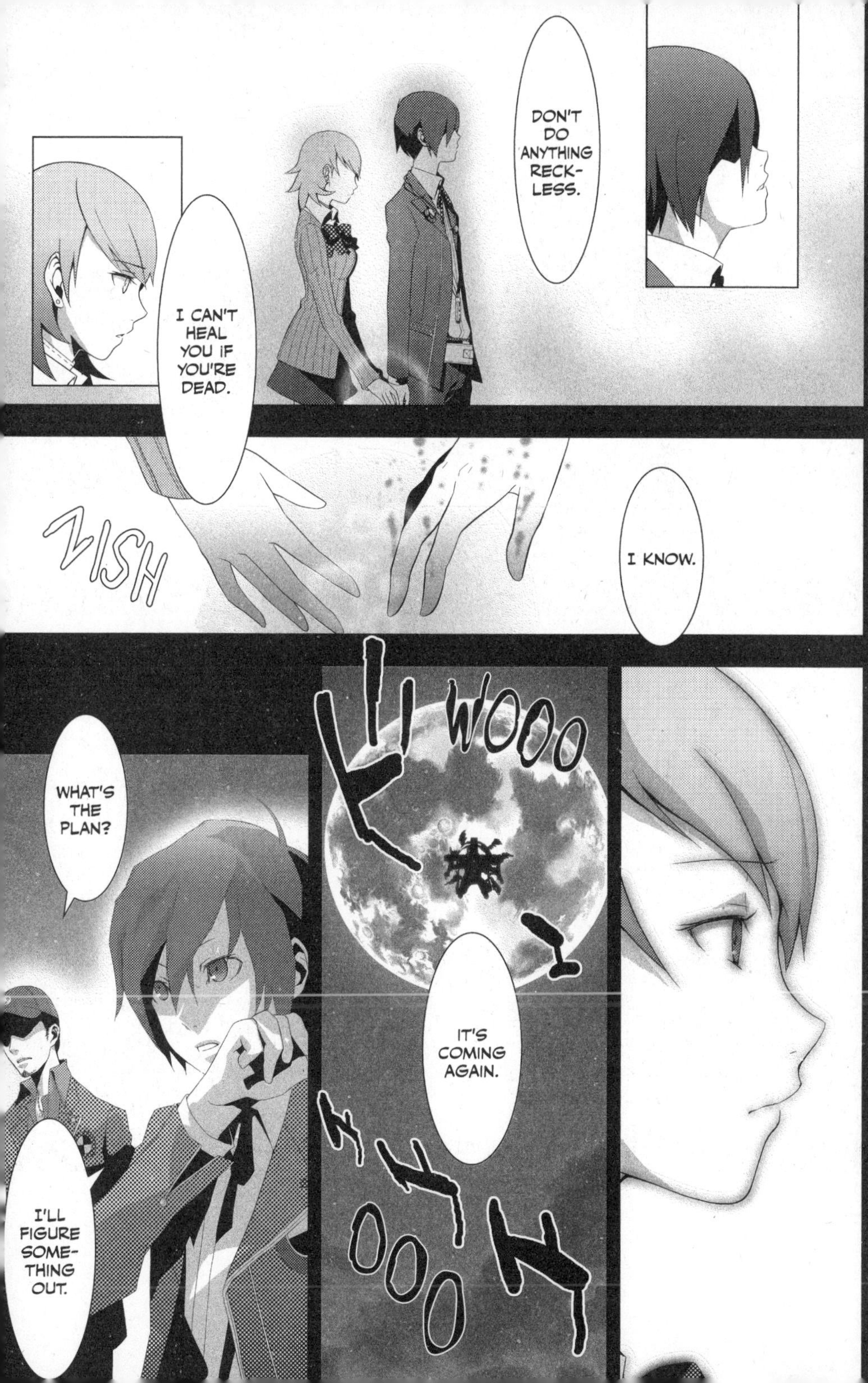
DON'T DO ANYTHING RECK-LESS.
I CAN'T HEAL YOU IF YOU'RE DEAD.
I KNOW.
ZISH
WOOO
IT'S COMING AGAIN.
OOO
WHAT'S THE PLAN?
I'LL FIGURE SOME-THING OUT.

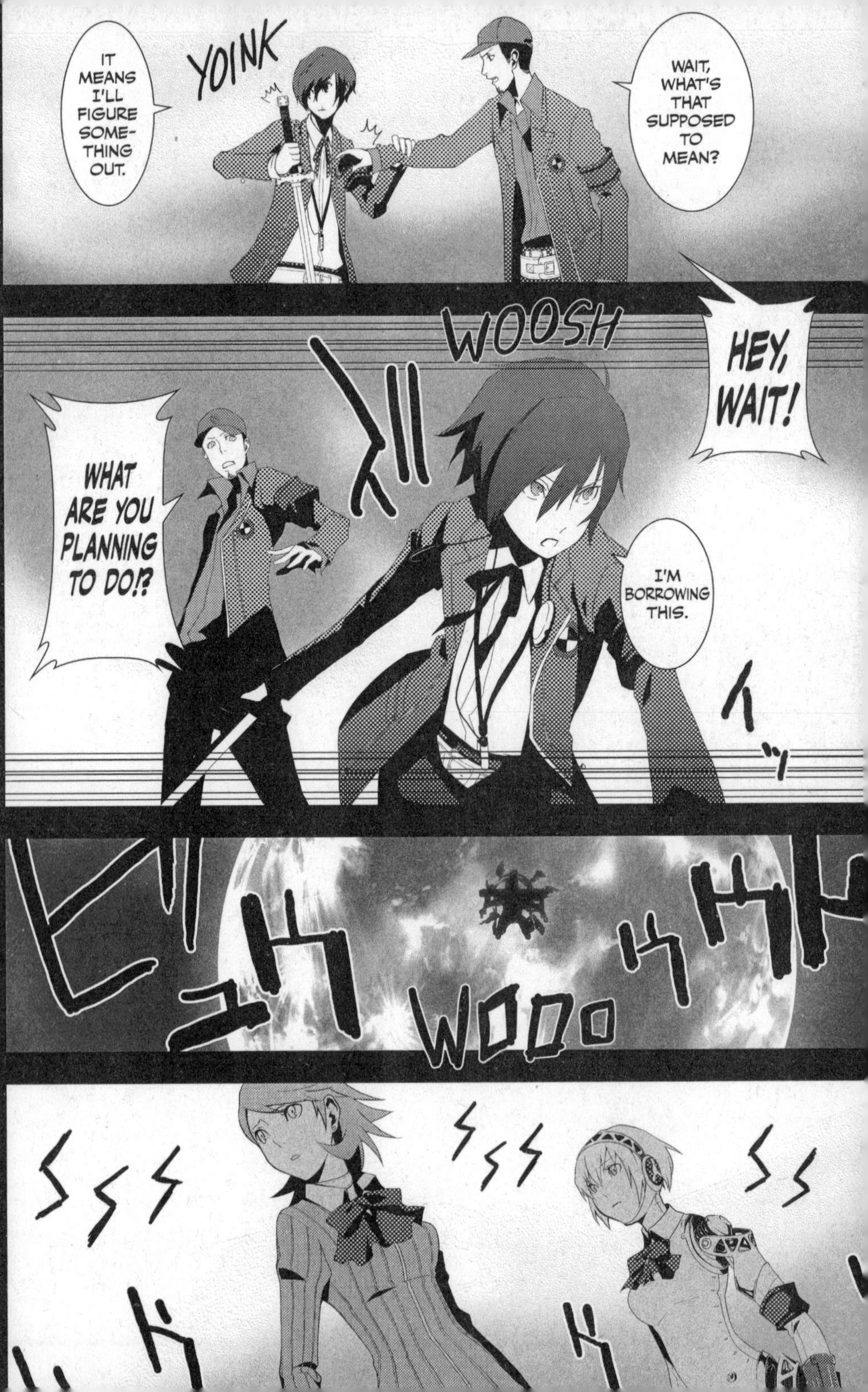
WAIT, WHAT'S THAT SUPPOSED TO MEAN?
YOINK
IT MEANS I'LL FIGURE SOMETHING OUT.
HEY, WAIT!
WOOSH
I'M BORROWING THIS.
WHAT ARE YOU PLANNING TO DO!?
WOOO

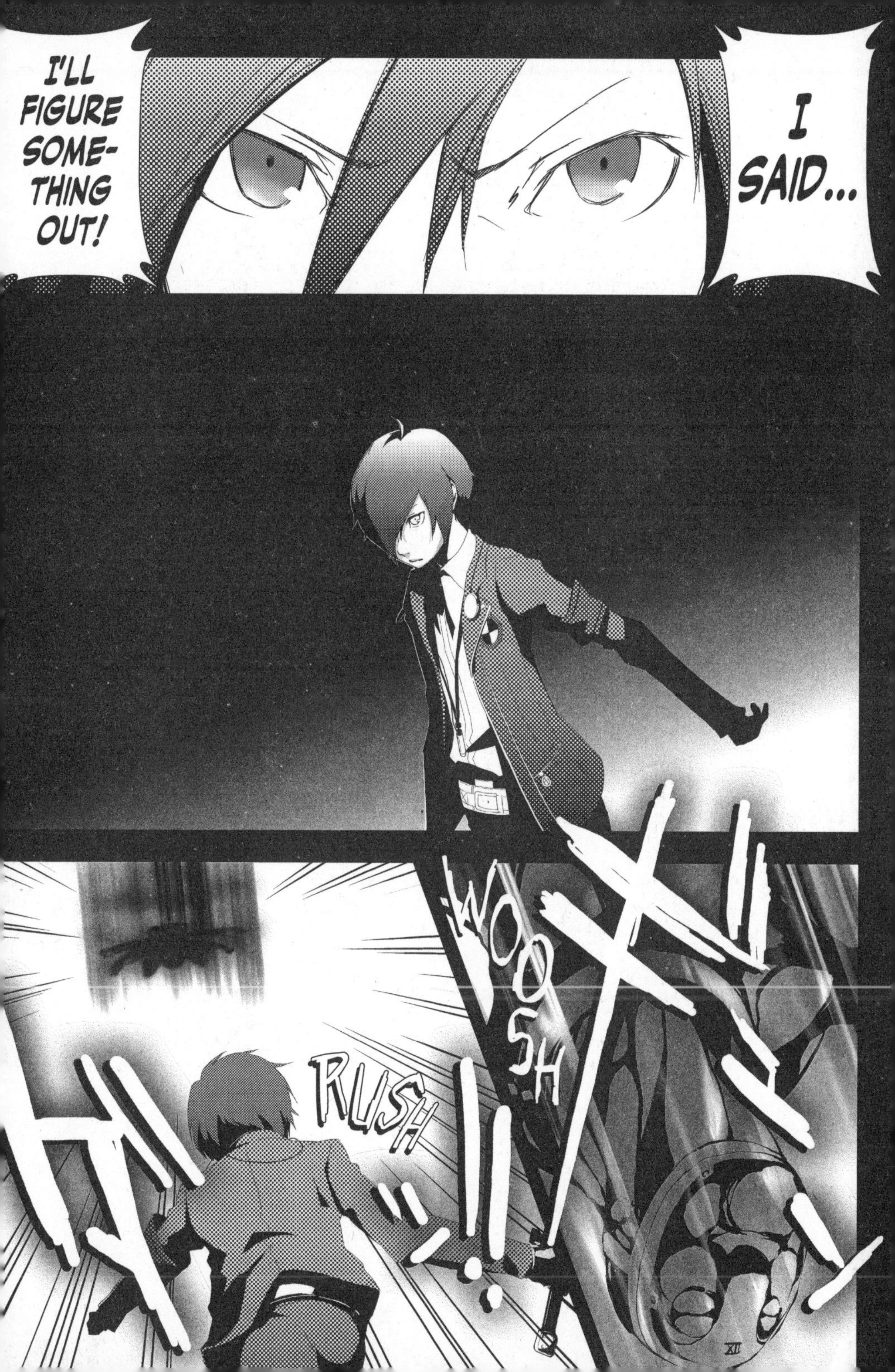
I SAID...
I'LL FIGURE SOME-THING OUT!
WOOSH
RUSH

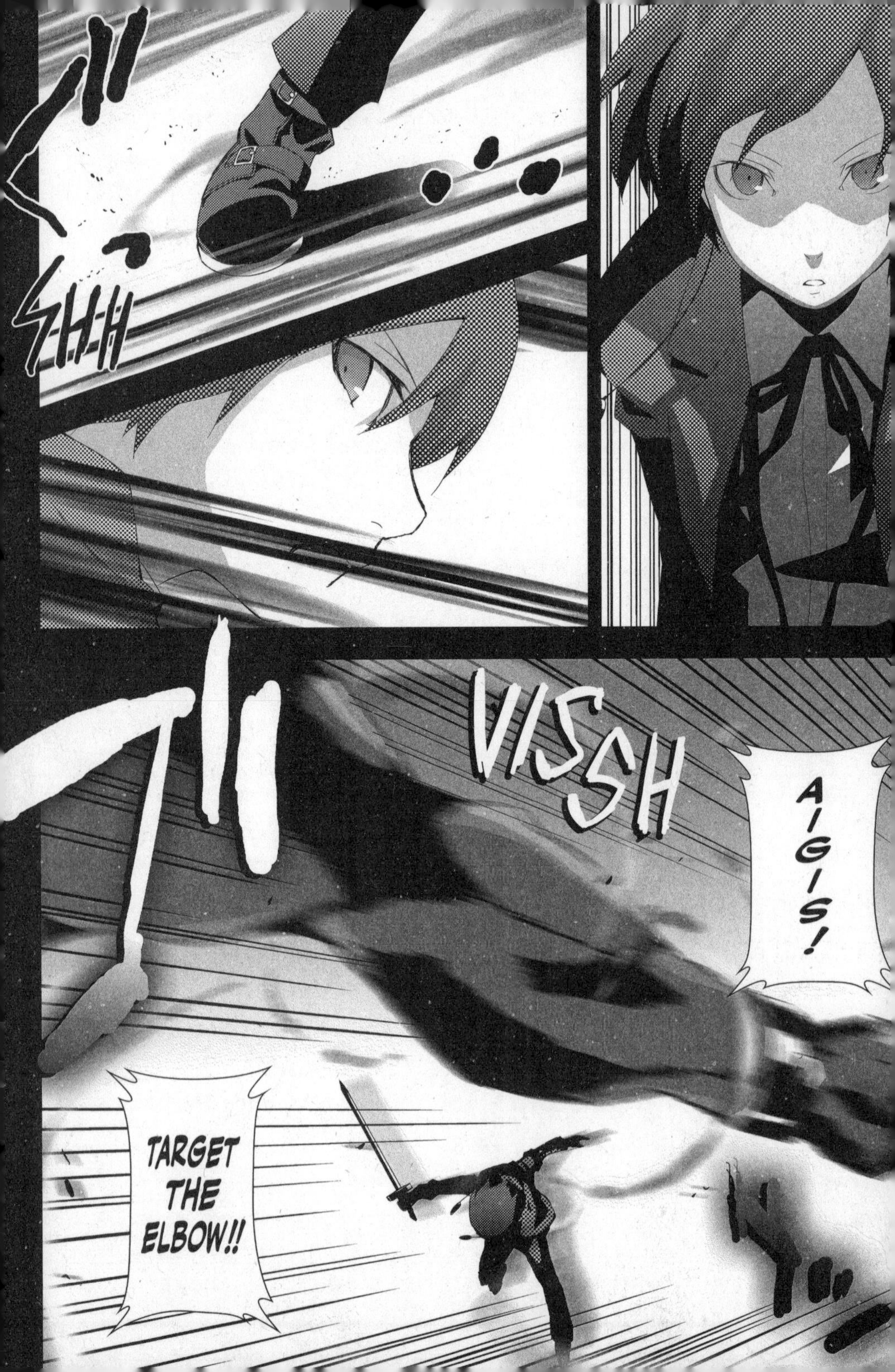
SHH
AIGIS!
VISSH
TARGET THE ELBOW!!

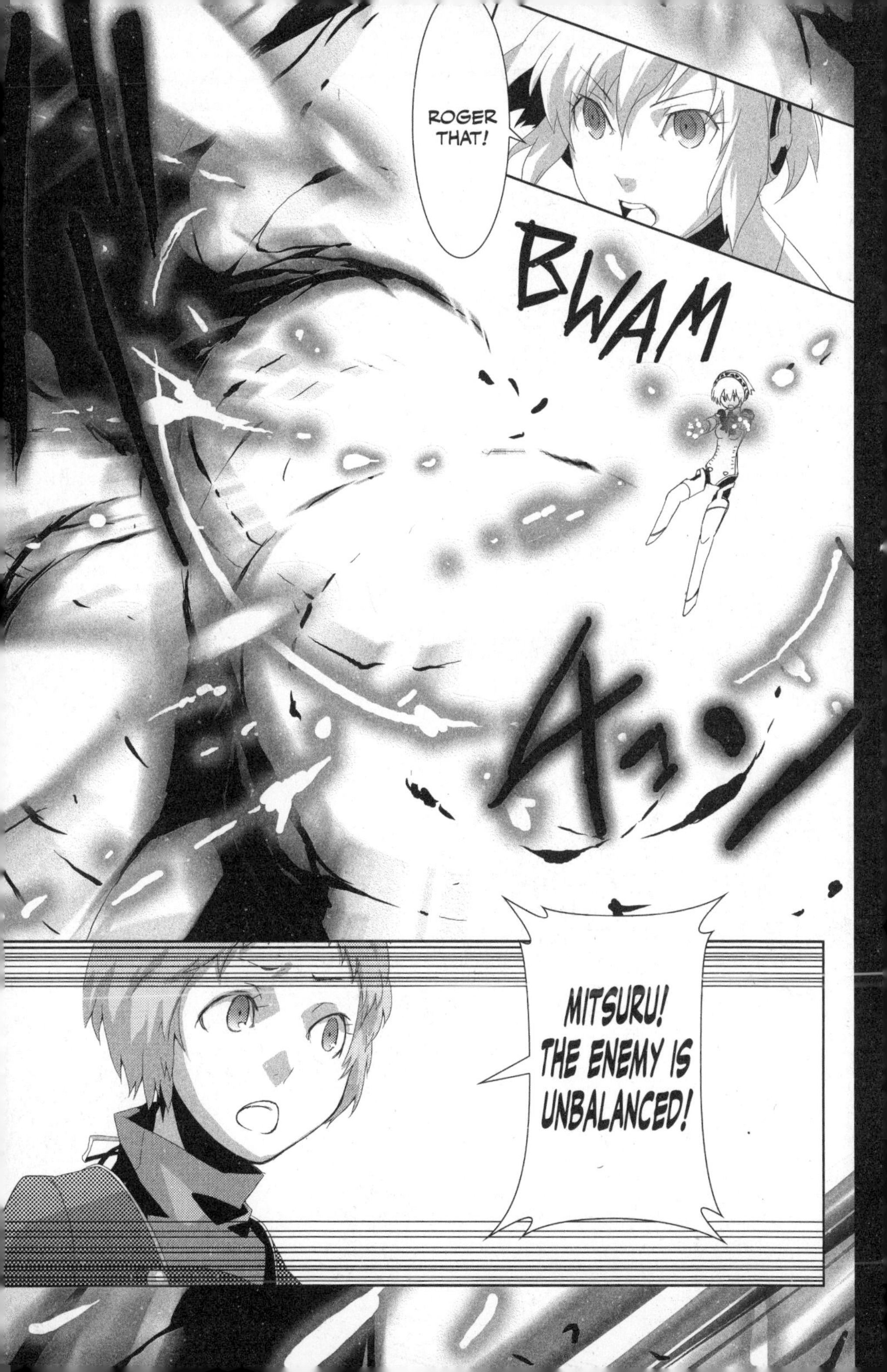
ROGER THAT!
BWAM
MITSURU! THE ENEMY IS UNBALANCED!

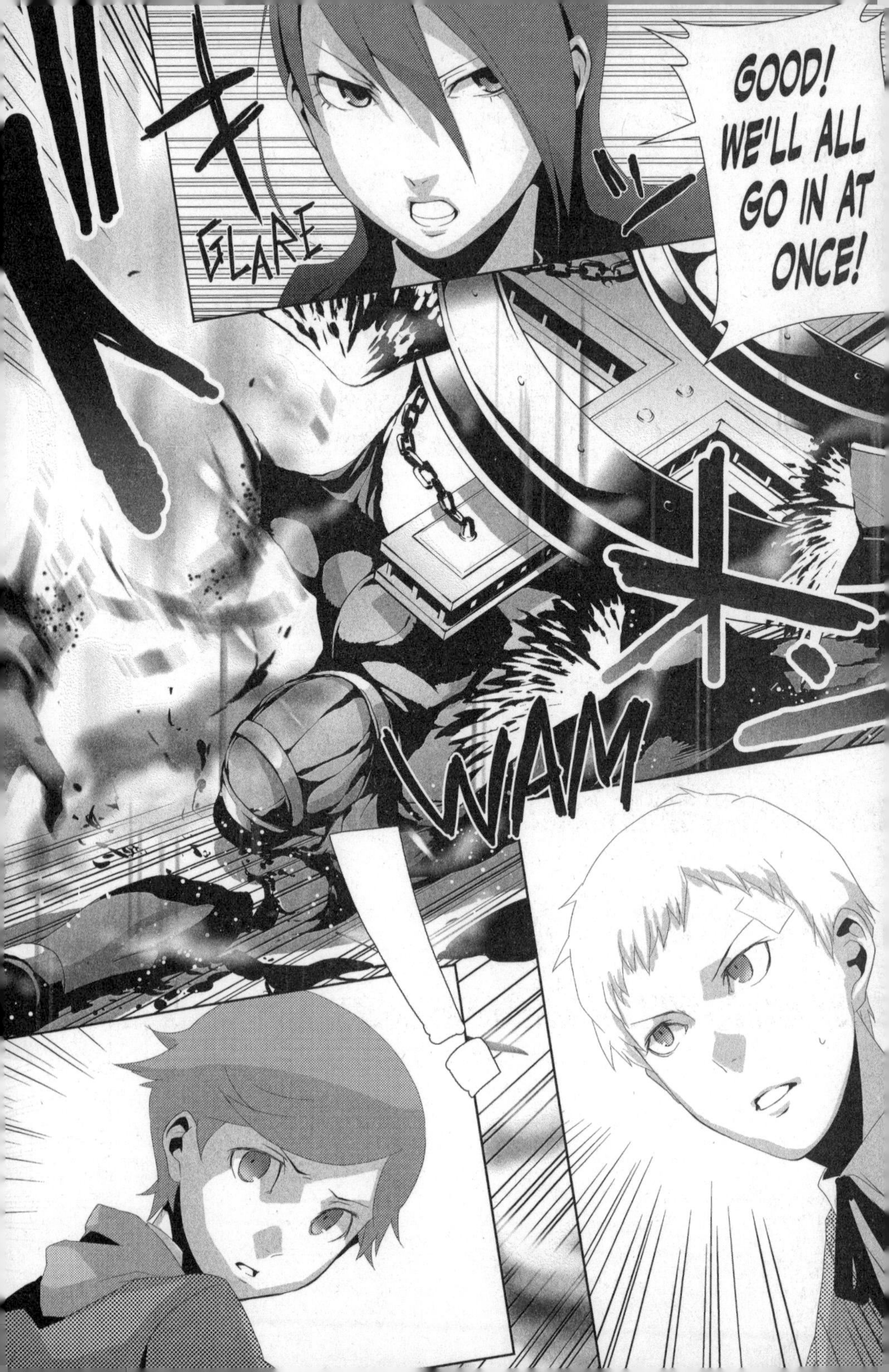
GOOD! WE'LL ALL GO IN AT ONCE!
GLARE
WAM

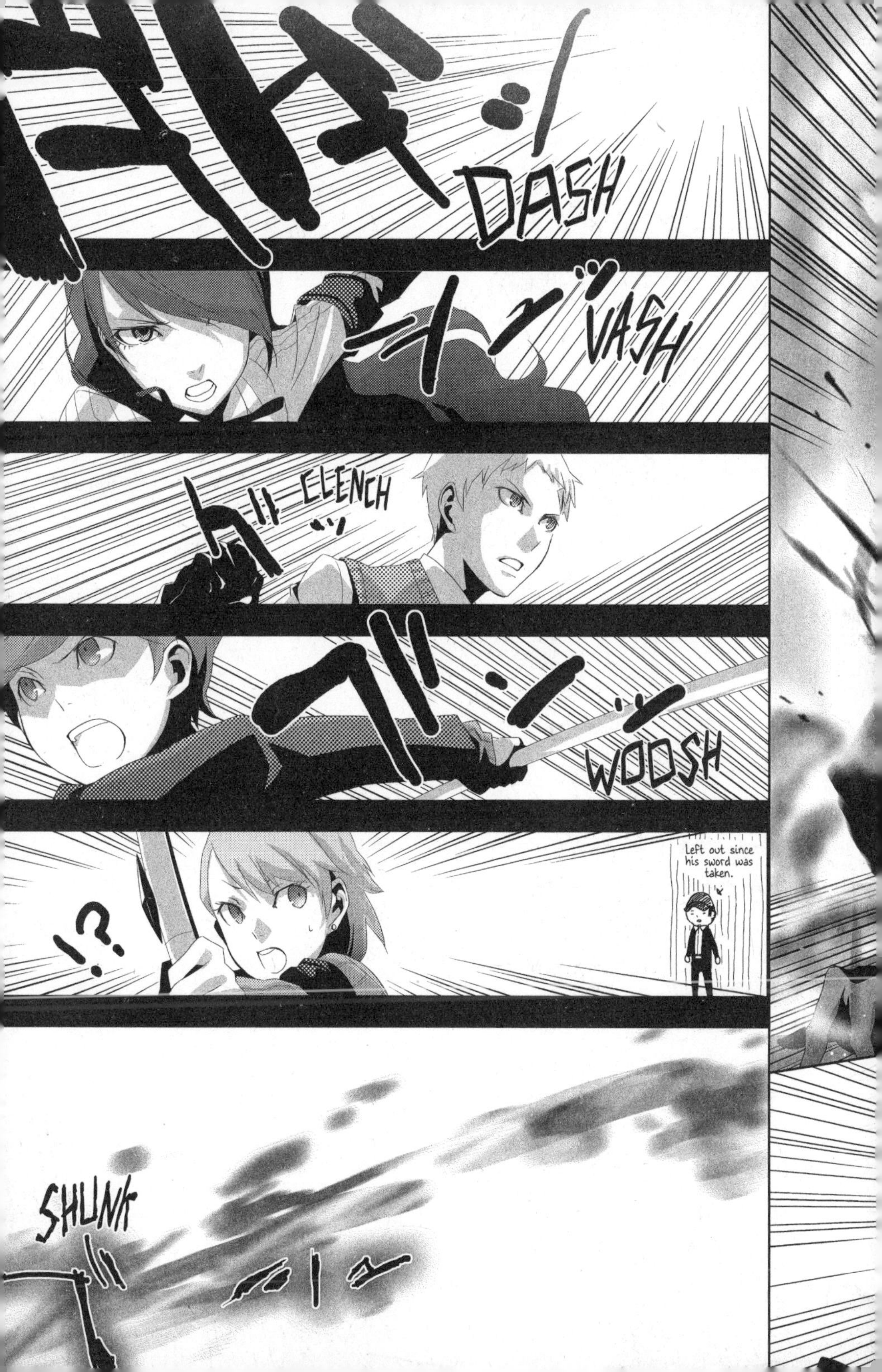
DASH
VASH
CLENCH
WOOSH
Left out since his sword was taken.
!?
SHUNK

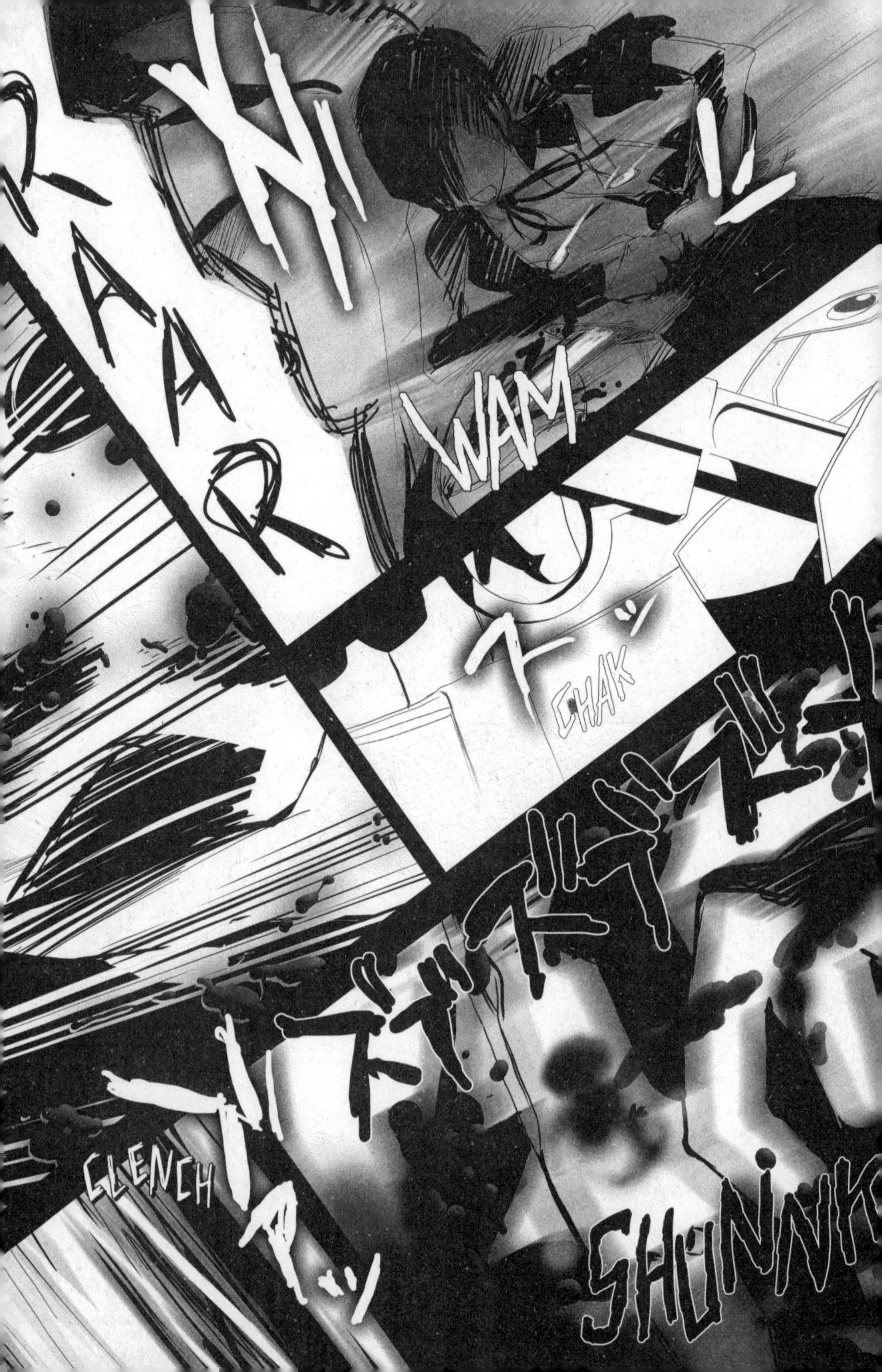
WAM
RAAR
CHAK
SHUNNK
CLENCH

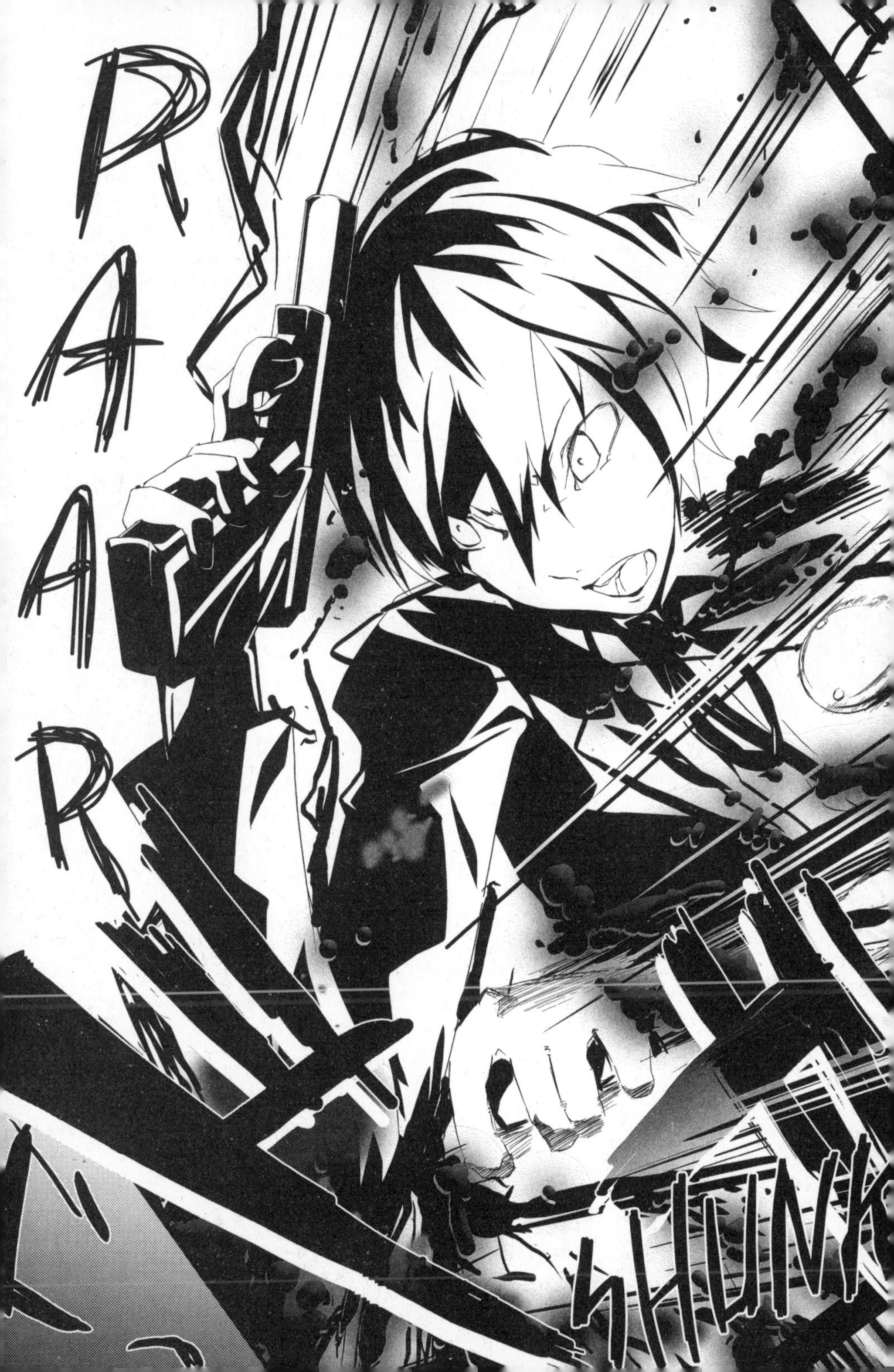
RAAAR
SHUNK

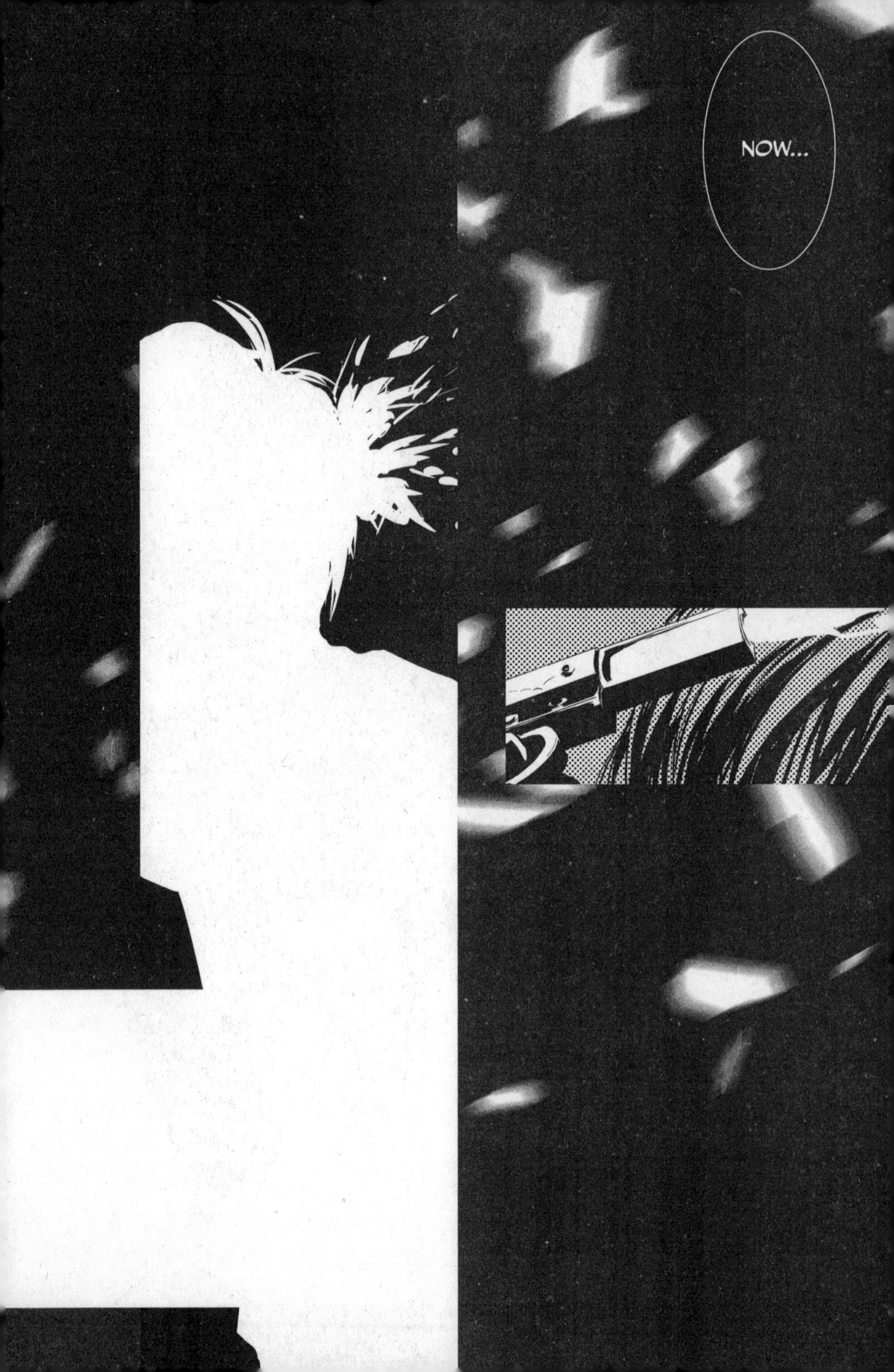
NOW...

IT
BEGINS.

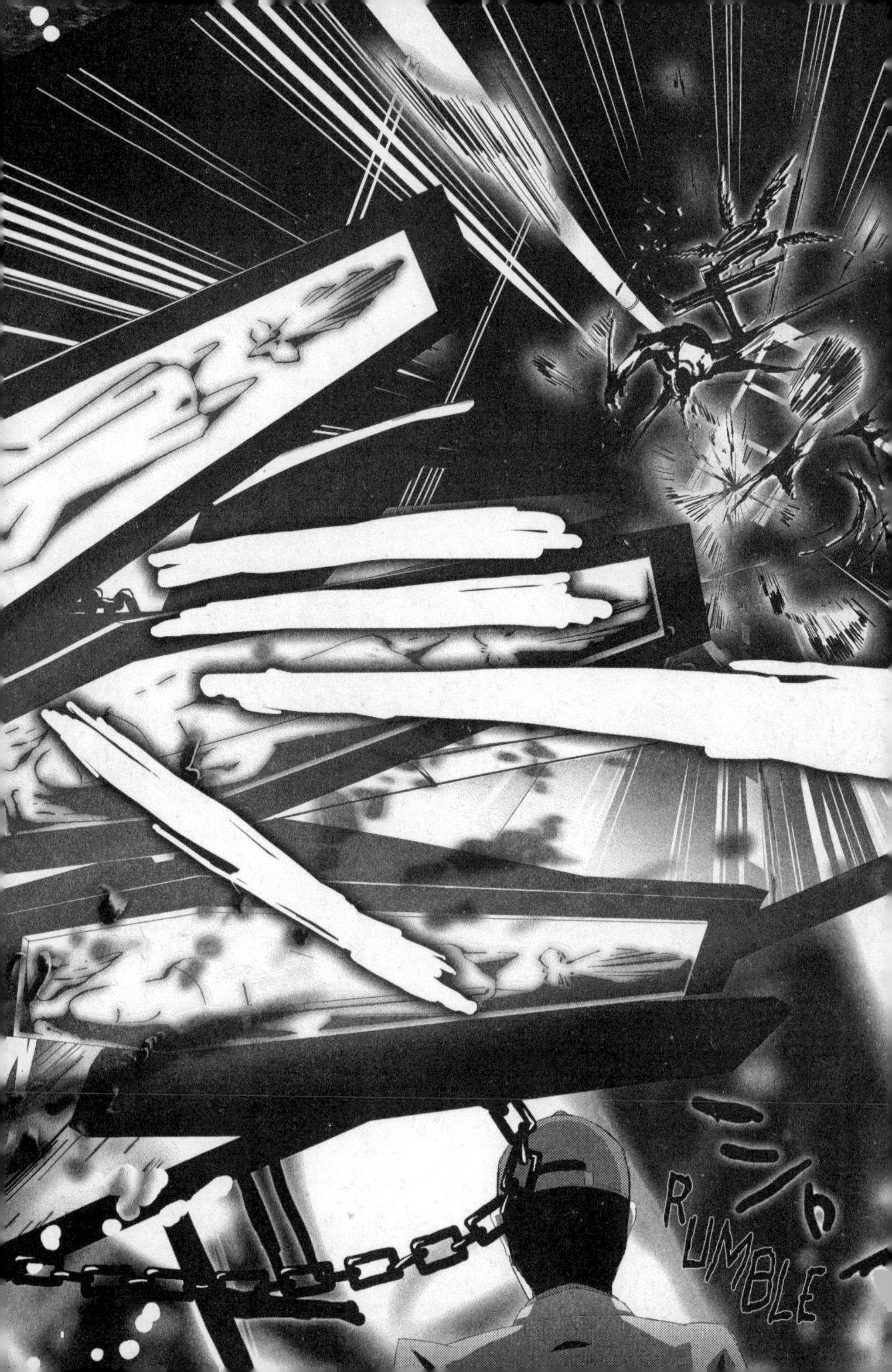
RUMBLE

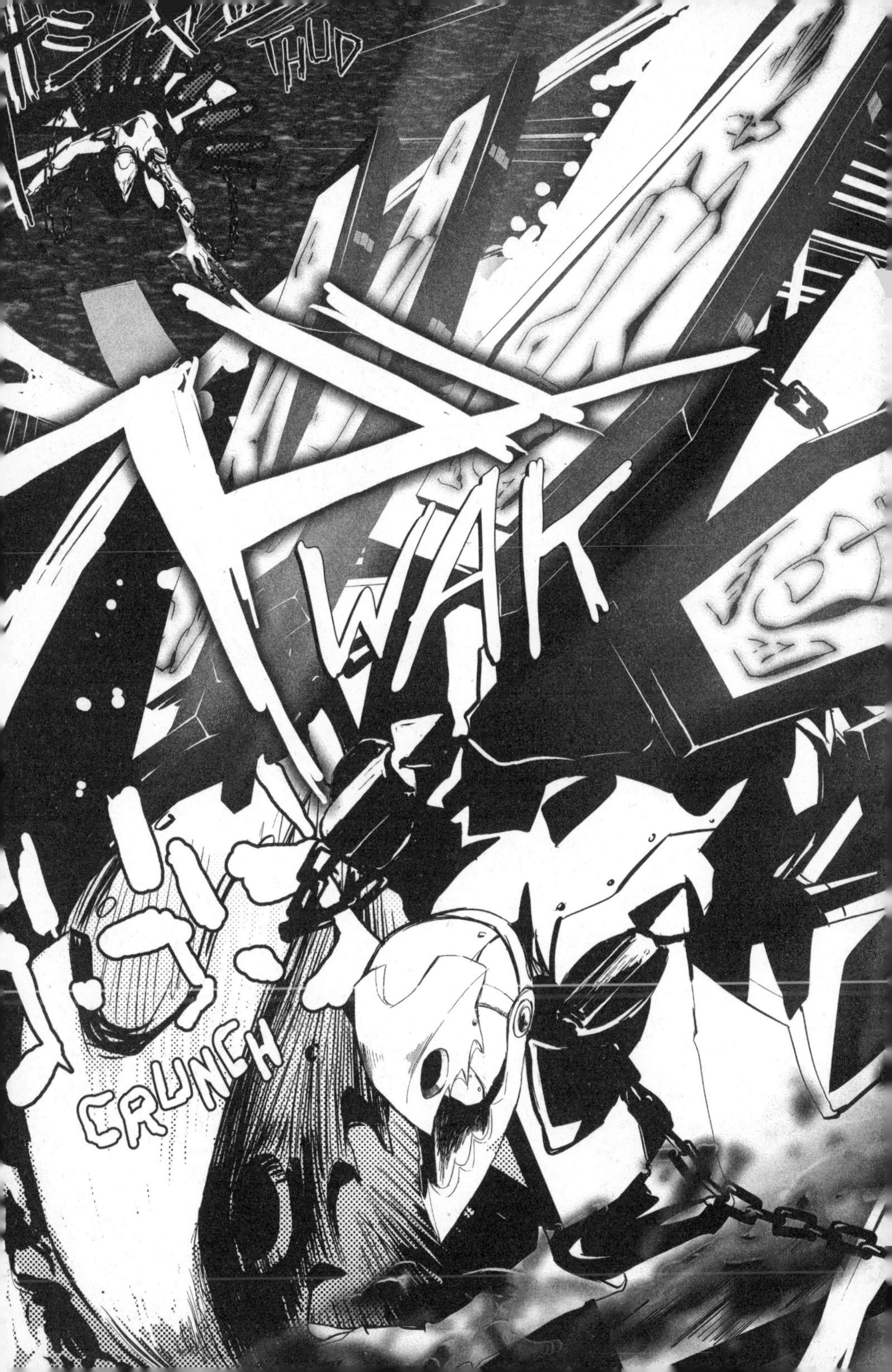
THUD
WAK
CRUNCH

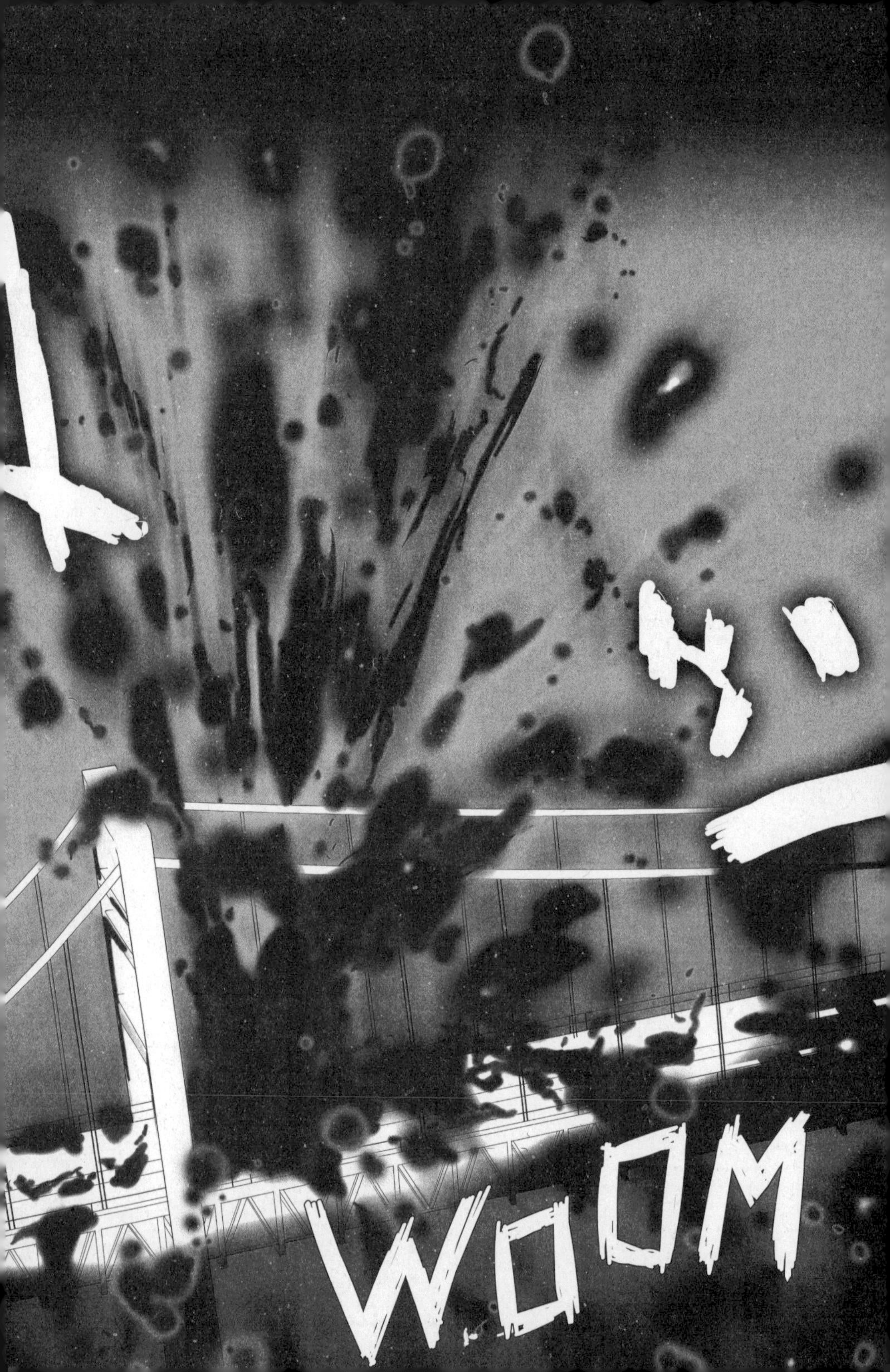
WOOM

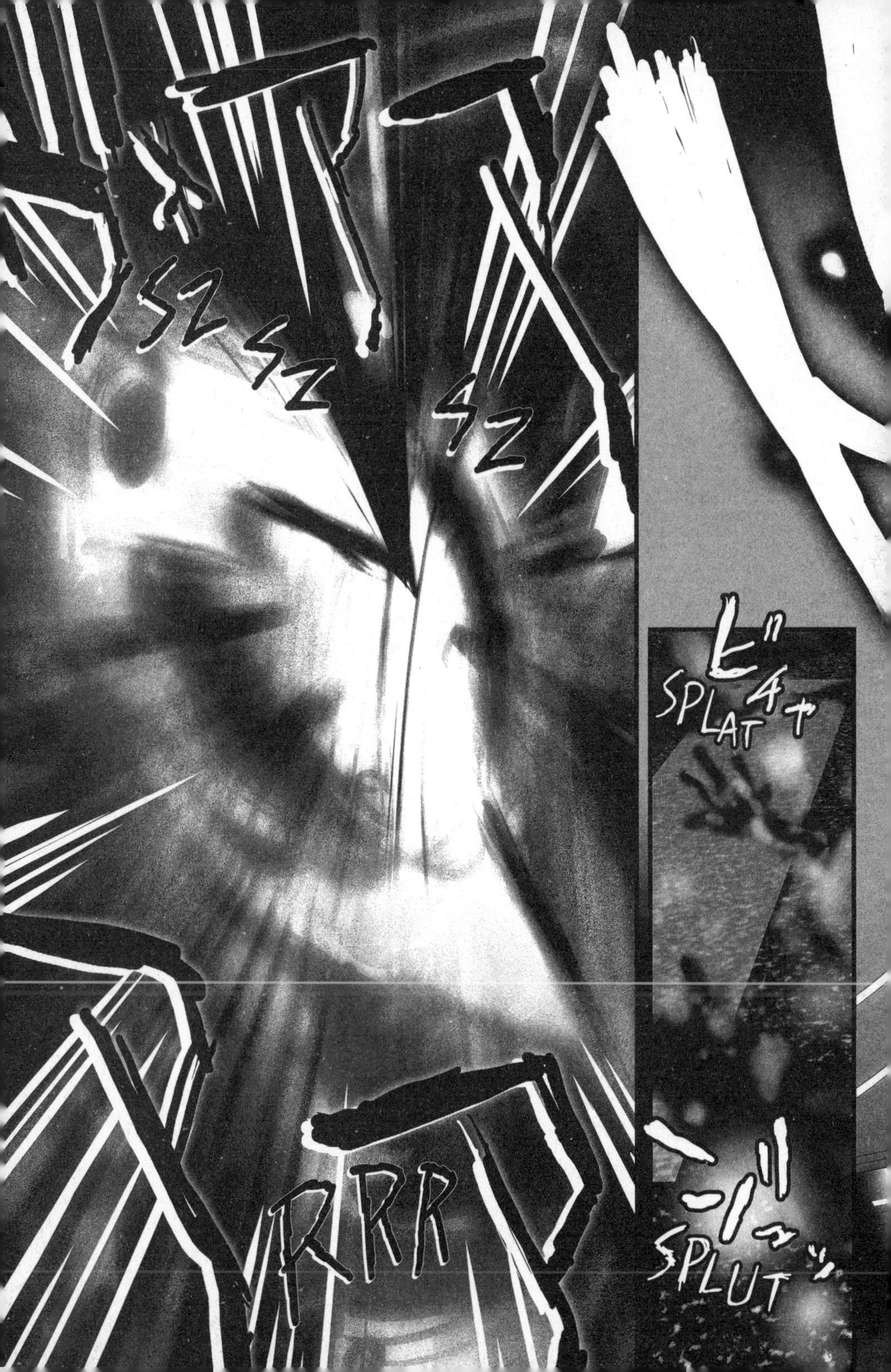
SPLAT
SPLUT
SZ SZ
SZ
RRR

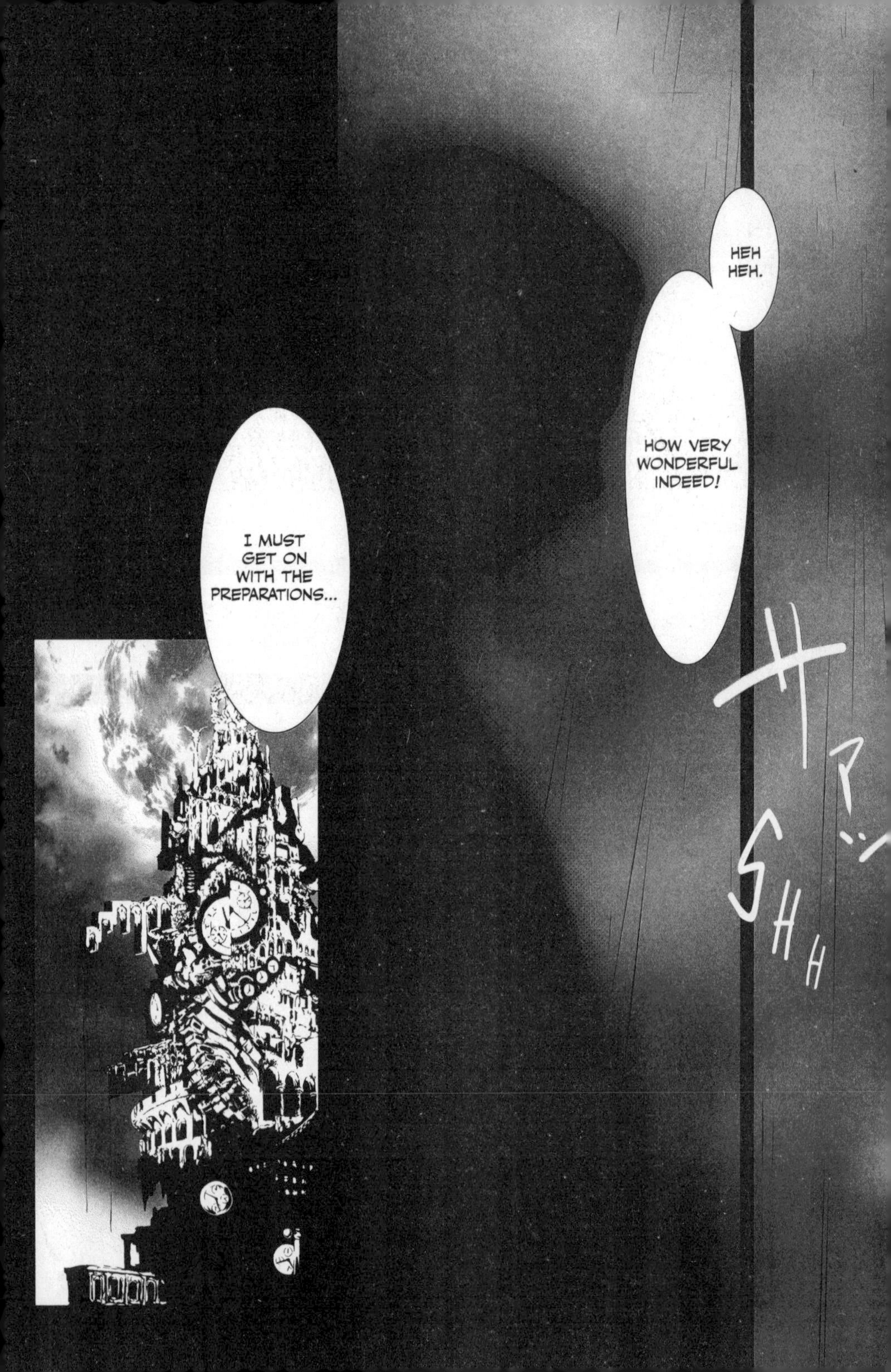
HEH HEH.
HOW VERY WONDERFUL INDEED!
SHH
I MUST GET ON WITH THE PREPARATIONS...

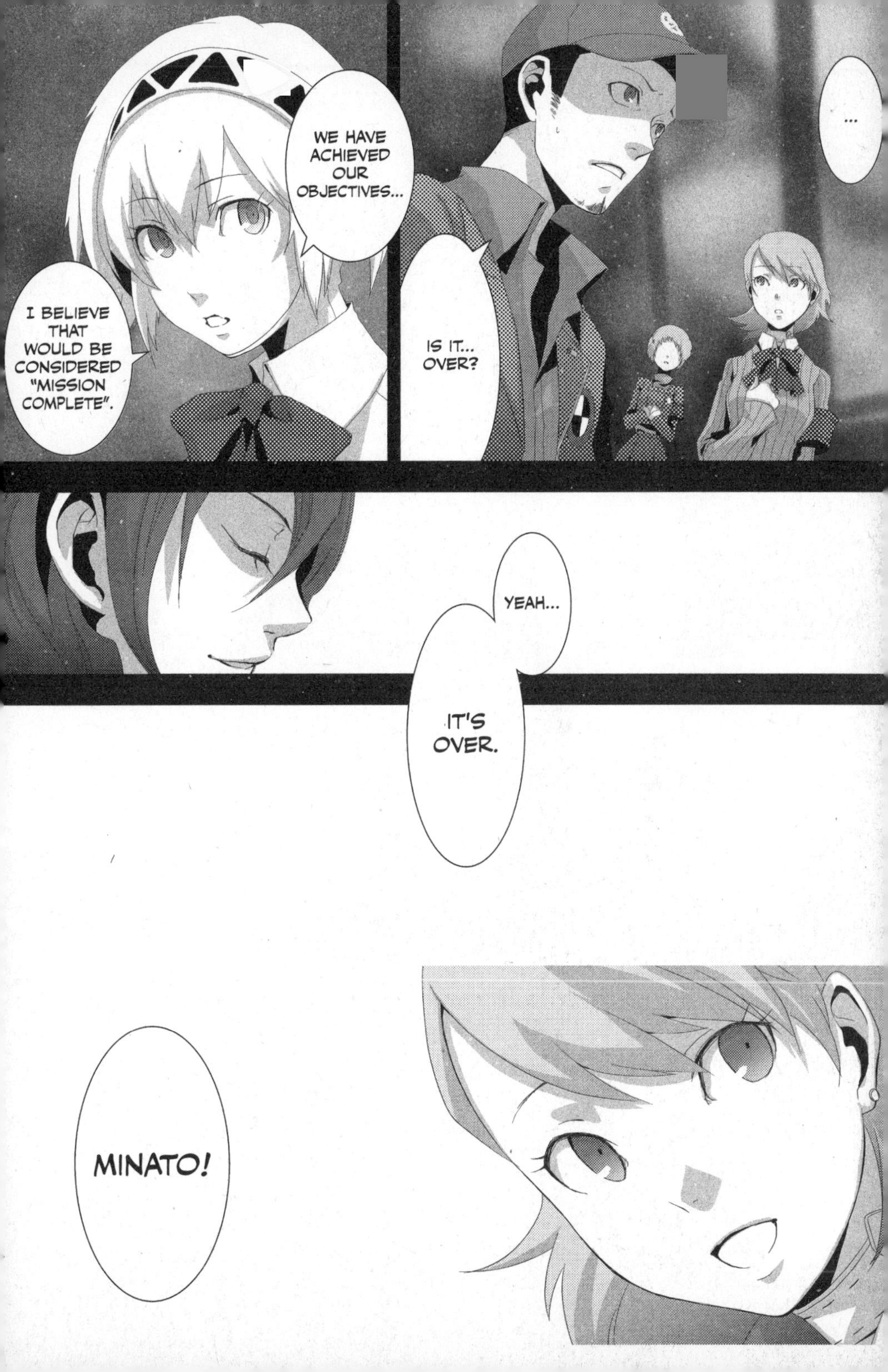
...
IS IT... OVER?
WE HAVE ACHIEVED OUR OBJECTIVES...
I BELIEVE THAT WOULD BE CONSIDERED "MISSION COMPLETE".
YEAH...
IT'S OVER.
MINATO!

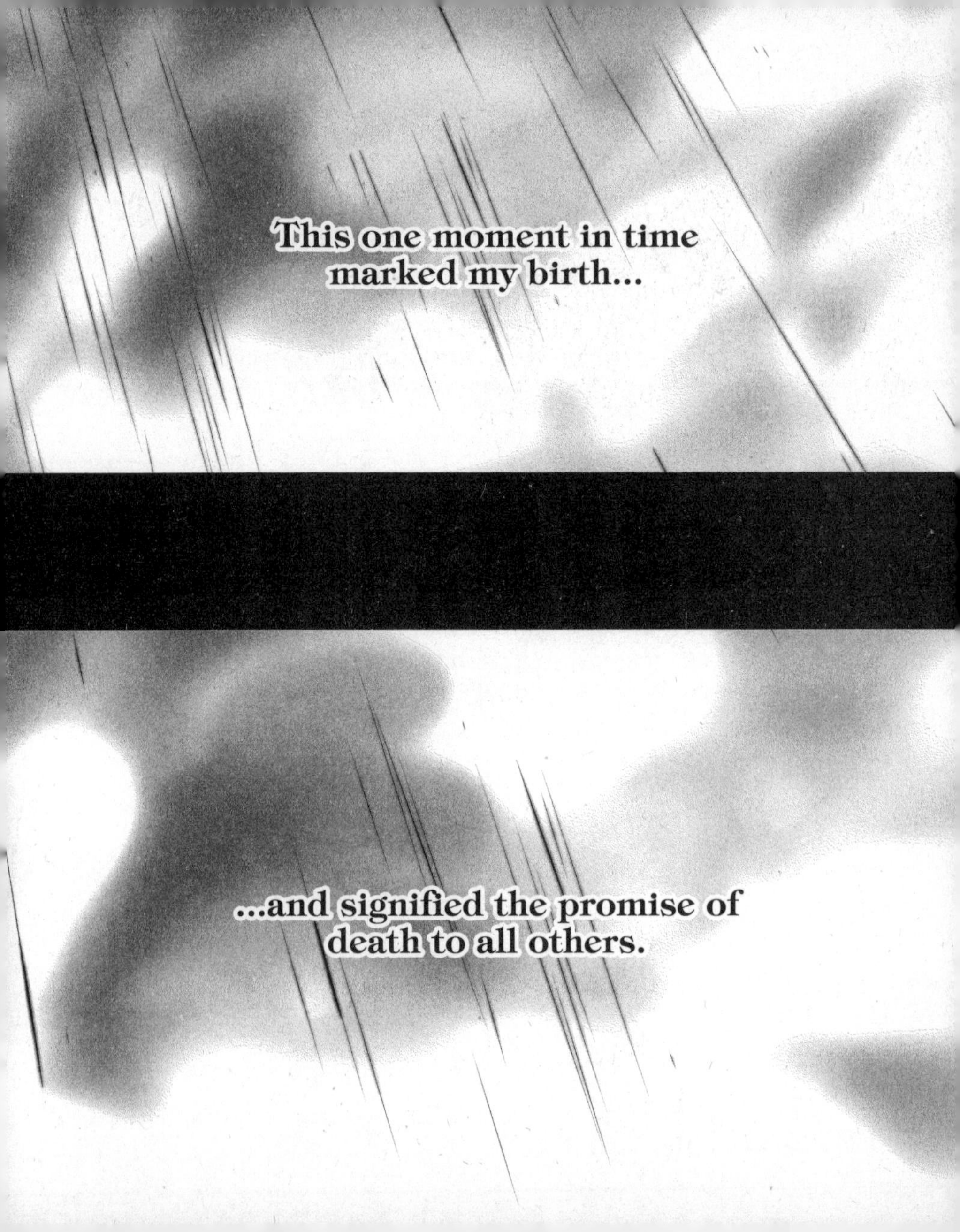
This one moment in time marked my birth...
...and signified the promise of death to all others.

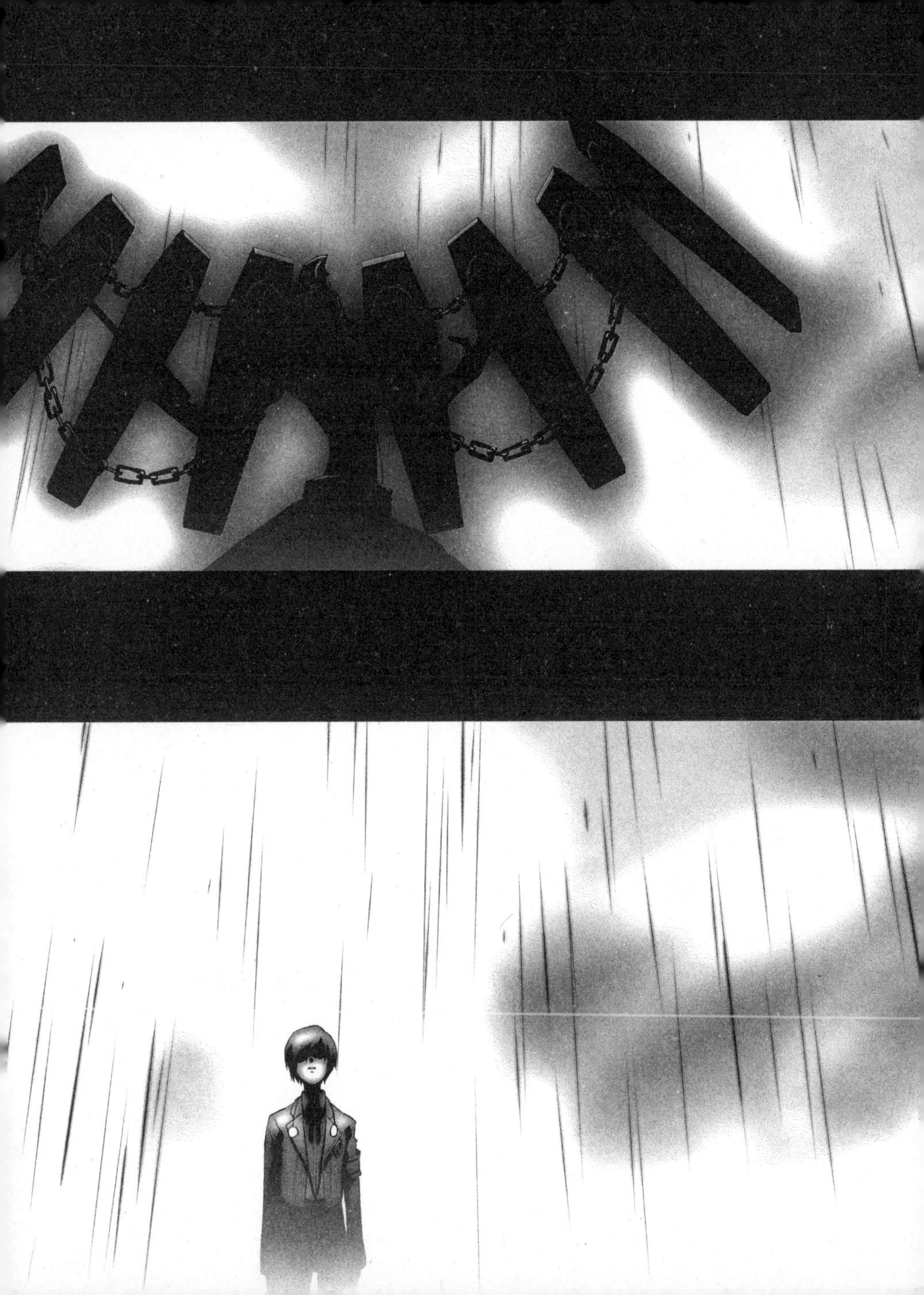

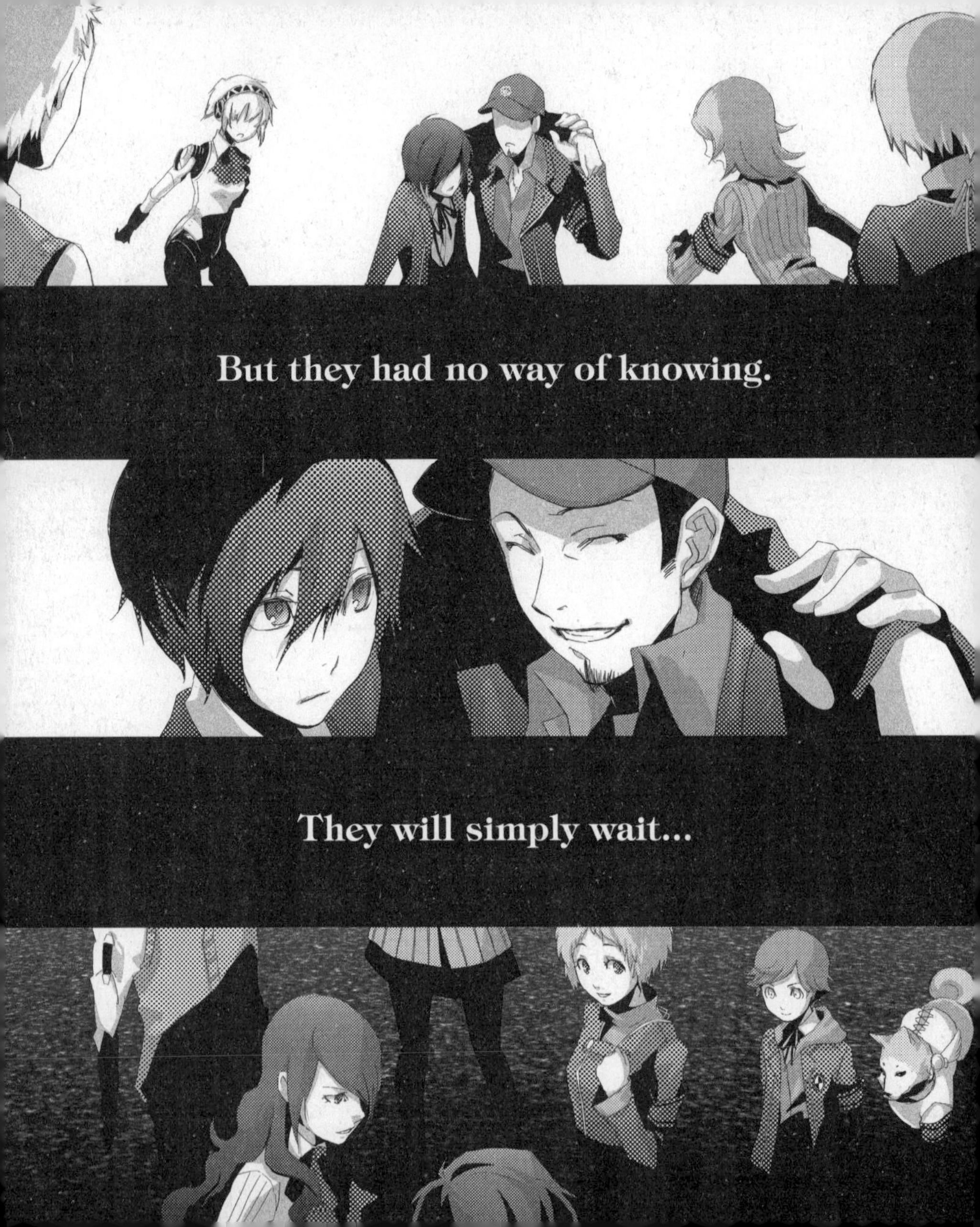
But they had no way of knowing.
They will simply wait...

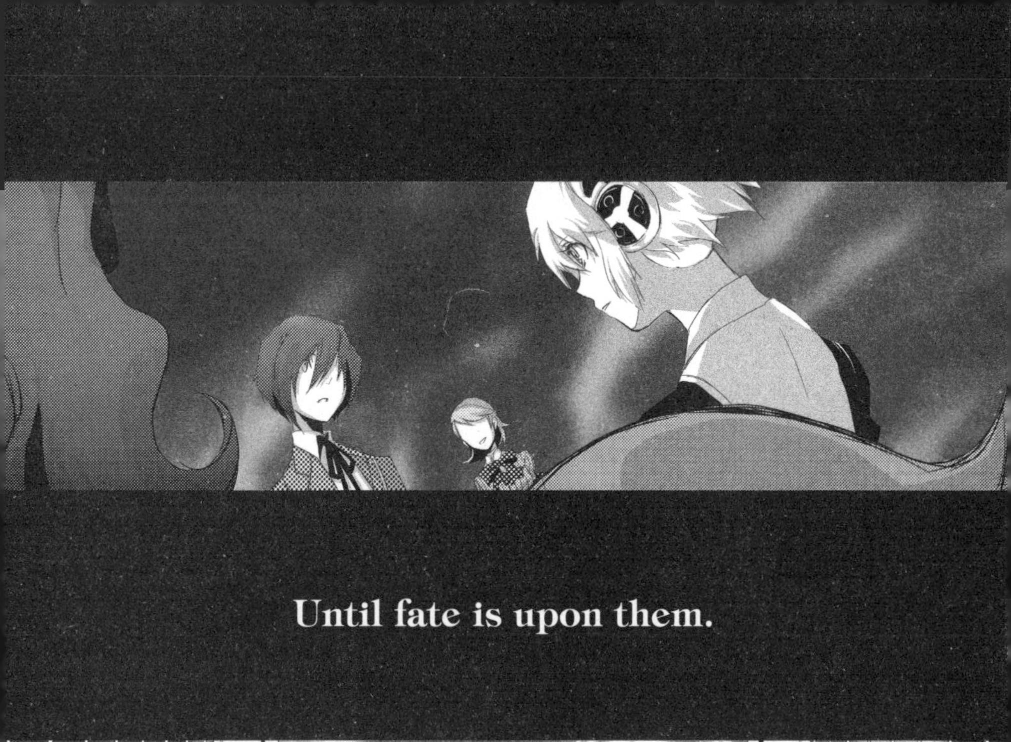

Until fate is upon them.

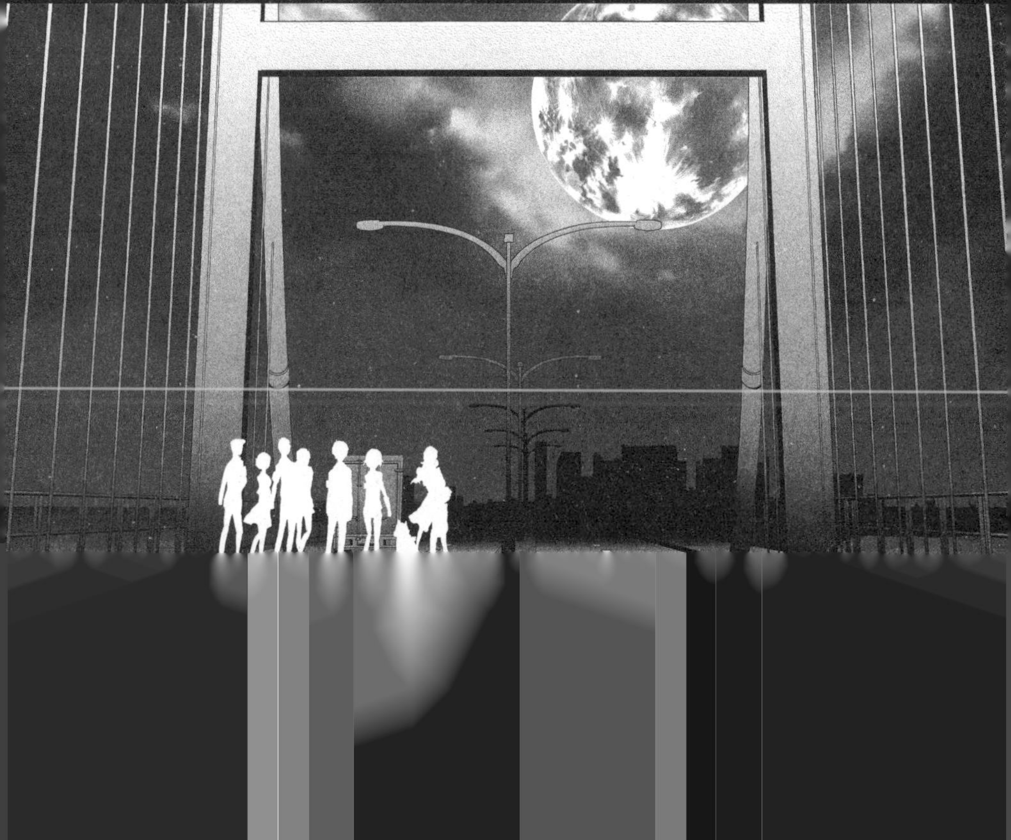

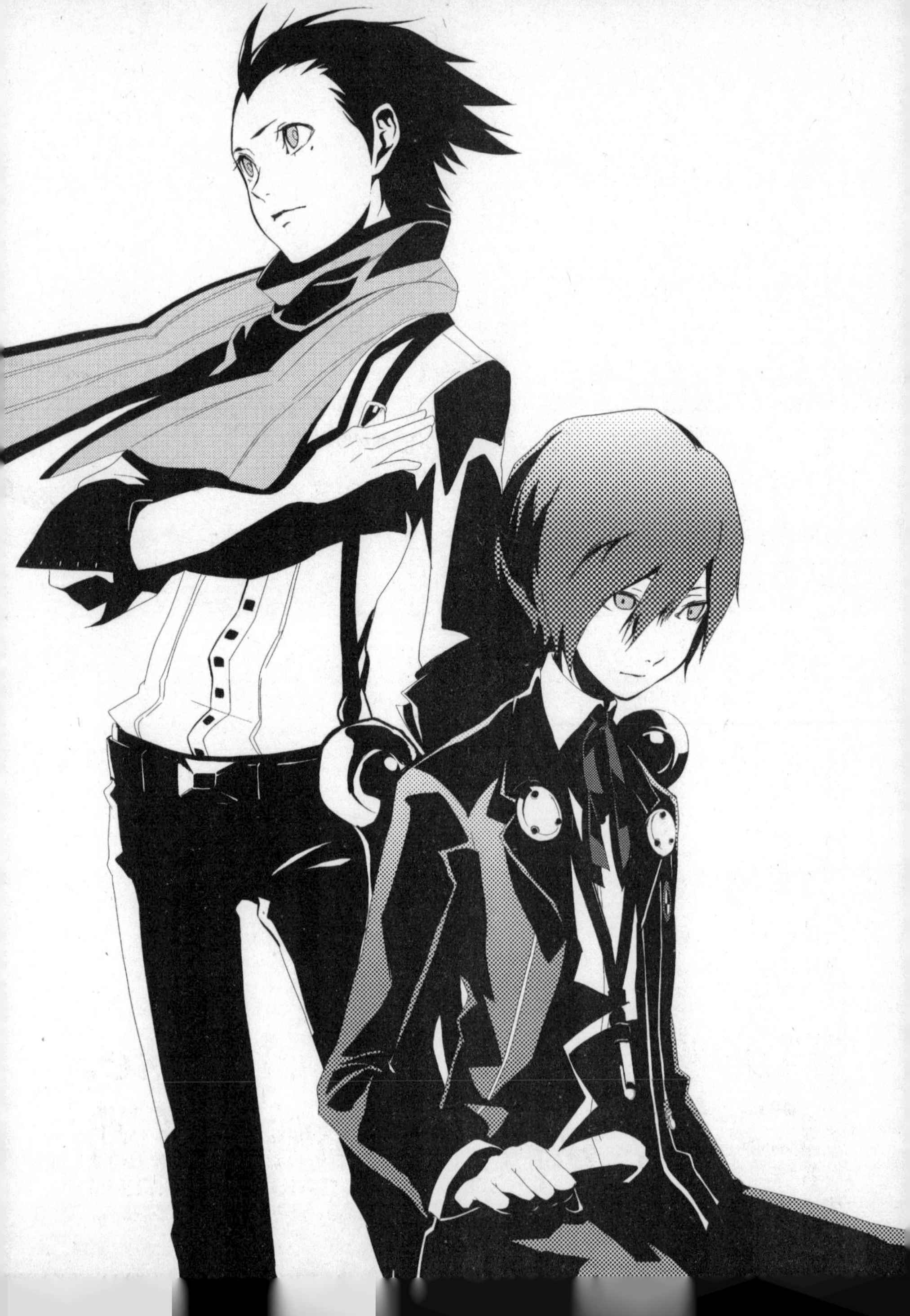

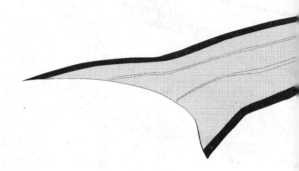

The fate that you choose.

PERSONA3

Prologue
#01 THE BEGINNING OF THE END

SHUJI SOGABE   ORIGINAL / ATLUS

Design&Finished : Studio Shortcake Screamer

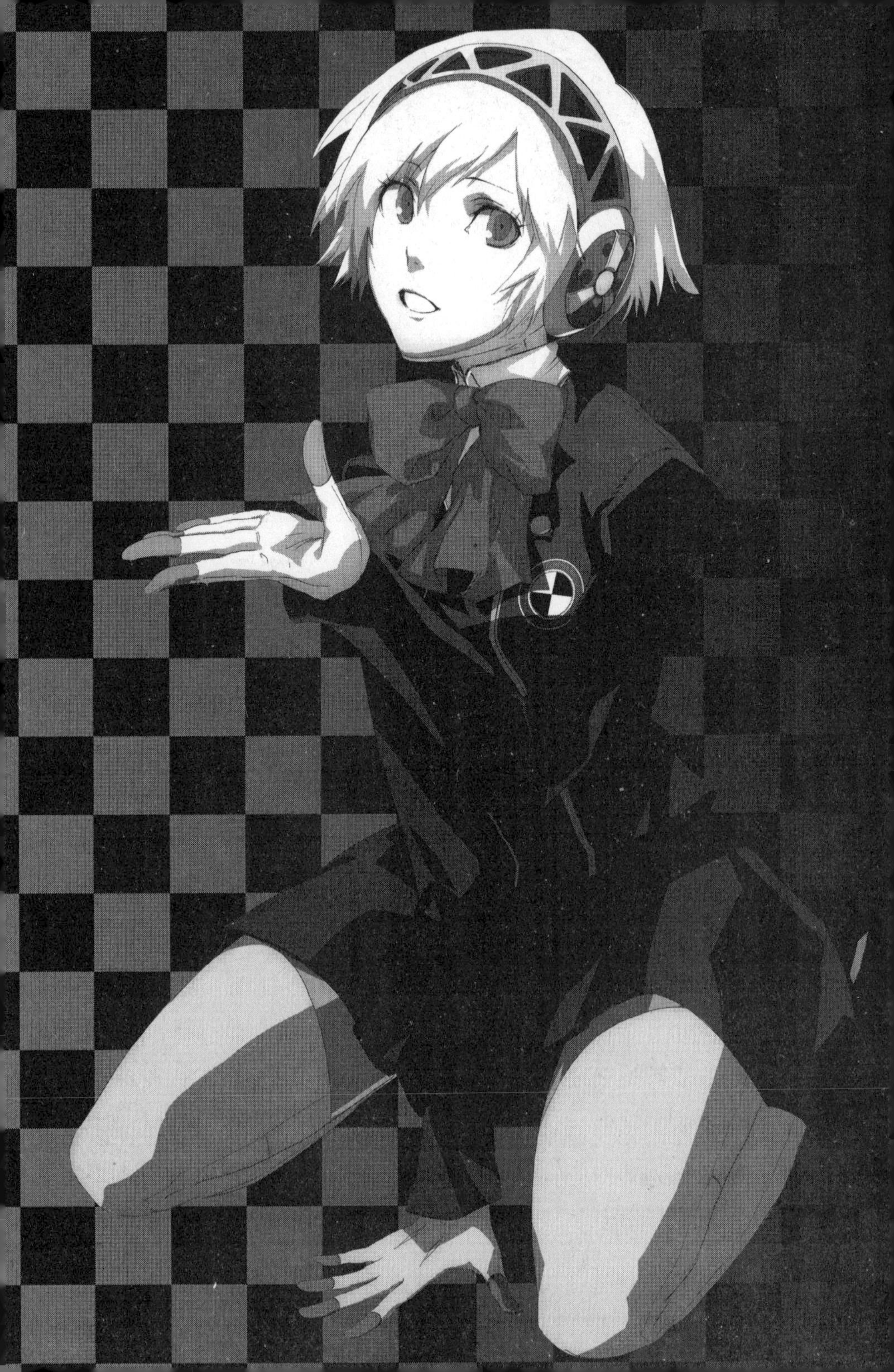

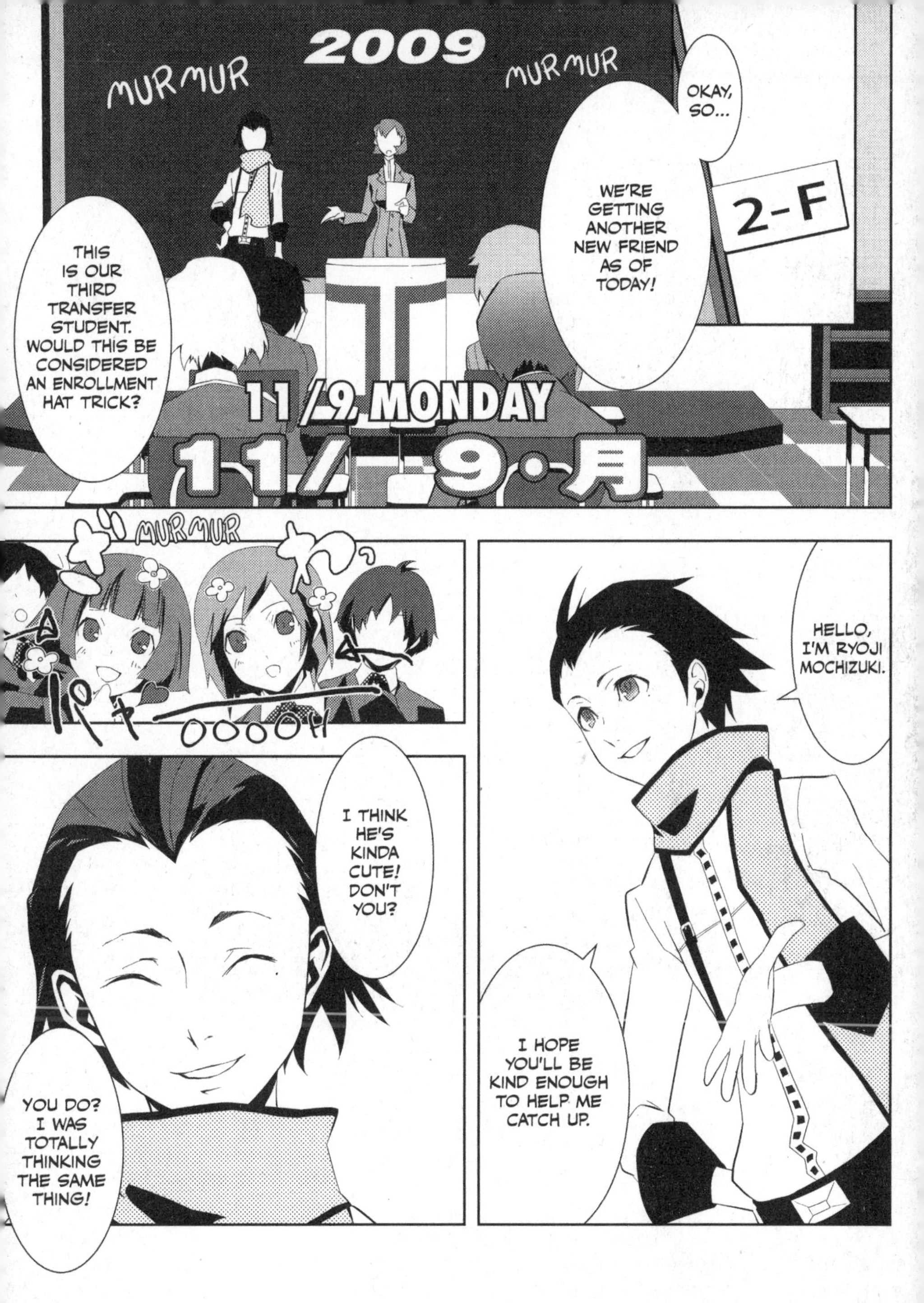
2009
MURMUR
MURMUR
2-F
OKAY, SO...
WE'RE GETTING ANOTHER NEW FRIEND AS OF TODAY!
THIS IS OUR THIRD TRANSFER STUDENT. WOULD THIS BE CONSIDERED AN ENROLLMENT HAT TRICK?
11/9 MONDAY
11/9・月
HELLO, I'M RYOJI MOCHIZUKI.
I HOPE YOU'LL BE KIND ENOUGH TO HELP ME CATCH UP.
MURMUR
OOOOH
I THINK HE'S KINDA CUTE! DON'T YOU?
YOU DO? I WAS TOTALLY THINKING THE SAME THING!

The Next Day

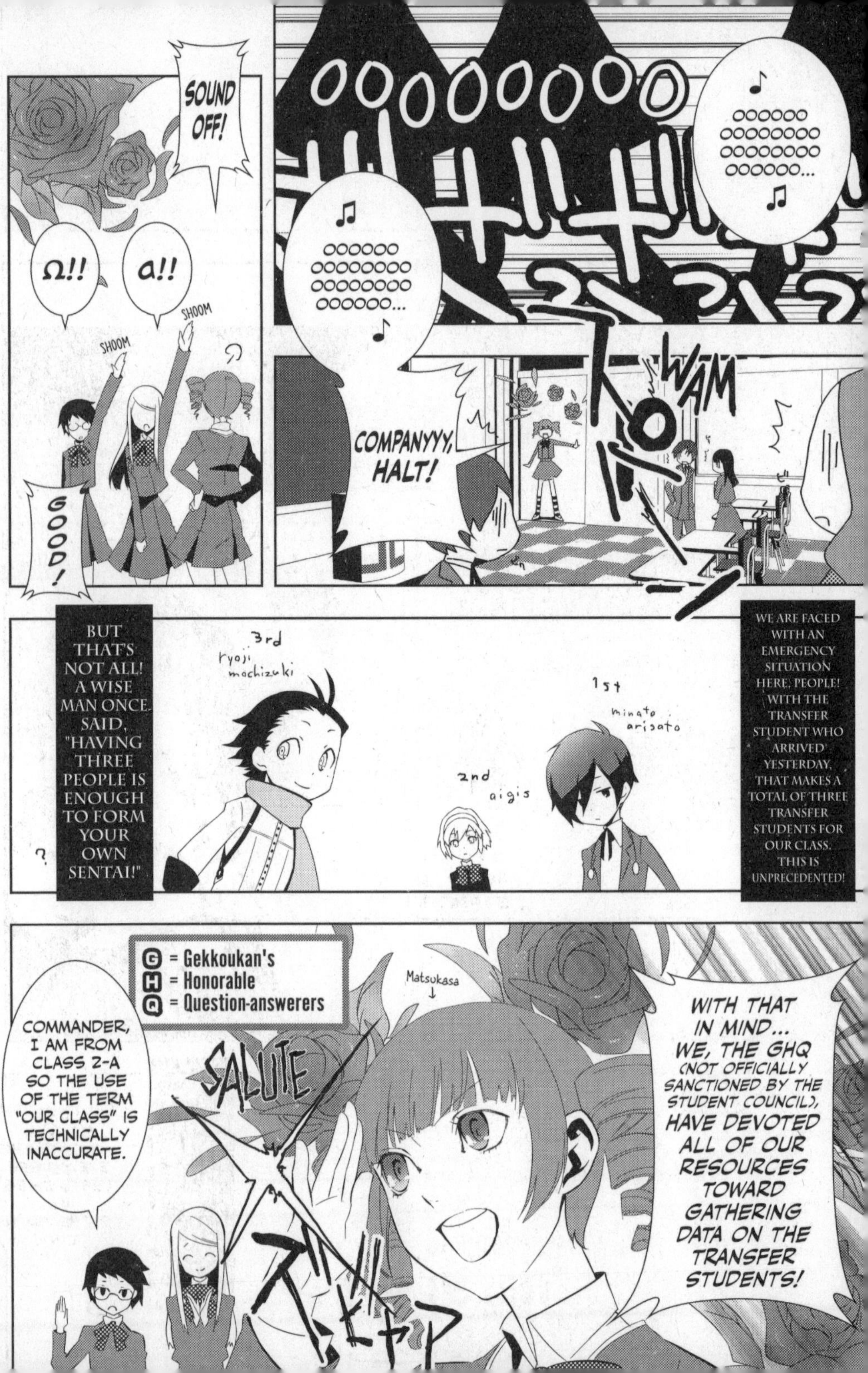
♪ OOOOOO OOOOOOOO OOOOOOOO OOOOOO... ♫
OOOOOOOO
♫ OOOOOO OOOOOOOO OOOOOOOO OOOOOO... ♪
COMPANYYY, HALT!
WAM
SOUND OFF!
Ω!!
α!!
SHOOM
SHOOM
GOOD!
WE ARE FACED WITH AN EMERGENCY SITUATION HERE, PEOPLE! WITH THE TRANSFER STUDENT WHO ARRIVED YESTERDAY, THAT MAKES A TOTAL OF THREE TRANSFER STUDENTS FOR OUR CLASS. THIS IS UNPRECEDENTED!
1st minato arisato
2nd aigis
3rd ryoji mochizuki
BUT THAT'S NOT ALL! A WISE MAN ONCE SAID, "HAVING THREE PEOPLE IS ENOUGH TO FORM YOUR OWN SENTAI!"
WITH THAT IN MIND... WE, THE GHQ (NOT OFFICIALLY SANCTIONED BY THE STUDENT COUNCIL), HAVE DEVOTED ALL OF OUR RESOURCES TOWARD GATHERING DATA ON THE TRANSFER STUDENTS!
Matsukasa ↓
SALUTE
G = Gekkoukan's
H = Honorable
Q = Question-answerers
COMMANDER, I AM FROM CLASS 2-A SO THE USE OF THE TERM "OUR CLASS" IS TECHNICALLY INACCURATE.

TRANSFER STUDENT #1

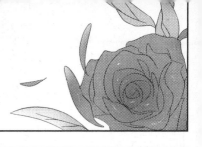

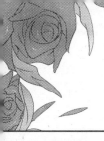

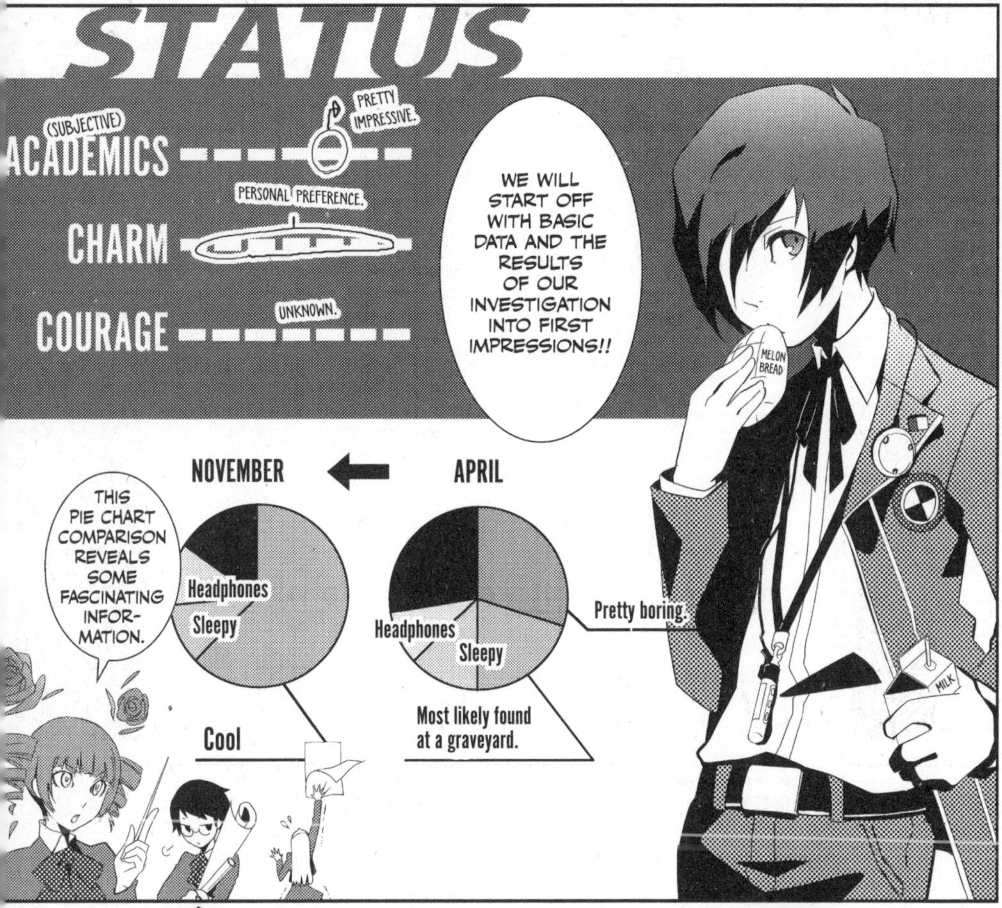
STATUS
WE WILL START OFF WITH BASIC DATA AND THE RESULTS OF OUR INVESTIGATION INTO FIRST IMPRESSIONS!!
(SUBJECTIVE)
ACADEMICS
PRETTY IMPRESSIVE.
CHARM
PERSONAL PREFERENCE.
COURAGE
UNKNOWN.
MELON BREAD
APRIL
NOVEMBER
Pretty boring.
Headphones
Sleepy
Most likely found at a graveyard.
Headphones
Sleepy
Cool
THIS PIE CHART COMPARISON REVEALS SOME FASCINATING INFOR-MATION.
MILK

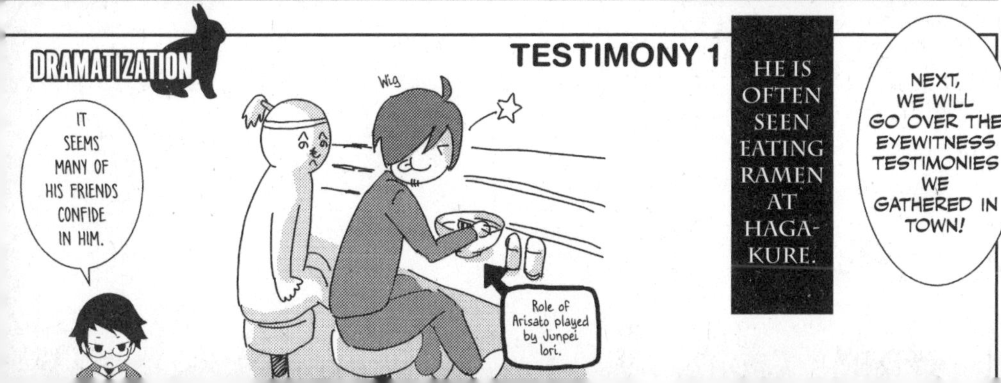
NEXT, WE WILL GO OVER THE EYEWITNESS TESTIMONIES WE GATHERED IN TOWN!
HE IS OFTEN SEEN EATING RAMEN AT HAGA-KURE.
TESTIMONY 1
Wig
Role of Arisato played by Junpei Iori.
DRAMATIZATION
IT SEEMS MANY OF HIS FRIENDS CONFIDE IN HIM.

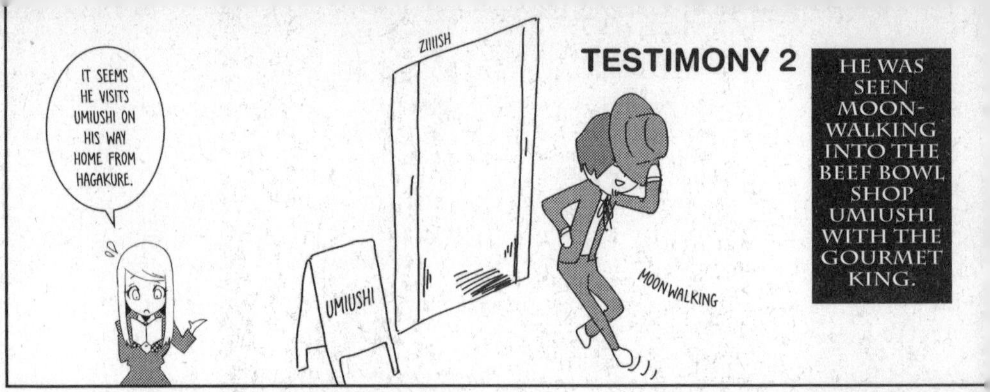
HE WAS SEEN MOON-WALKING INTO THE BEEF BOWL SHOP UMIUSHI WITH THE GOURMET KING.
TESTIMONY 2
MOONWALKING
ZIIIISH
UMIUSHI
IT SEEMS HE VISITS UMIUSHI ON HIS WAY HOME FROM HAGAKURE.

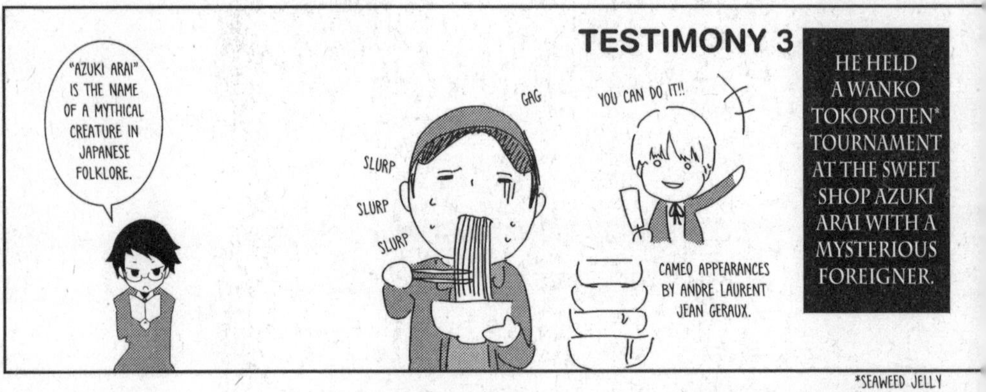
HE HELD A WANKO TOKOROTEN* TOURNAMENT AT THE SWEET SHOP AZUKI ARAI WITH A MYSTERIOUS FOREIGNER.
TESTIMONY 3
YOU CAN DO IT!!
CAMEO APPEARANCES BY ANDRE LAURENT JEAN GERAUX.
GAG
SLURP
SLURP
SLURP
"AZUKI ARAI" IS THE NAME OF A MYTHICAL CREATURE IN JAPANESE FOLKLORE.

*SEAWEED JELLY

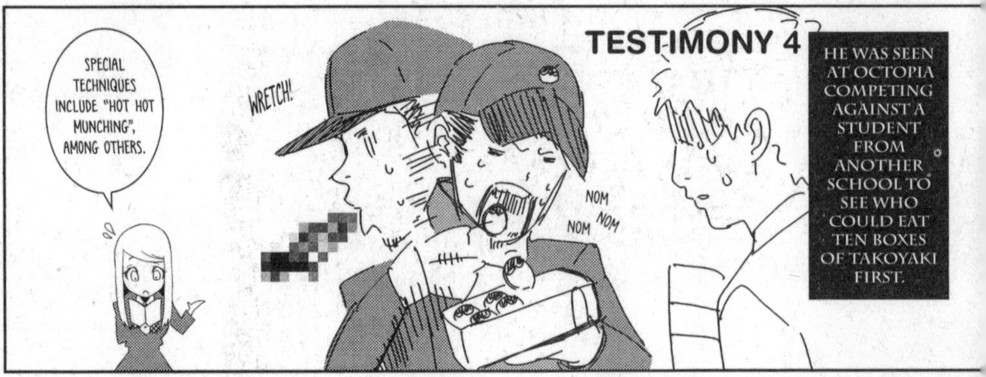
HE WAS SEEN AT OCTOPIA COMPETING AGAINST A STUDENT FROM ANOTHER SCHOOL TO SEE WHO COULD EAT TEN BOXES OF TAKOYAKI FIRST.
TESTIMONY 4
NOM
NOM
NOM
WRETCH!
SPECIAL TECHNIQUES INCLUDE "HOT HOT MUNCHING", AMONG OTHERS.

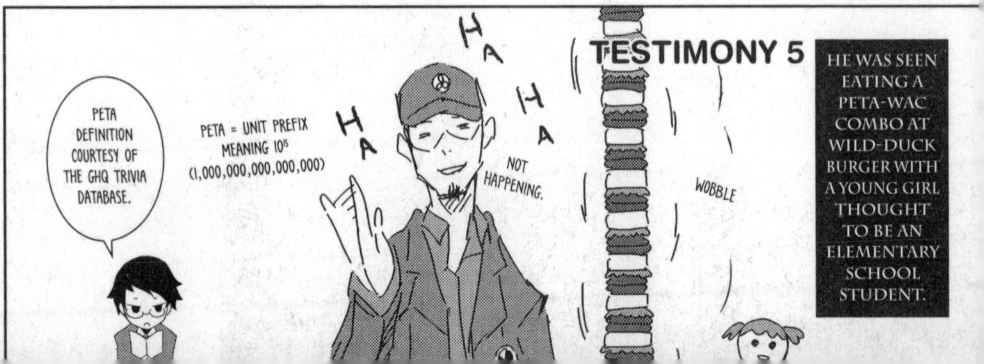
HE WAS SEEN EATING A PETA-WAC COMBO AT WILD-DUCK BURGER WITH A YOUNG GIRL THOUGHT TO BE AN ELEMENTARY SCHOOL STUDENT.
TESTIMONY 5
WOBBLE
HA
HA
HA
HA
NOT HAPPENING.
HA
HA
PETA = UNIT PREFIX MEANING 10^{15} (1,000,000,000,000,000)
PETA DEFINITION COURTESY OF THE GHQ TRIVIA DATABASE.

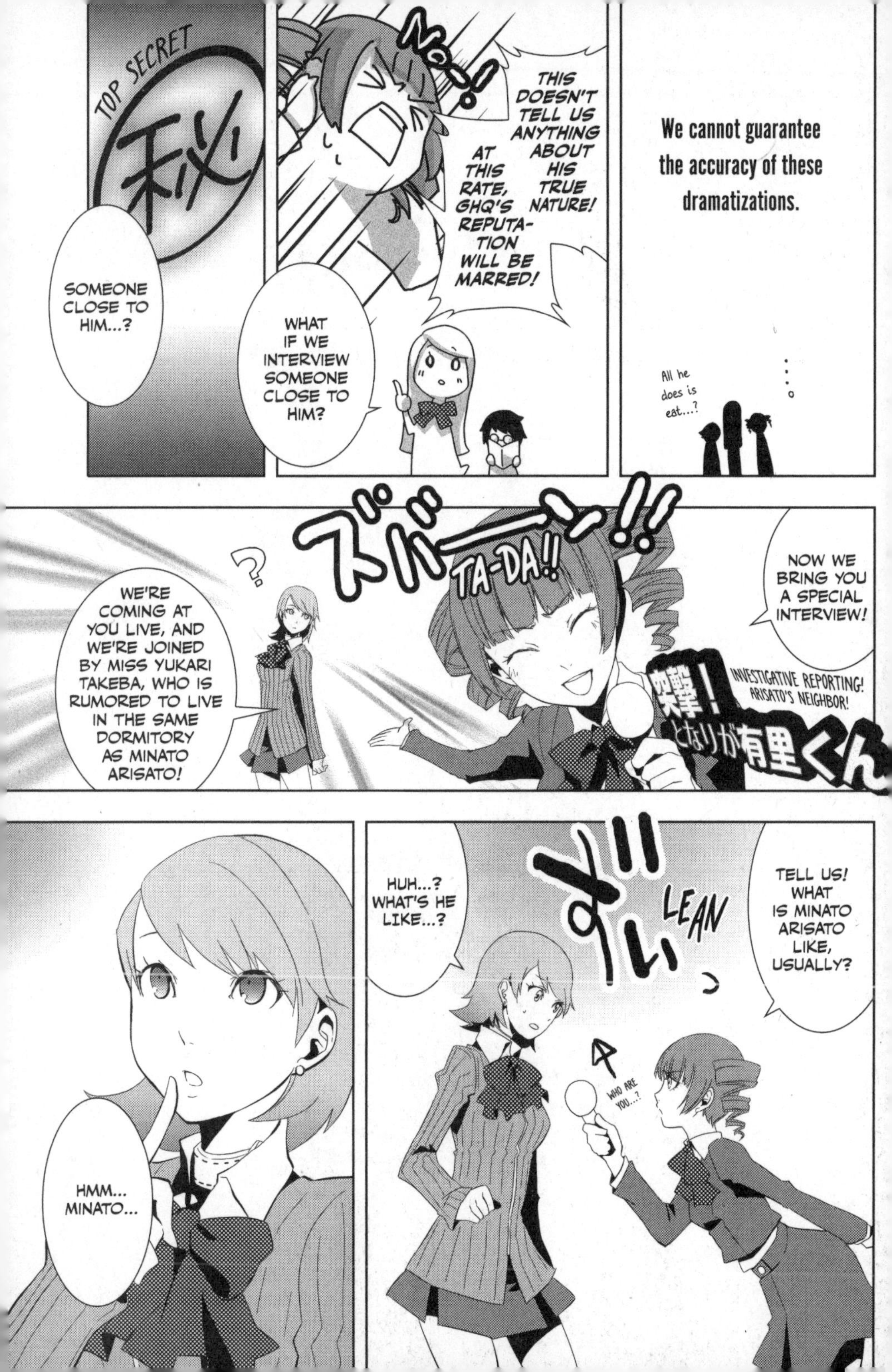
We cannot guarantee the accuracy of these dramatizations.
All he does is eat...?
...
NO--!!
THIS DOESN'T TELL US ANYTHING ABOUT HIS TRUE NATURE!
AT THIS RATE, GHQ'S REPUTATION WILL BE MARRED!
WHAT IF WE INTERVIEW SOMEONE CLOSE TO HIM?
TOP SECRET
秘
SOMEONE CLOSE TO HIM...?
NOW WE BRING YOU A SPECIAL INTERVIEW!
ズバーン!!
TA-DA!!
突撃！となりが有里くん
INVESTIGATIVE REPORTING! ARISATO'S NEIGHBOR!
?
WE'RE COMING AT YOU LIVE, AND WE'RE JOINED BY MISS YUKARI TAKEBA, WHO IS RUMORED TO LIVE IN THE SAME DORMITORY AS MINATO ARISATO!
TELL US! WHAT IS MINATO ARISATO LIKE, USUALLY?
ずい
LEAN
WHO ARE YOU...?
HUH...? WHAT'S HE LIKE...?
HMM... MINATO...

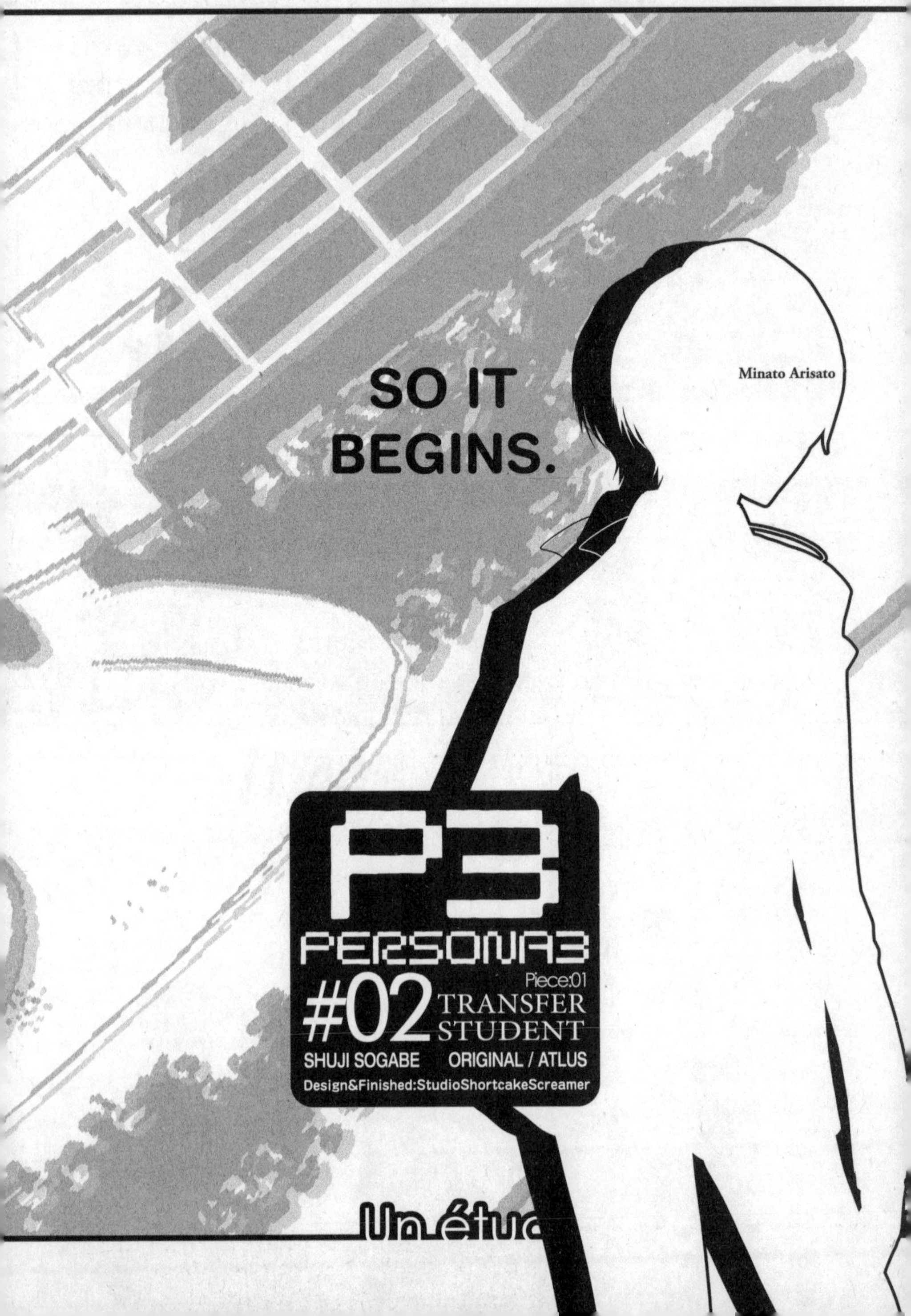
SO IT BEGINS.
Minato Arisato
P3
PERSONA3
#02
Piece:01
TRANSFER STUDENT
SHUJI SOGABE
ORIGINAL / ATLUS
Design&Finished:StudioShortcakeScreamer

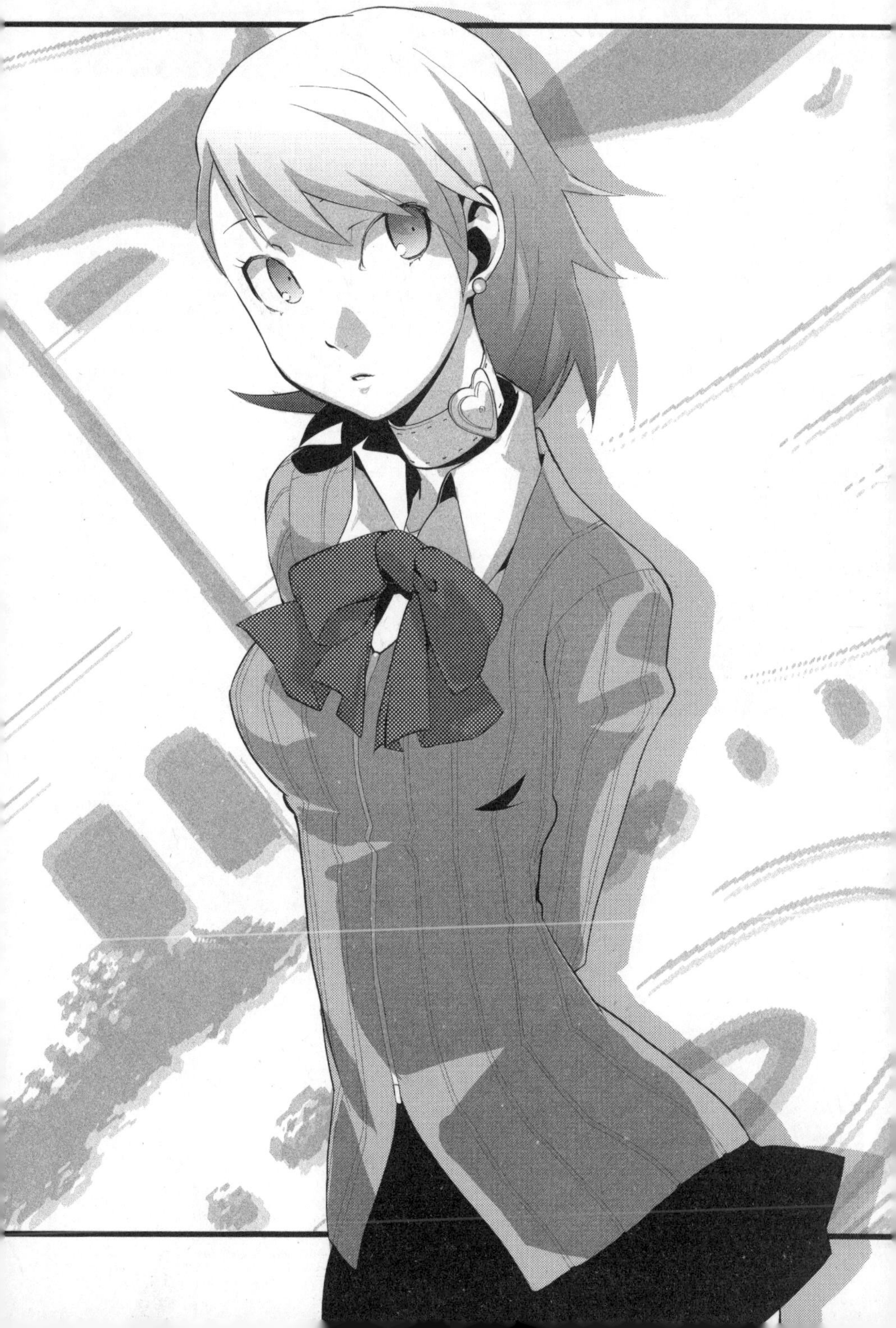

4/6 MONDAY

eamless do
cking clock
walk away from
a soundless room
Windless
night, moonligh
elts M
ostly shadow

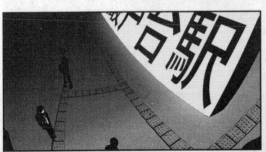

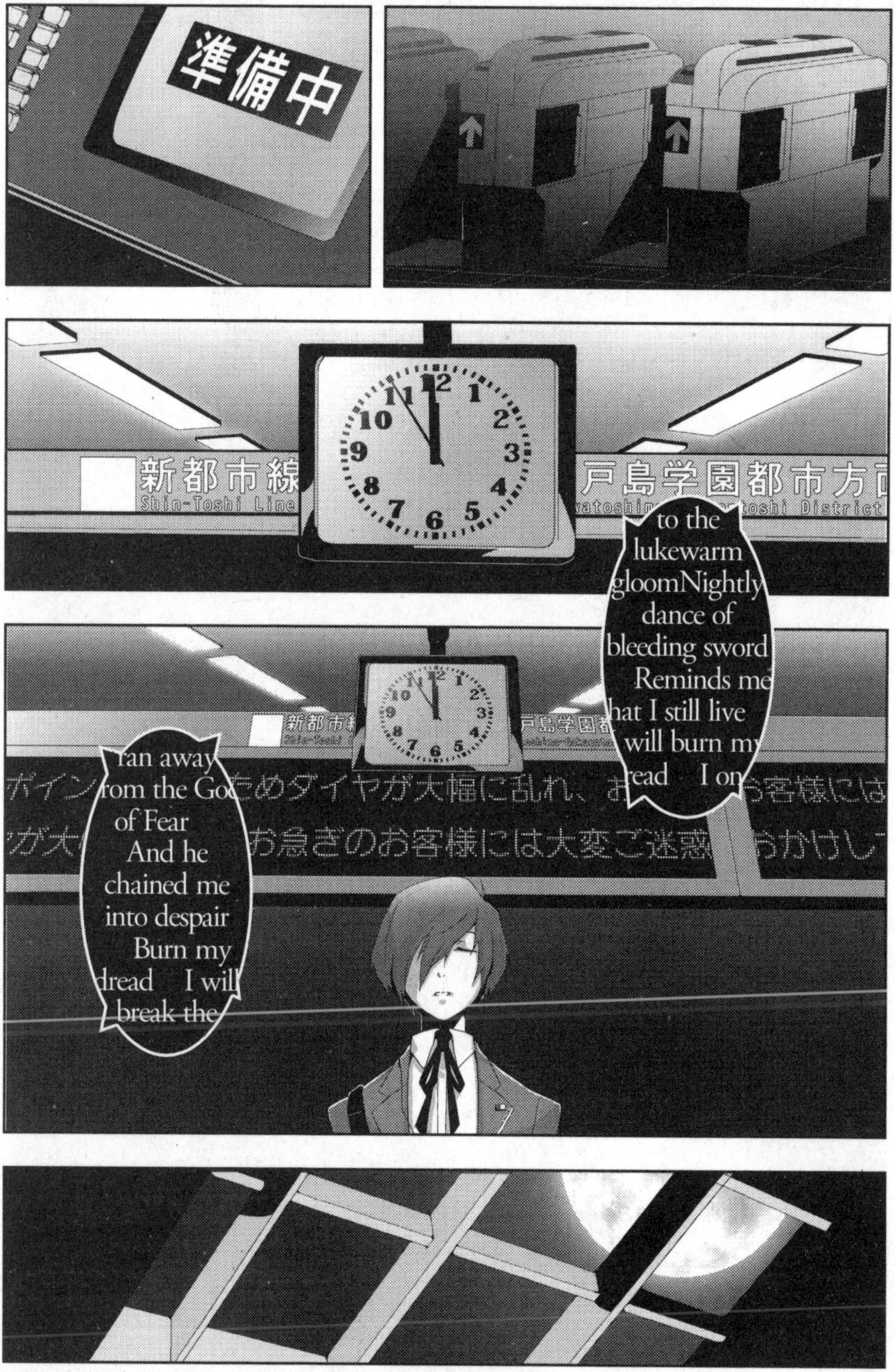
準備中
新都市線
Shin-Toshi Line
戸島学園都市方
toshi District
to the lukewarm gloomNightly dance of bleeding sword Reminds me hat I still live will burn my read I on
ため ダイヤが大幅に乱れ、お お客様には
お急ぎのお客様には大変ご迷惑 おかけし
ran away rom the Go of Fear And he chained me into despair Burn my dread I will break the

 新都市線 戸島学園都市方面
Shin-Toshi Line Toshima Gakuentoshi District

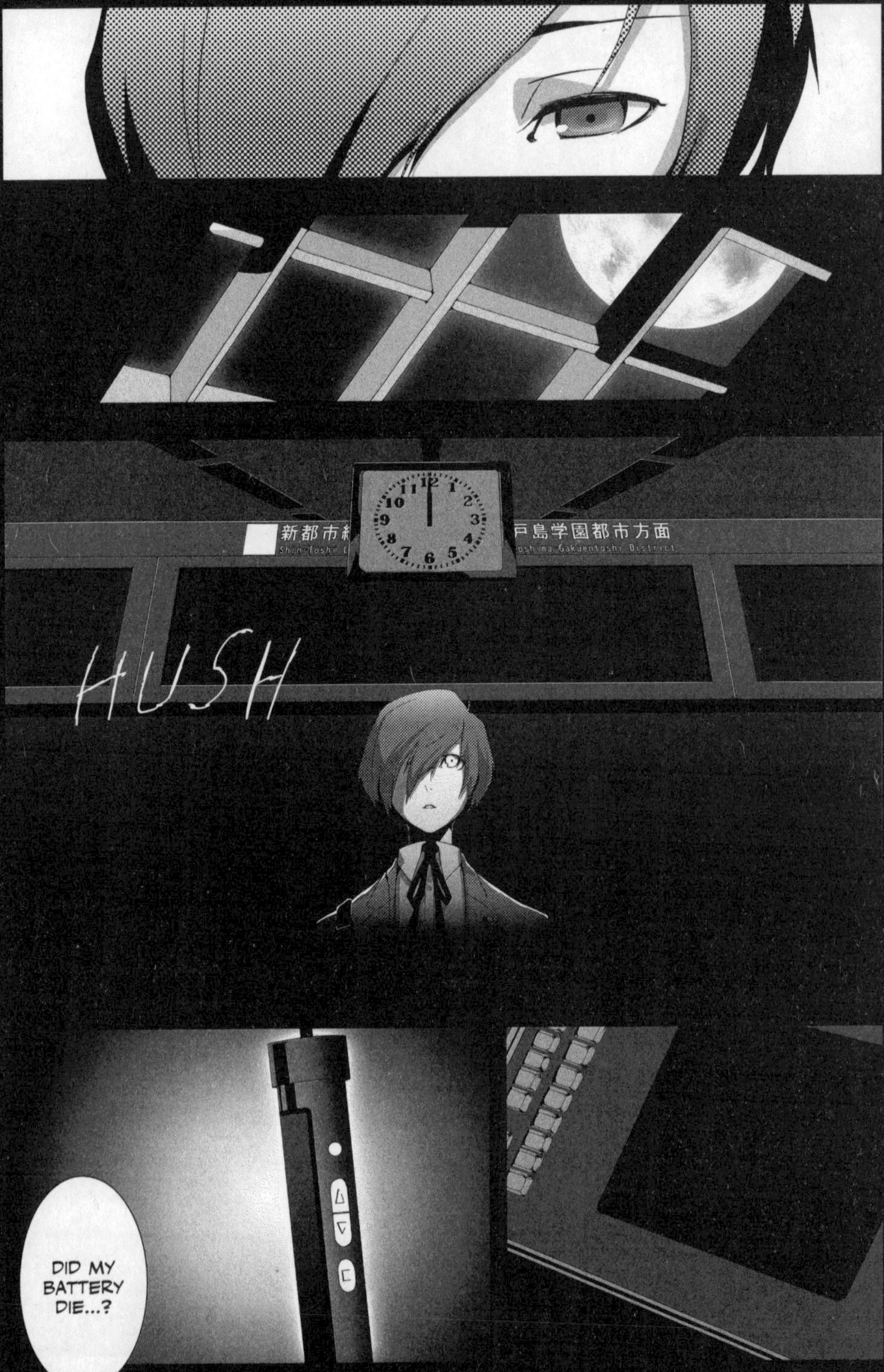

HUSH

DID MY
BATTERY
DIE...?

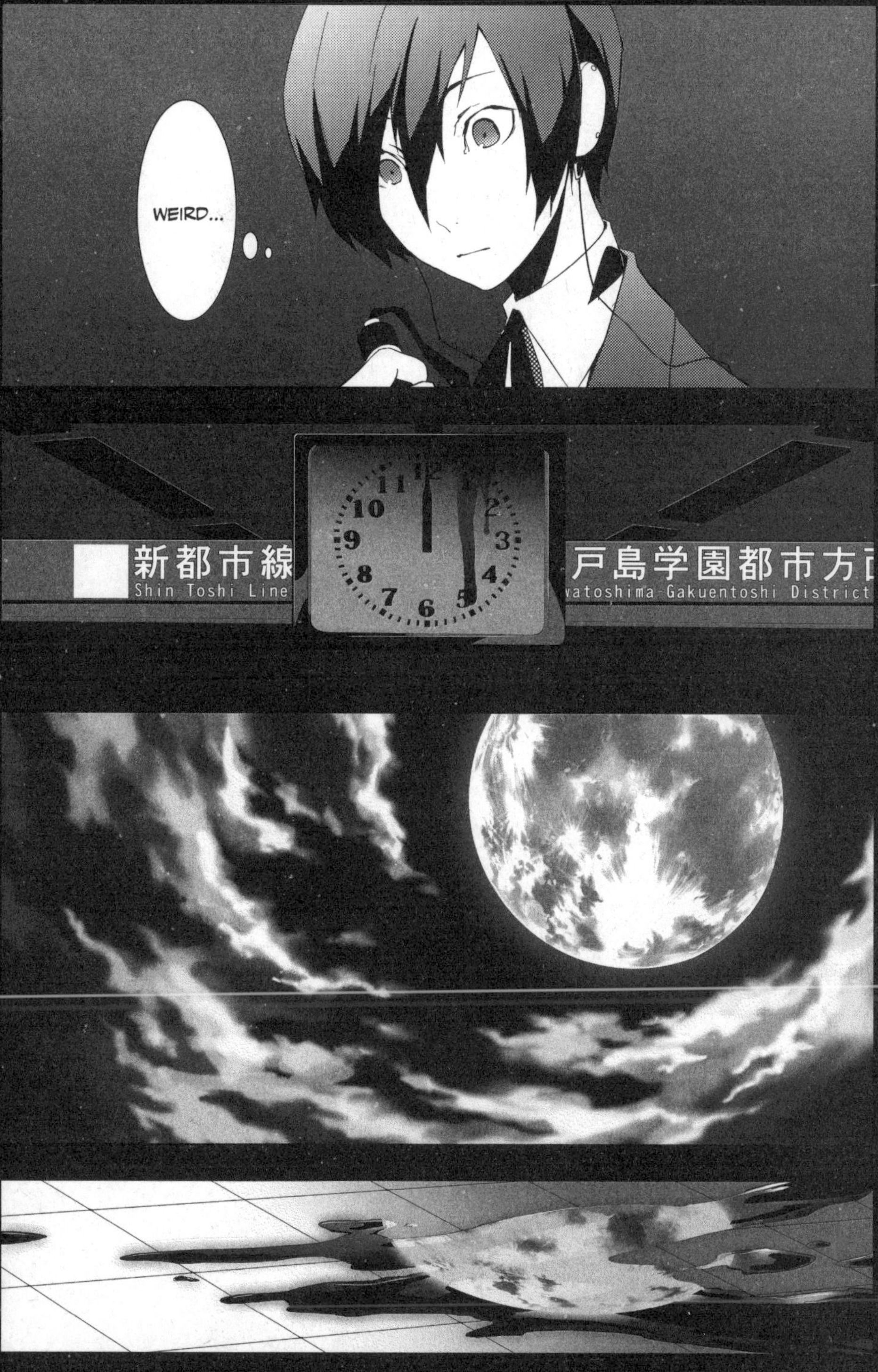
WEIRD...
新都市線
Shin-Toshi Line
戸島学園都市方
watoshima-Gakuentoshi District

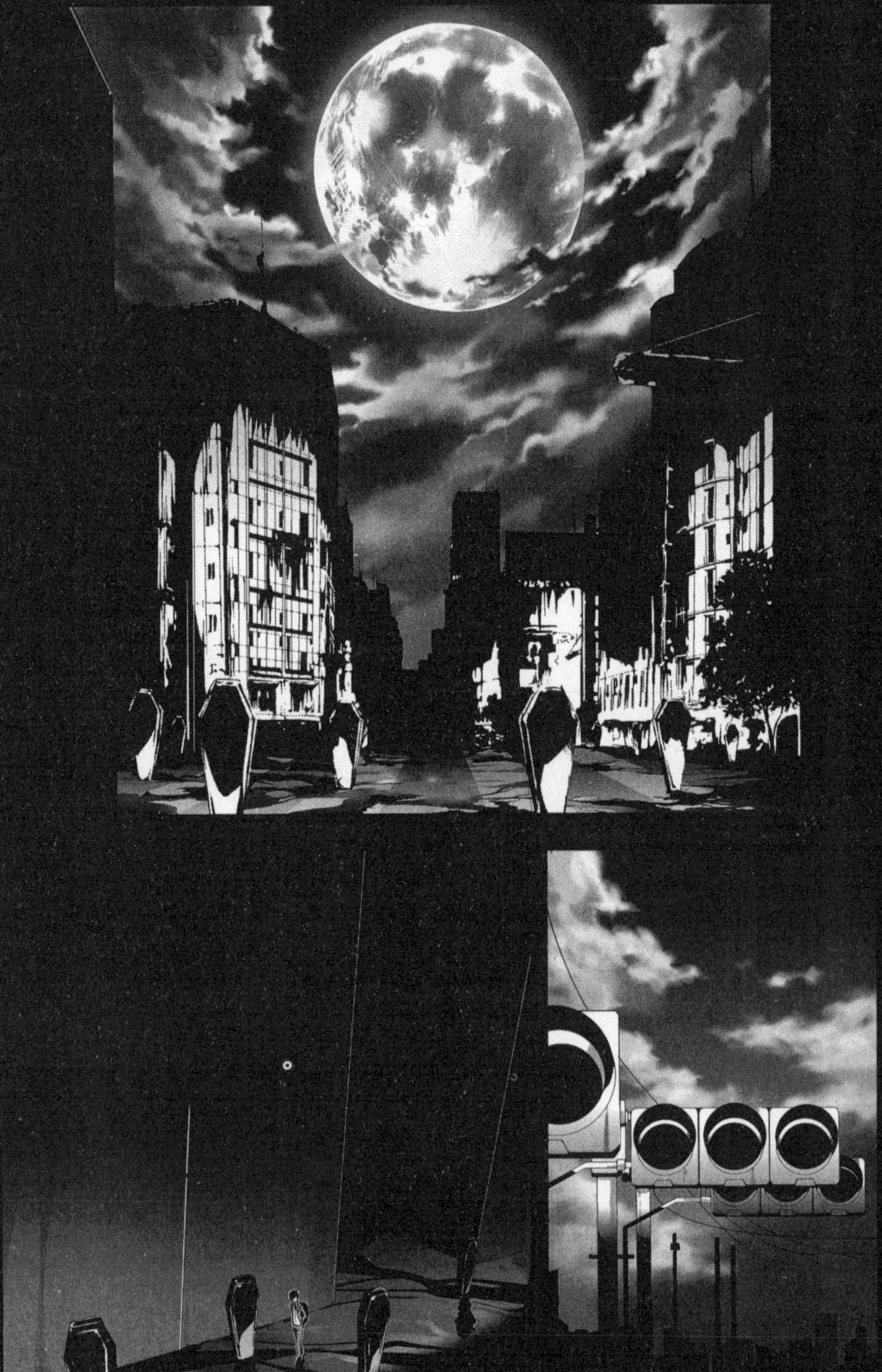

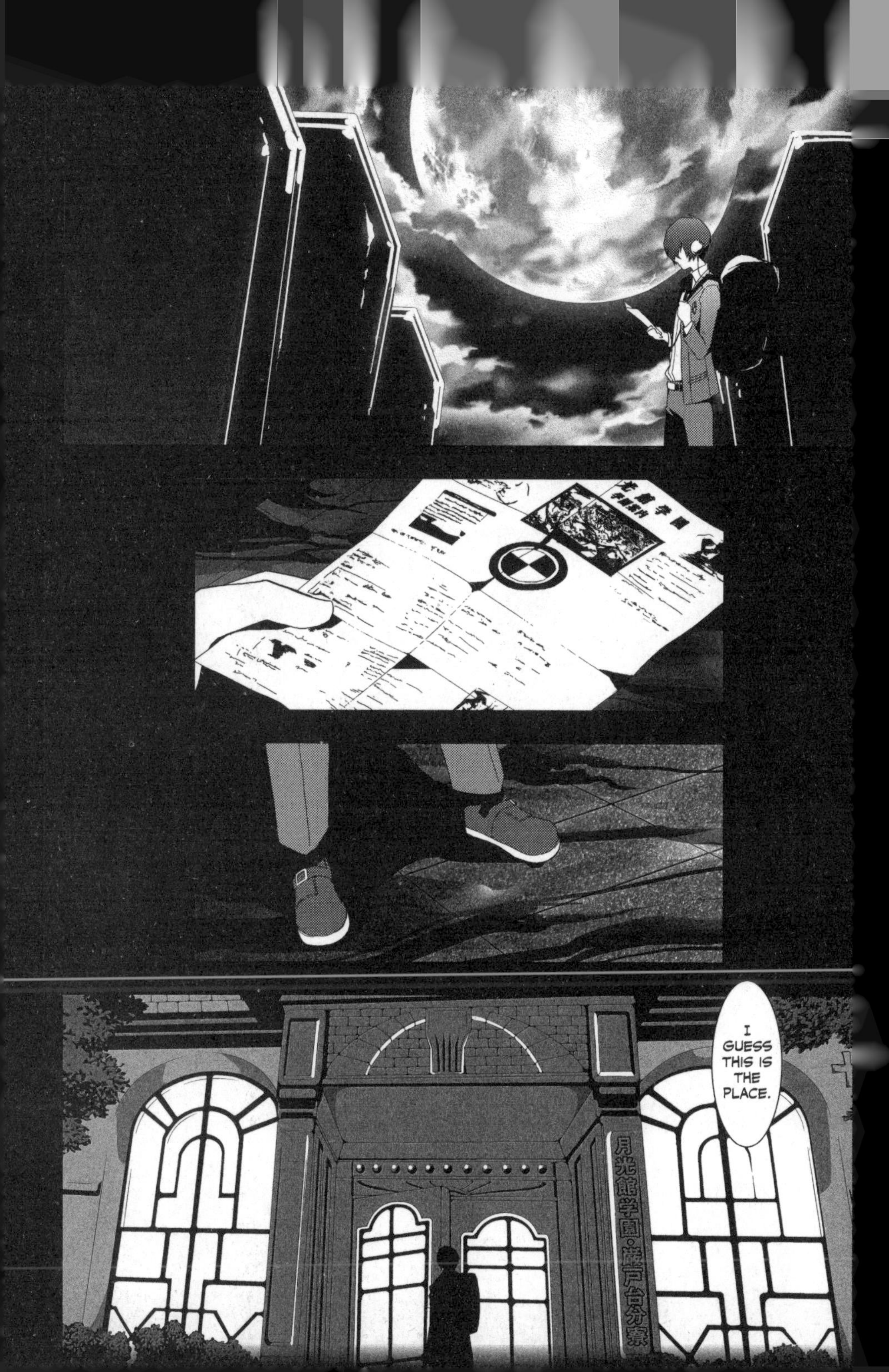
I GUESS THIS IS THE PLACE.
月光館学園・巌戸台分寮

YOU'RE LATE.

I'VE BEEN WAITING A LONG TIME FOR YOU.

IF YOU WISH TO PROCEED...

YOU MUST SIGN YOUR NAME THERE.

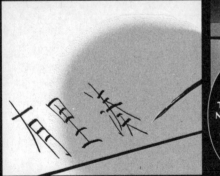

IT IS A BINDING CONTRACT,

BUT THERE'S NO NEED TO WORRY.

IT SIMPLY STATES THAT YOU ALONE WILL BE HELD RESPONSIBLE

FOR YOUR DECISIONS AND ACTIONS BEYOND THIS POINT...

PRETTY STANDARD STUFF.

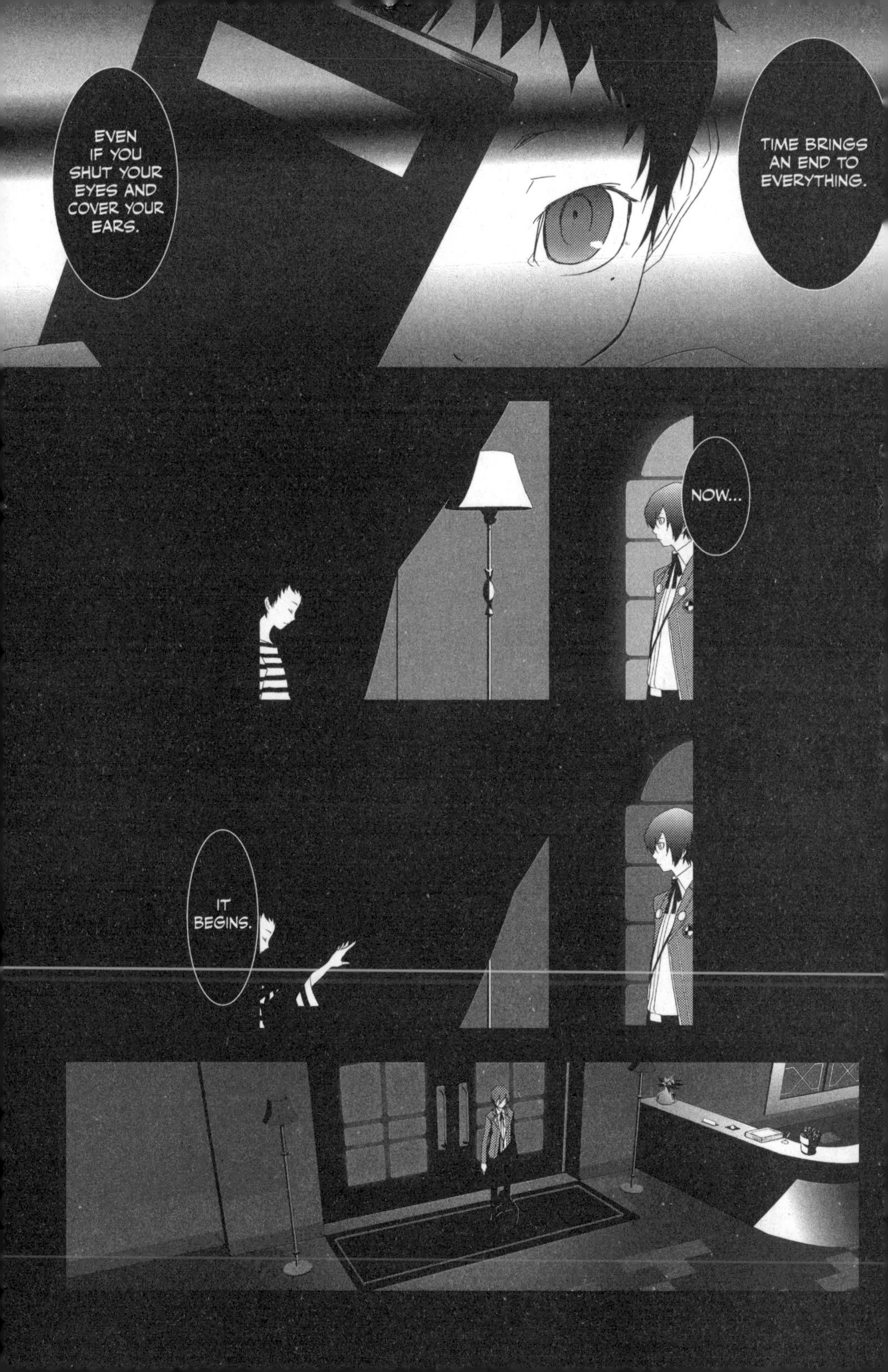

TIME BRINGS AN END TO EVERYTHING.
EVEN IF YOU SHUT YOUR EYES AND COVER YOUR EARS.
NOW...
IT BEGINS.

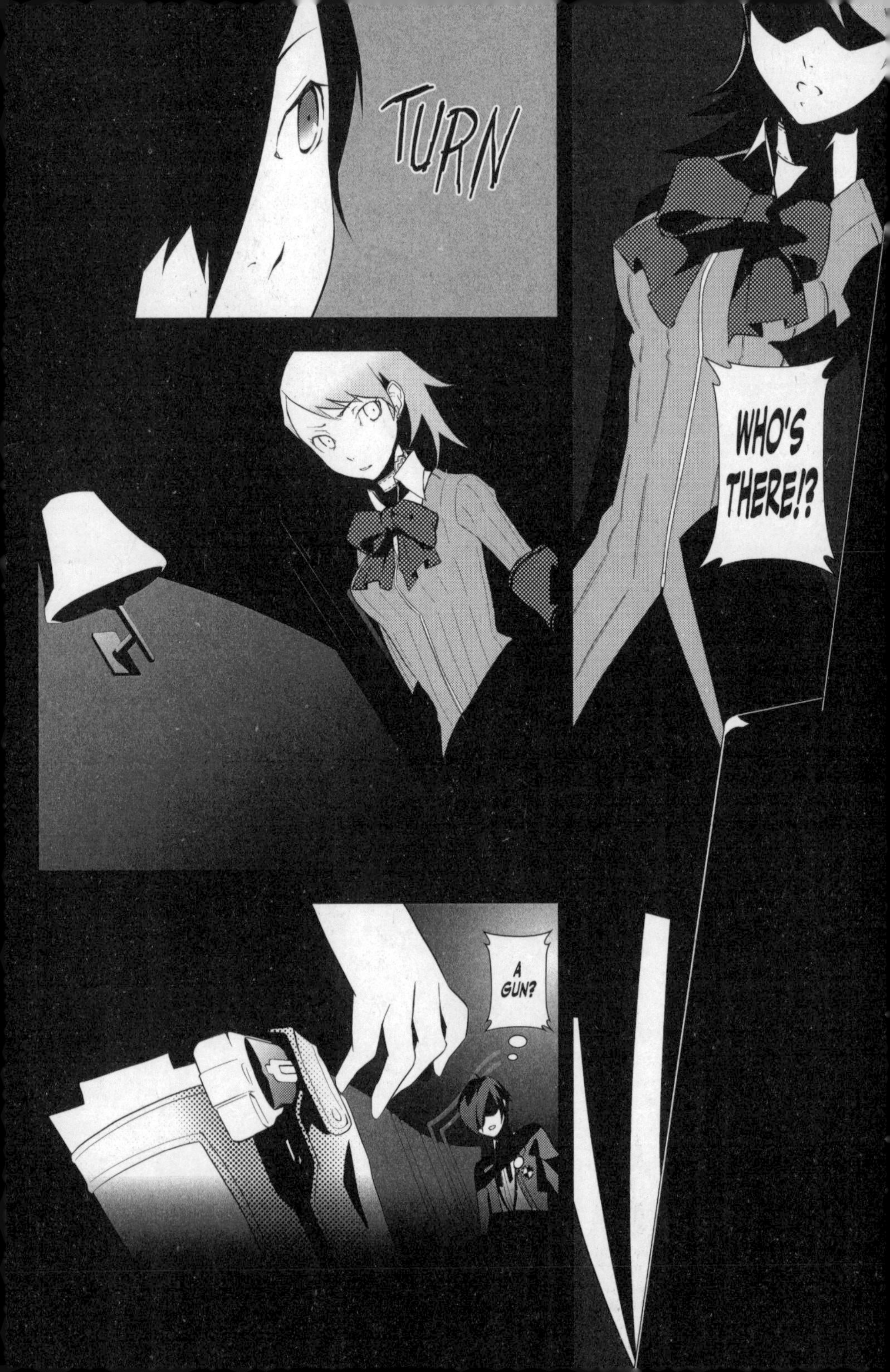
WHO'S THERE!?
TURN
A GUN?

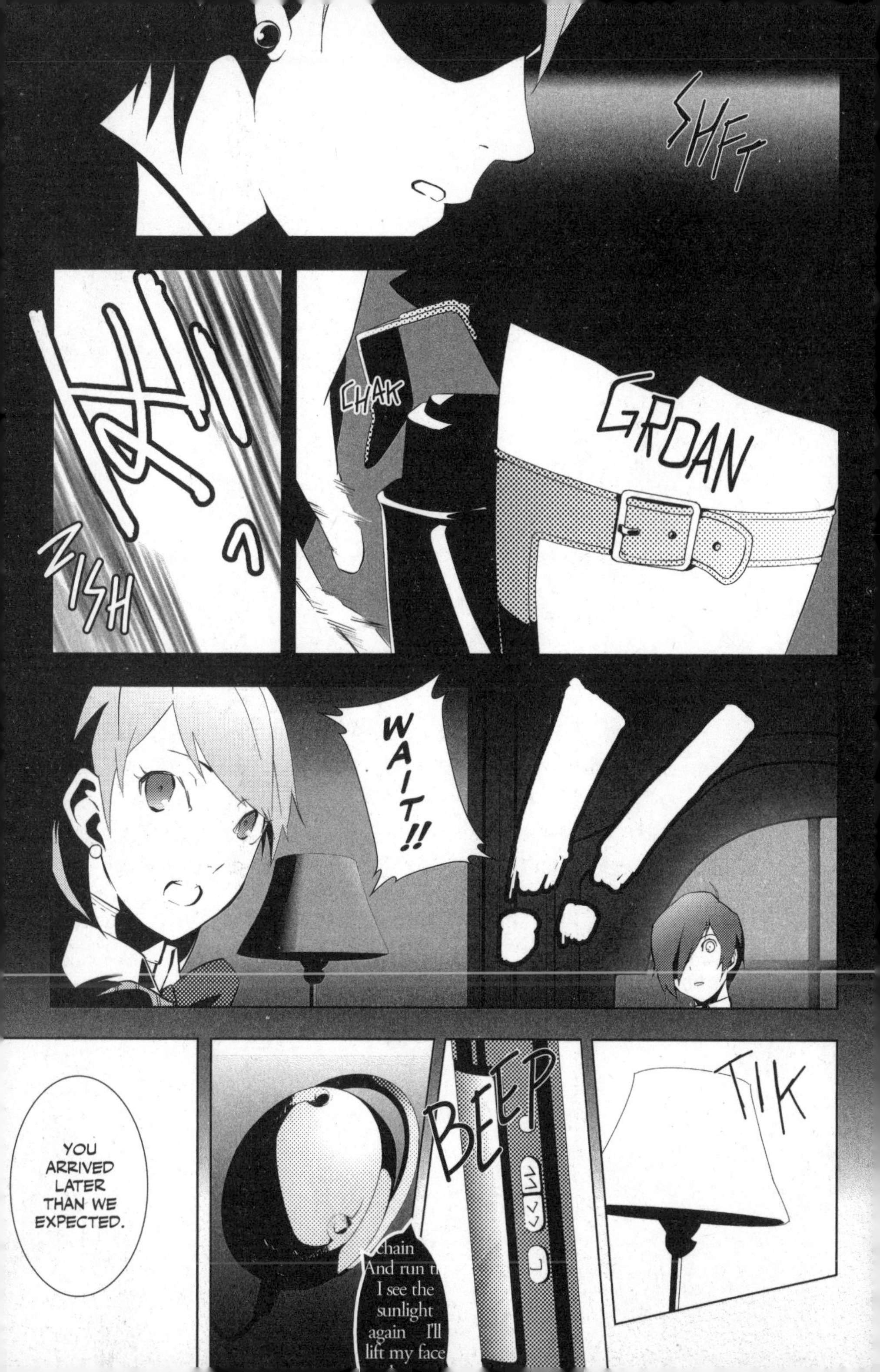

SHFT
GRDAN
CHAK
ZISH
WAIT!!
TIK
BEEP
chain
I see the sunlight again I'll lift my face
YOU ARRIVED LATER THAN WE EXPECTED.

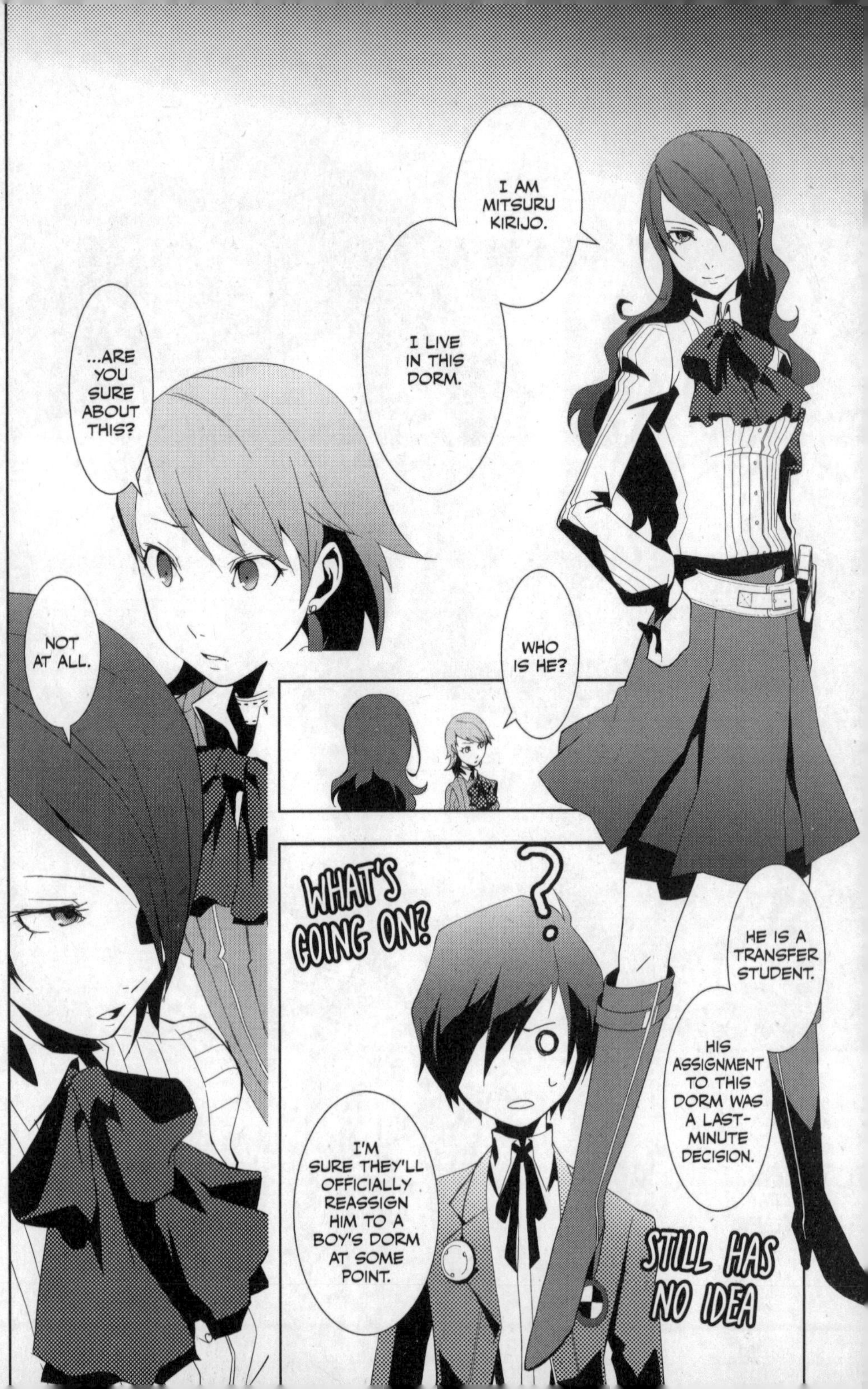
I AM MITSURU KIRIJO.
I LIVE IN THIS DORM.
WHO IS HE?
HE IS A TRANSFER STUDENT.
HIS ASSIGNMENT TO THIS DORM WAS A LAST-MINUTE DECISION.
WHAT'S GOING ON?
I'M SURE THEY'LL OFFICIALLY REASSIGN HIM TO A BOY'S DORM AT SOME POINT.
STILL HAS NO IDEA
...ARE YOU SURE ABOUT THIS?
NOT AT ALL.

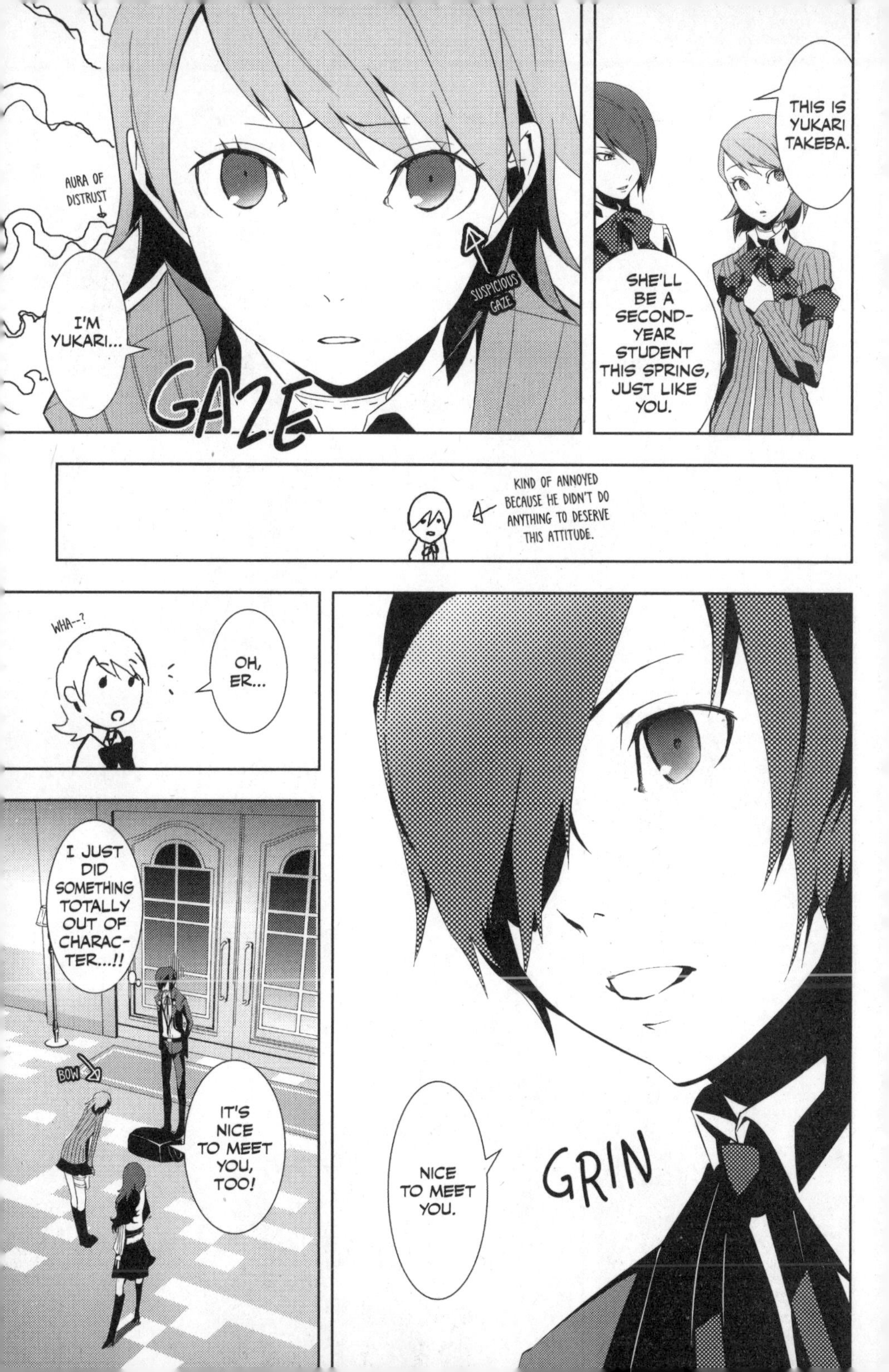
THIS IS YUKARI TAKEBA.
SHE'LL BE A SECOND-YEAR STUDENT THIS SPRING, JUST LIKE YOU.
AURA OF DISTRUST
I'M YUKARI...
SUSPICIOUS GAZE
GAZE
KIND OF ANNOYED BECAUSE HE DIDN'T DO ANYTHING TO DESERVE THIS ATTITUDE.
GRIN
NICE TO MEET YOU.
WHA--?
OH, ER...
I JUST DID SOMETHING TOTALLY OUT OF CHARAC-TER...!!
BOW
IT'S NICE TO MEET YOU, TOO!

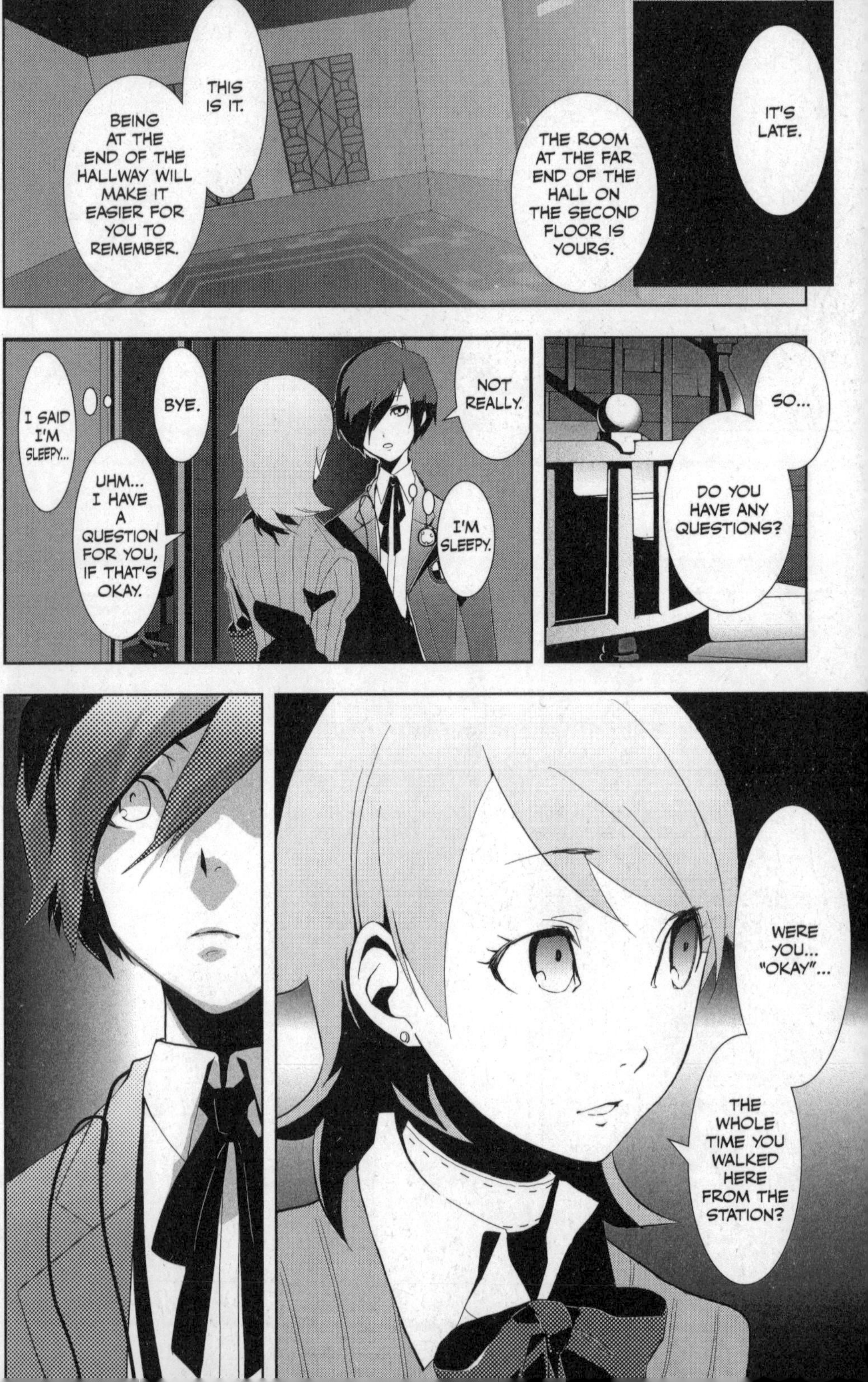
IT'S LATE.
THE ROOM AT THE FAR END OF THE HALL ON THE SECOND FLOOR IS YOURS.
THIS IS IT.
BEING AT THE END OF THE HALLWAY WILL MAKE IT EASIER FOR YOU TO REMEMBER.
SO...
DO YOU HAVE ANY QUESTIONS?
NOT REALLY.
I'M SLEEPY.
BYE.
UHM... I HAVE A QUESTION FOR YOU, IF THAT'S OKAY.
I SAID I'M SLEEPY...
WERE YOU... "OKAY"...
THE WHOLE TIME YOU WALKED HERE FROM THE STATION?

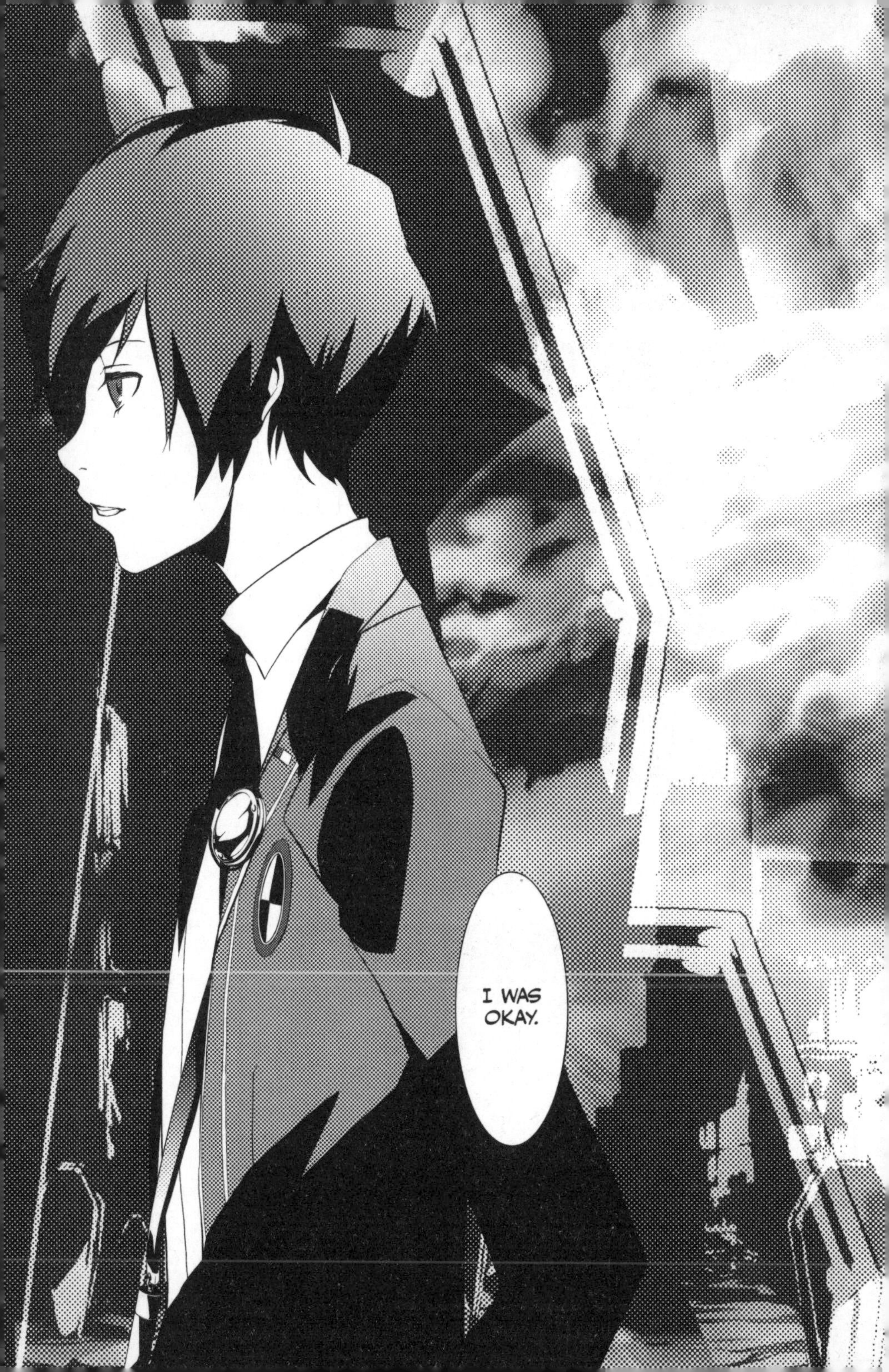
I WAS OKAY.

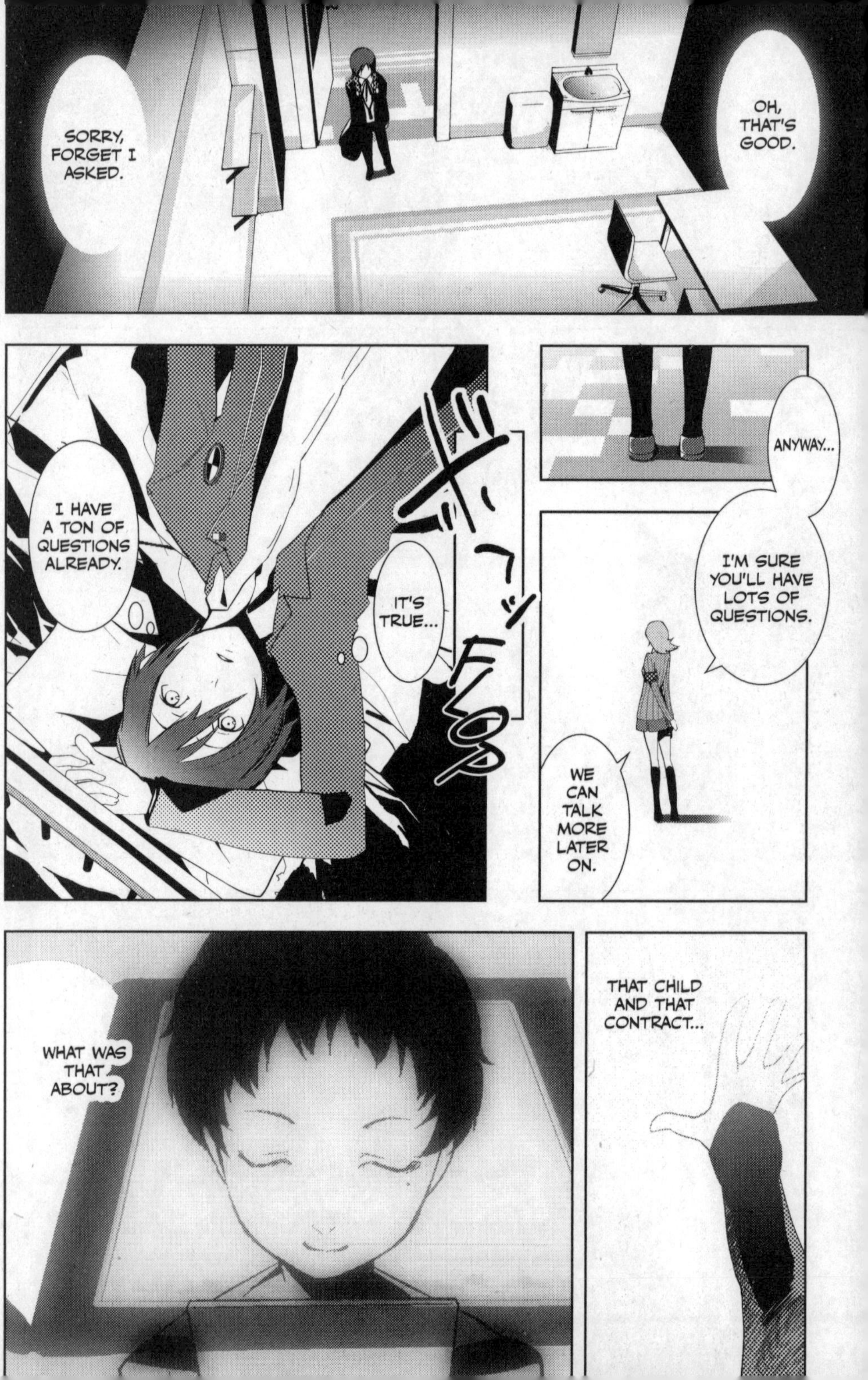
OH, THAT'S GOOD.
SORRY, FORGET I ASKED.
ANYWAY...
I'M SURE YOU'LL HAVE LOTS OF QUESTIONS.
WE CAN TALK MORE LATER ON.
FLOP
IT'S TRUE...
I HAVE A TON OF QUESTIONS ALREADY.
THAT CHILD AND THAT CONTRACT...
WHAT WAS THAT ABOUT?

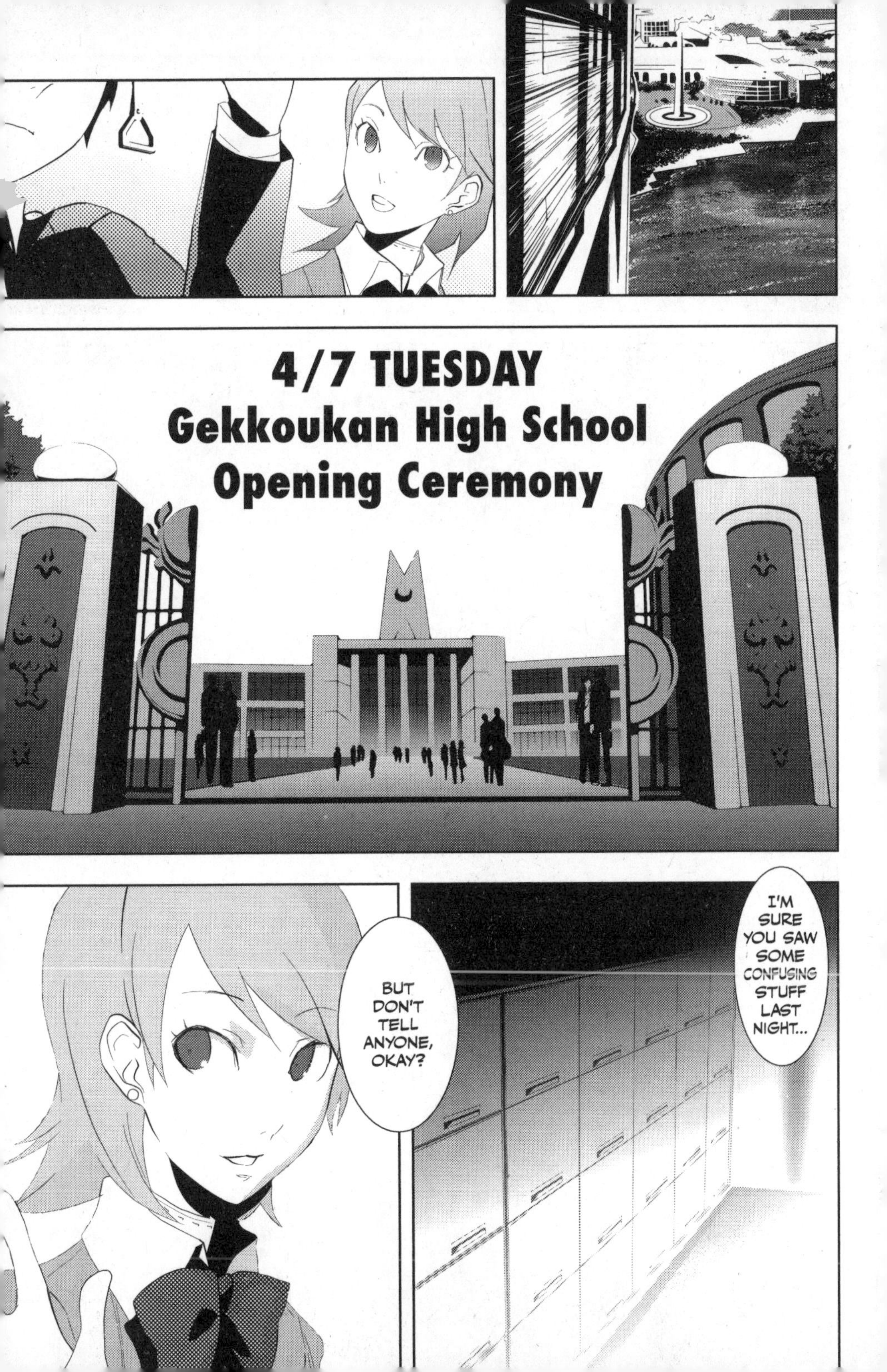
4/7 TUESDAY
Gekkoukan High School
Opening Ceremony
I'M SURE YOU SAW SOME CONFUSING STUFF LAST NIGHT...
BUT DON'T TELL ANYONE, OKAY?

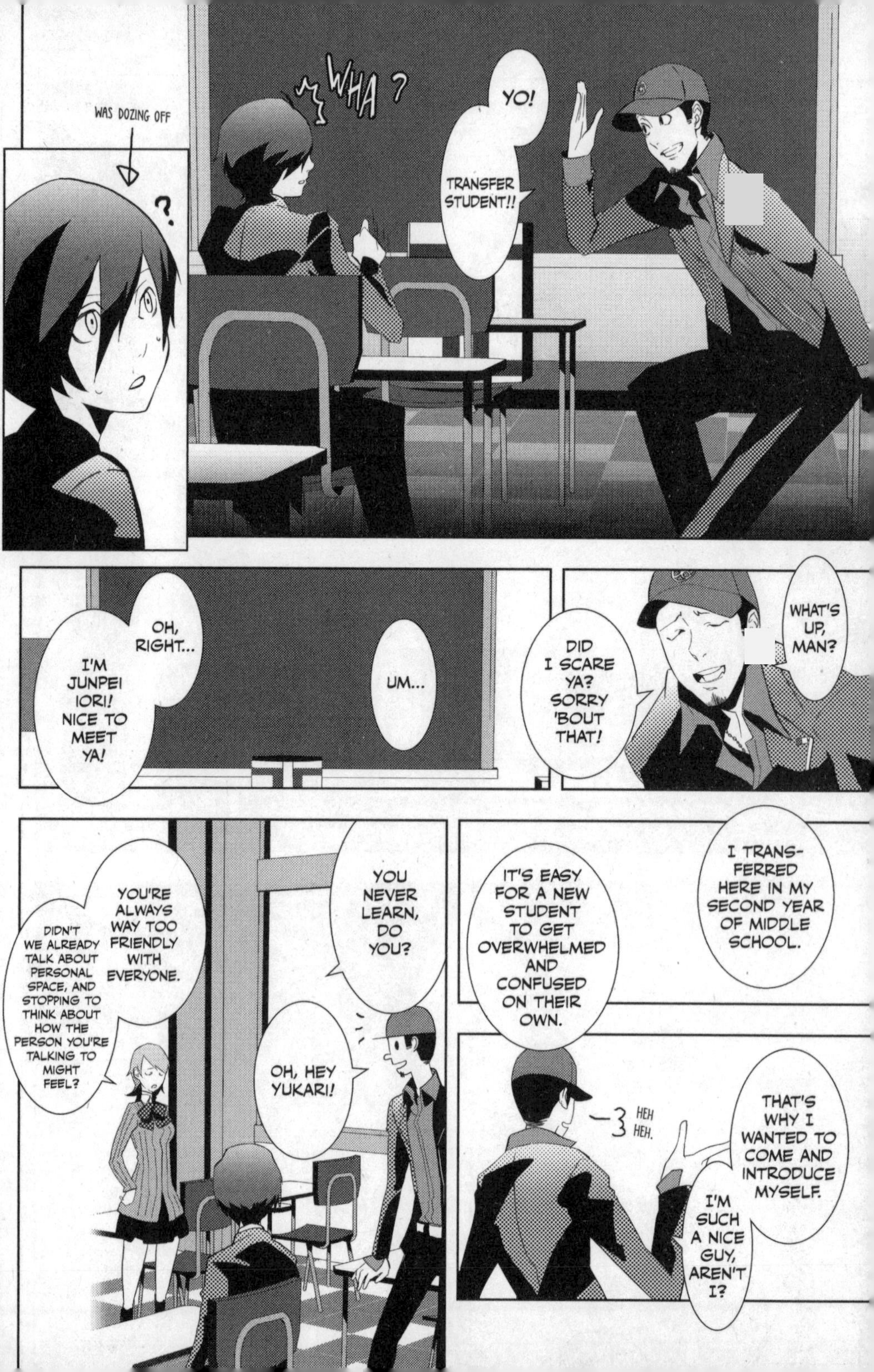

YO!
TRANSFER STUDENT!!
WHA ?
WAS DOZING OFF
?
WHAT'S UP, MAN?
DID I SCARE YA? SORRY 'BOUT THAT!
UM...
OH, RIGHT...
I'M JUNPEI IORI! NICE TO MEET YA!
I TRANS-FERRED HERE IN MY SECOND YEAR OF MIDDLE SCHOOL.
IT'S EASY FOR A NEW STUDENT TO GET OVERWHELMED AND CONFUSED ON THEIR OWN.
THAT'S WHY I WANTED TO COME AND INTRODUCE MYSELF.
I'M SUCH A NICE GUY, AREN'T I?
HEH HEH.
YOU NEVER LEARN, DO YOU?
OH, HEY YUKARI!
YOU'RE ALWAYS WAY TOO FRIENDLY WITH EVERYONE.
DIDN'T WE ALREADY TALK ABOUT PERSONAL SPACE, AND STOPPING TO THINK ABOUT HOW THE PERSON YOU'RE TALKING TO MIGHT FEEL?

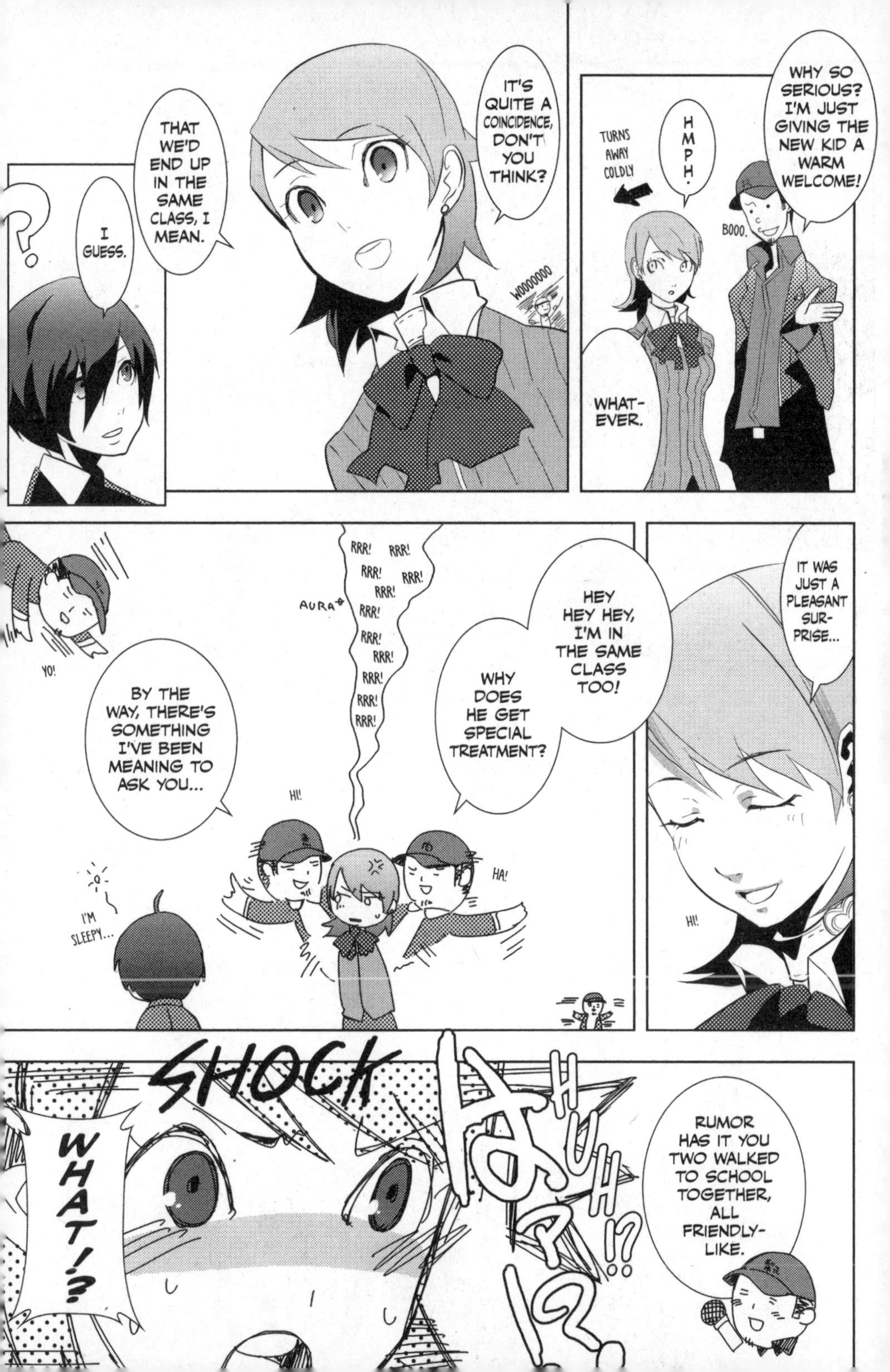
WHY SO SERIOUS? I'M JUST GIVING THE NEW KID A WARM WELCOME!
BOOO.
HMPH.
TURNS AWAY COLDLY
WHATEVER.
IT'S QUITE A COINCIDENCE, DON'T YOU THINK?
WOOOOOOO
THAT WE'D END UP IN THE SAME CLASS, I MEAN.
I GUESS.
IT WAS JUST A PLEASANT SURPRISE...
HI!
HEY HEY HEY, I'M IN THE SAME CLASS TOO!
WHY DOES HE GET SPECIAL TREATMENT?
AURA
RRR! RRR! RRR! RRR! RRR! RRR! RRR! RRR! RRR! RRR! RRR!
HI!
HA!
YO!
BY THE WAY, THERE'S SOMETHING I'VE BEEN MEANING TO ASK YOU...
I'M SLEEPY...
RUMOR HAS IT YOU TWO WALKED TO SCHOOL TOGETHER, ALL FRIENDLY-LIKE.
HUH!?
SHOCK
WHAT!?

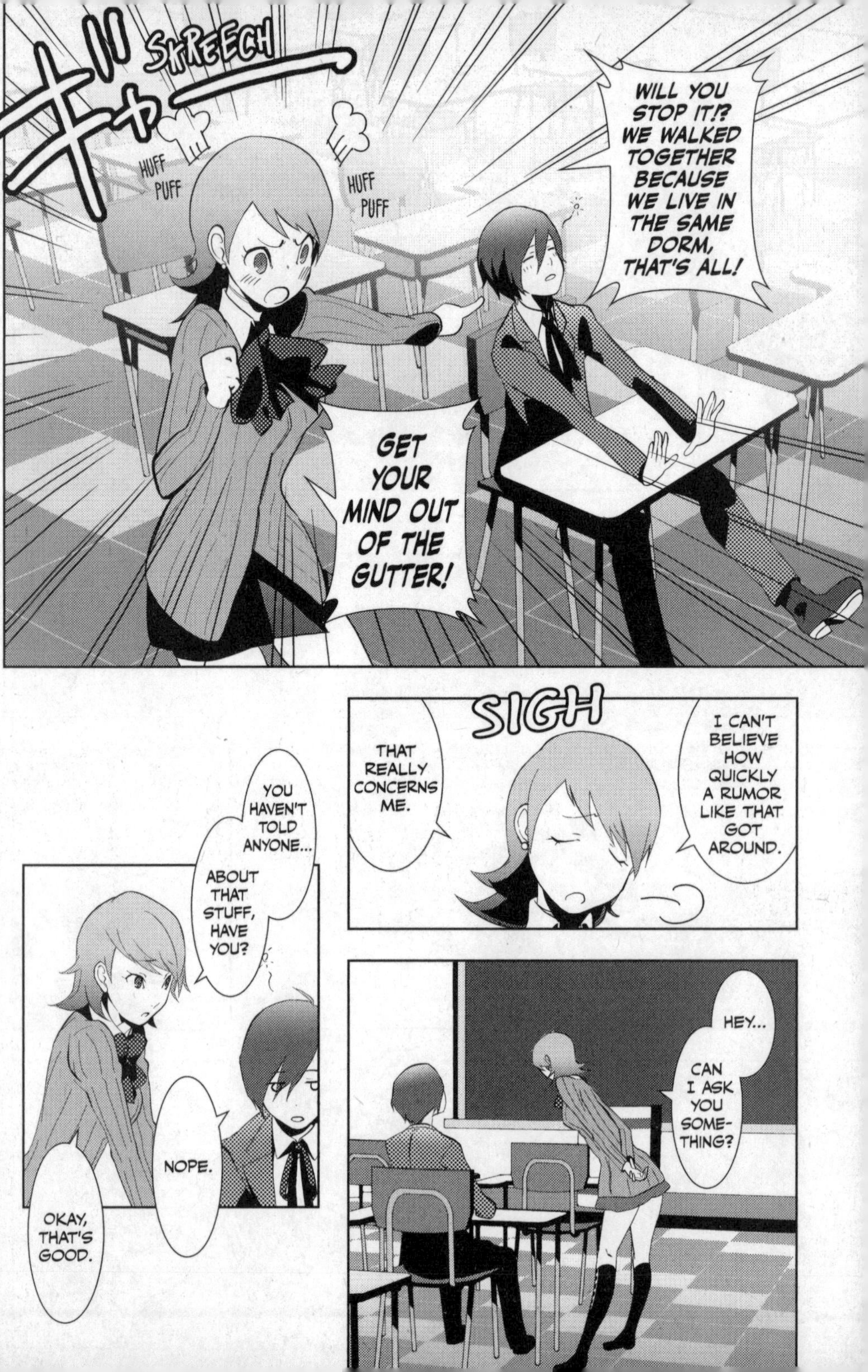
SKREECH
HUFF PUFF
HUFF PUFF
WILL YOU STOP IT!? WE WALKED TOGETHER BECAUSE WE LIVE IN THE SAME DORM, THAT'S ALL!
GET YOUR MIND OUT OF THE GUTTER!
SIGH
I CAN'T BELIEVE HOW QUICKLY A RUMOR LIKE THAT GOT AROUND.
THAT REALLY CONCERNS ME.
HEY...
CAN I ASK YOU SOME-THING?
YOU HAVEN'T TOLD ANYONE...
ABOUT THAT STUFF, HAVE YOU?
NOPE.
OKAY, THAT'S GOOD.

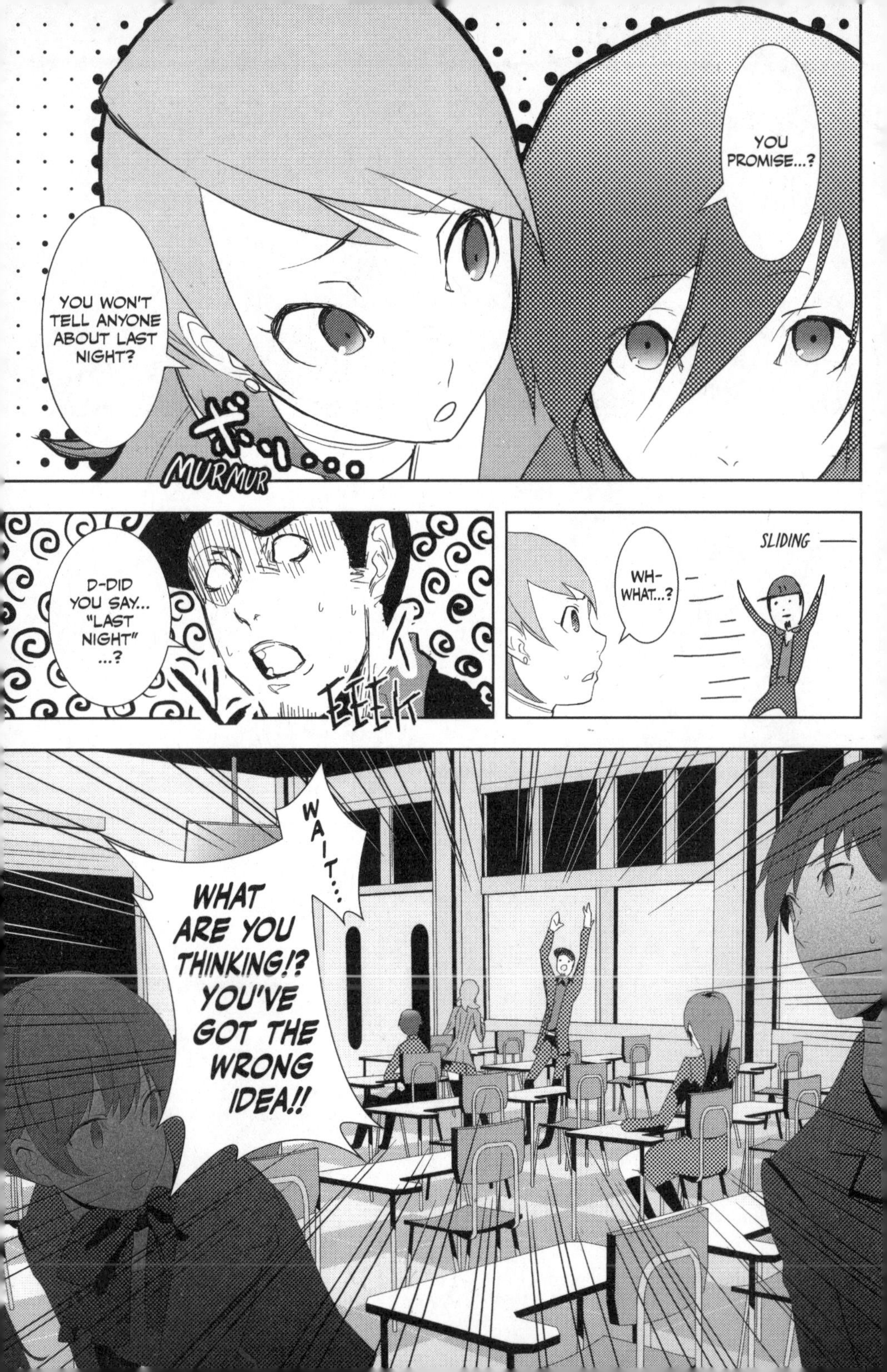
YOU PROMISE...?
YOU WON'T TELL ANYONE ABOUT LAST NIGHT?
MURMUR
SLIDING
WH- WHAT...?
D-DID YOU SAY... "LAST NIGHT" ...?
EEEK
WAIT...
WHAT ARE YOU THINKING!? YOU'VE GOT THE WRONG IDEA!!

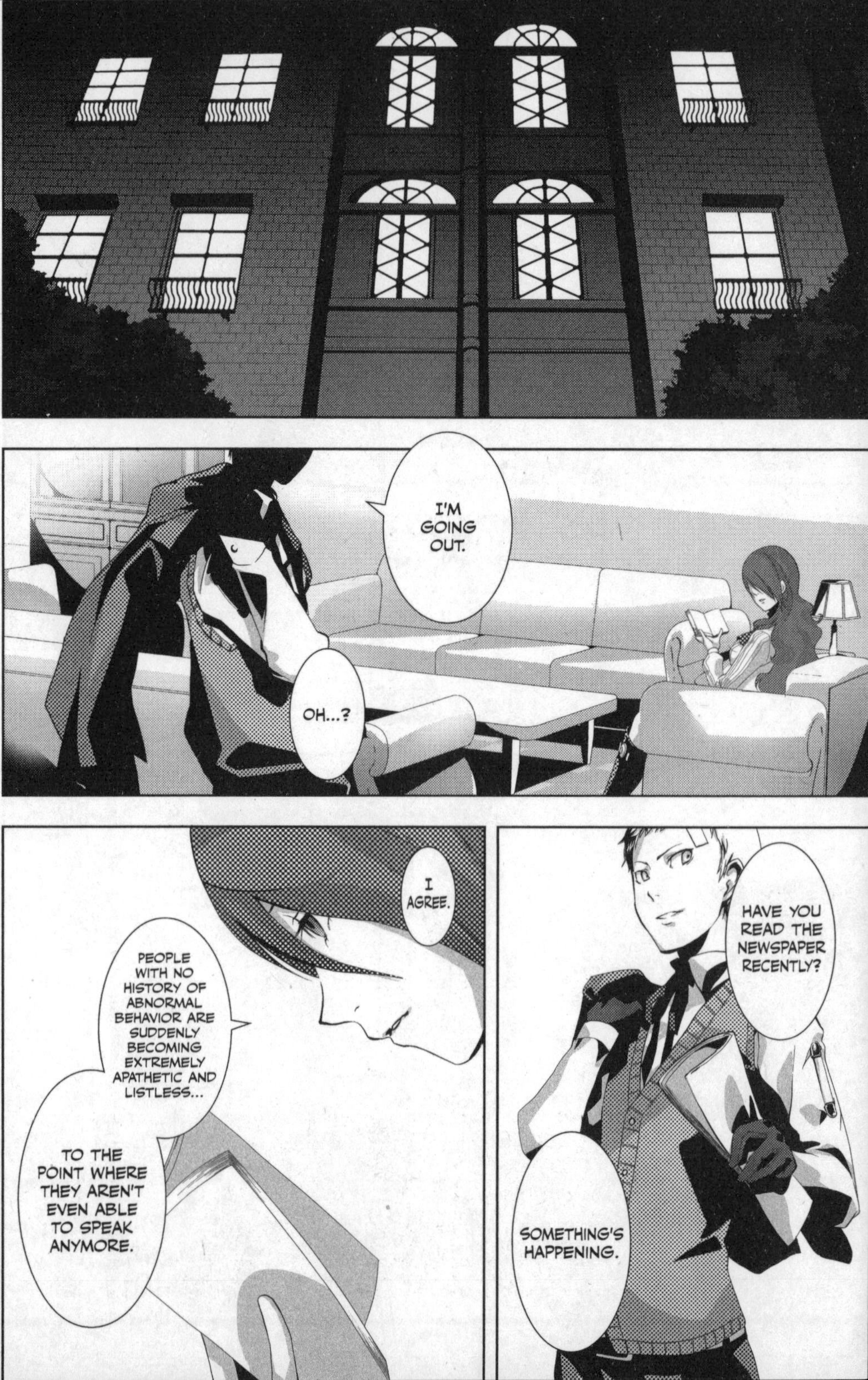
I'M GOING OUT.
OH...?
HAVE YOU READ THE NEWSPAPER RECENTLY?
SOMETHING'S HAPPENING.
I AGREE.
PEOPLE WITH NO HISTORY OF ABNORMAL BEHAVIOR ARE SUDDENLY BECOMING EXTREMELY APATHETIC AND LISTLESS...
TO THE POINT WHERE THEY AREN'T EVEN ABLE TO SPEAK ANYMORE.

IT'S QUITE AN EPIDEMIC.

THE NEWSPAPER IS SUGGESTING THAT IT'S A CONDITION BROUGHT ON BY STRESS.

AS IF.

IT'S GOTTA BE THEIR DOING.

WHAT FUN WOULD IT BE OTHERWISE?

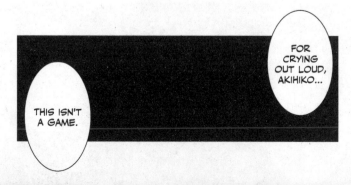

FOR CRYING OUT LOUD, AKIHIKO...

THIS ISN'T A GAME.

4/8 WEDNESDAY

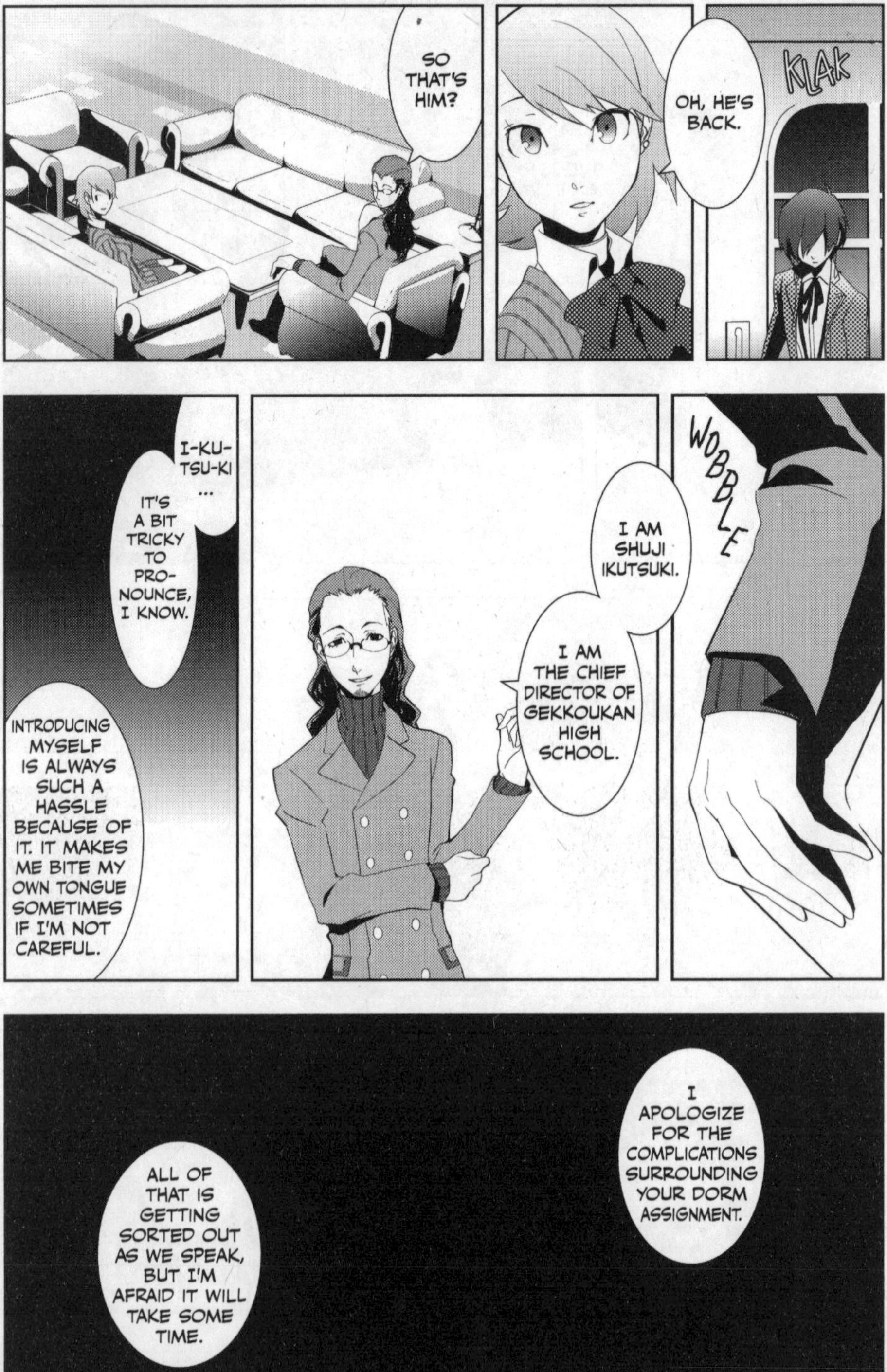
KLAK
OH, HE'S BACK.
SO THAT'S HIM?
WOBBLE
I AM SHUJI IKUTSUKI.
I AM THE CHIEF DIRECTOR OF GEKKOUKAN HIGH SCHOOL.
I-KU-TSU-KI ...
IT'S A BIT TRICKY TO PRO-NOUNCE, I KNOW.
INTRODUCING MYSELF IS ALWAYS SUCH A HASSLE BECAUSE OF IT. IT MAKES ME BITE MY OWN TONGUE SOMETIMES IF I'M NOT CAREFUL.
I APOLOGIZE FOR THE COMPLICATIONS SURROUNDING YOUR DORM ASSIGNMENT.
ALL OF THAT IS GETTING SORTED OUT AS WE SPEAK, BUT I'M AFRAID IT WILL TAKE SOME TIME.

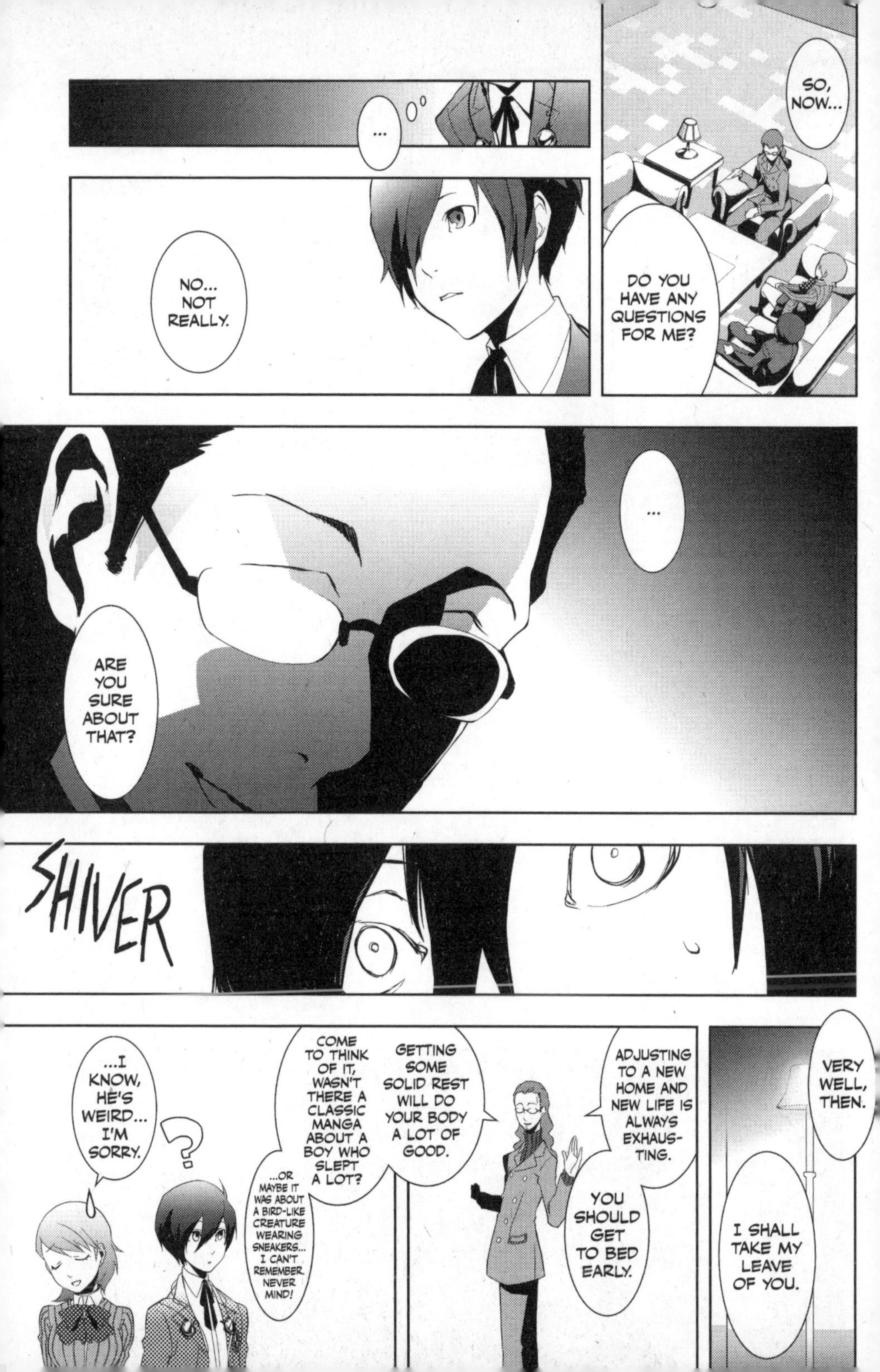
SO, NOW...
DO YOU HAVE ANY QUESTIONS FOR ME?
...
NO... NOT REALLY.
...
ARE YOU SURE ABOUT THAT?
SHIVER
VERY WELL, THEN.
I SHALL TAKE MY LEAVE OF YOU.
ADJUSTING TO A NEW HOME AND NEW LIFE IS ALWAYS EXHAUS-TING.
YOU SHOULD GET TO BED EARLY.
GETTING SOME SOLID REST WILL DO YOUR BODY A LOT OF GOOD.
COME TO THINK OF IT, WASN'T THERE A CLASSIC MANGA ABOUT A BOY WHO SLEPT A LOT?
...OR MAYBE IT WAS ABOUT A BIRD-LIKE CREATURE WEARING SNEAKERS... I CAN'T REMEMBER. NEVER MIND!
?
...I KNOW, HE'S WEIRD... I'M SORRY.

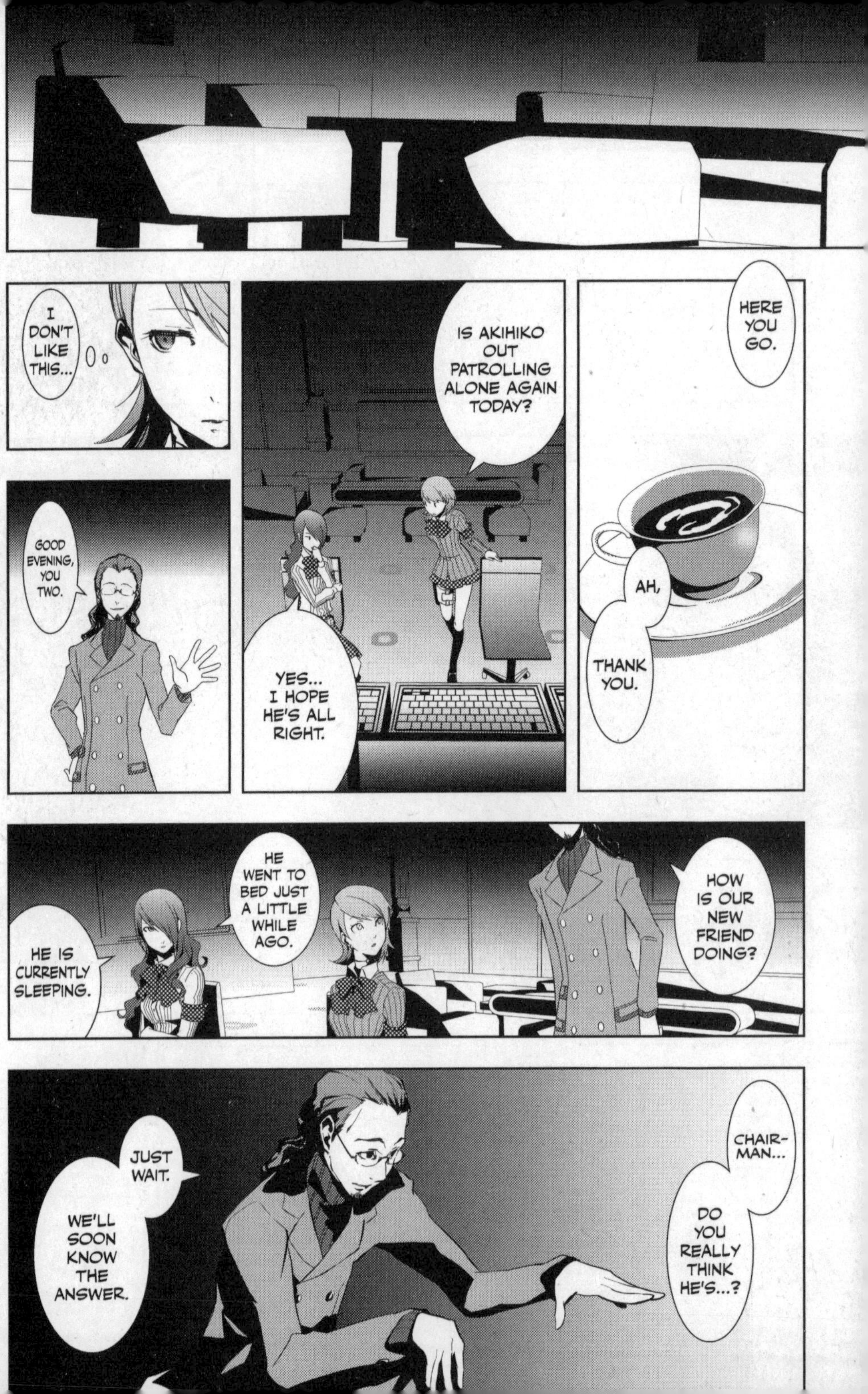
HERE YOU GO.
AH,
THANK YOU.
IS AKIHIKO OUT PATROLLING ALONE AGAIN TODAY?
YES... I HOPE HE'S ALL RIGHT.
I DON'T LIKE THIS...
GOOD EVENING, YOU TWO.
HOW IS OUR NEW FRIEND DOING?
HE WENT TO BED JUST A LITTLE WHILE AGO.
HE IS CURRENTLY SLEEPING.
CHAIR-MAN...
DO YOU REALLY THINK HE'S...?
JUST WAIT.
WE'LL SOON KNOW THE ANSWER.

THE DARK HOUR...

...IS NEARLY UPON US.

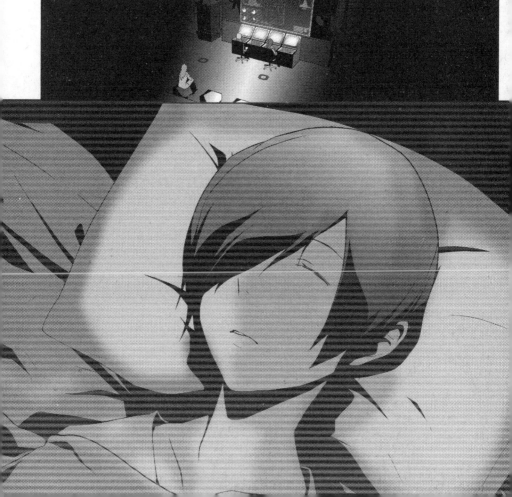

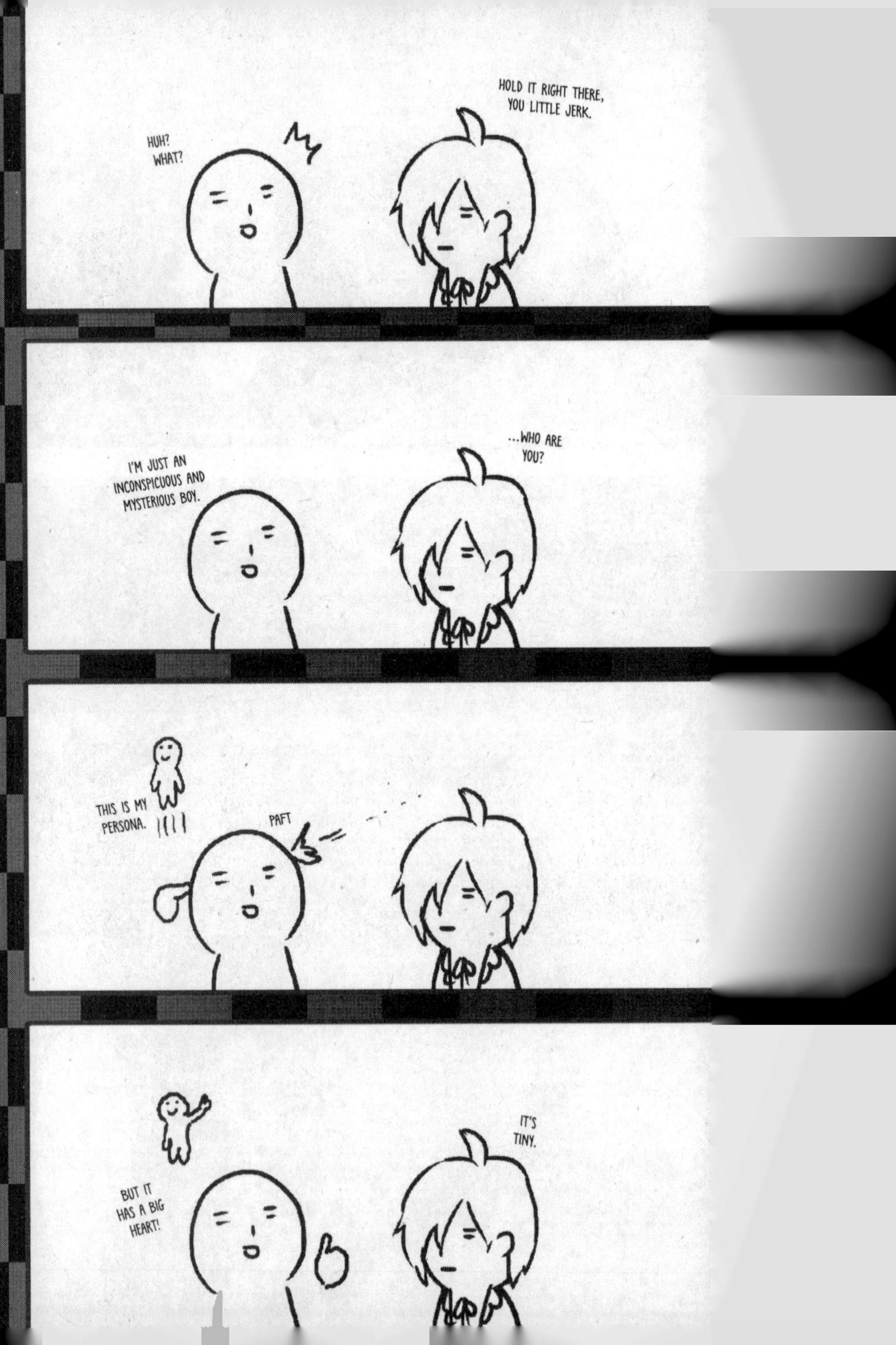
HOLD IT RIGHT THERE, YOU LITTLE JERK.
HUH? WHAT?
...WHO ARE YOU?
I'M JUST AN INCONSPICUOUS AND MYSTERIOUS BOY.
PAFT
THIS IS MY PERSONA.
IT'S TINY.
BUT IT HAS A BIG HEART!

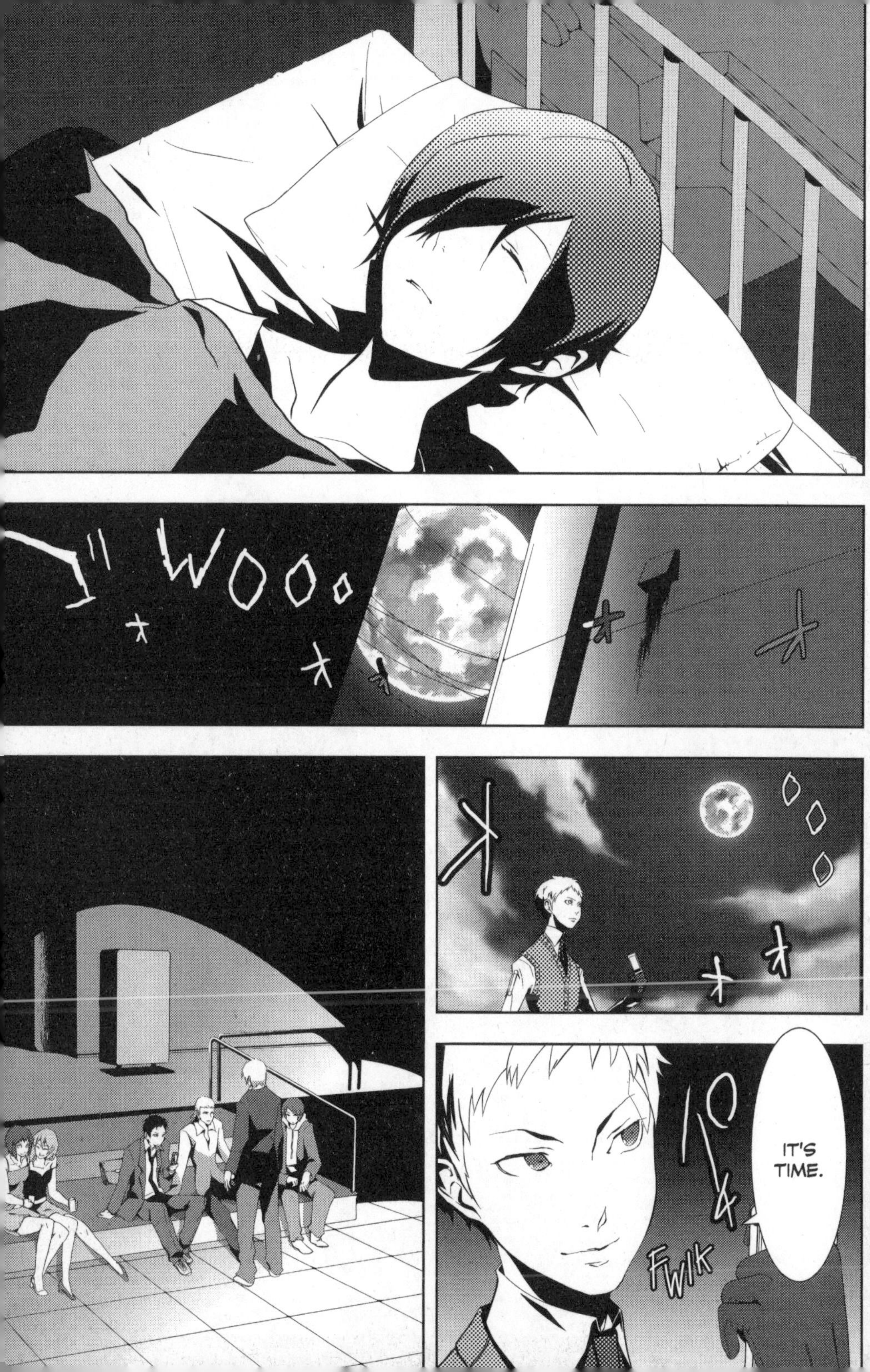
WOOO
IT'S TIME.
FWIK

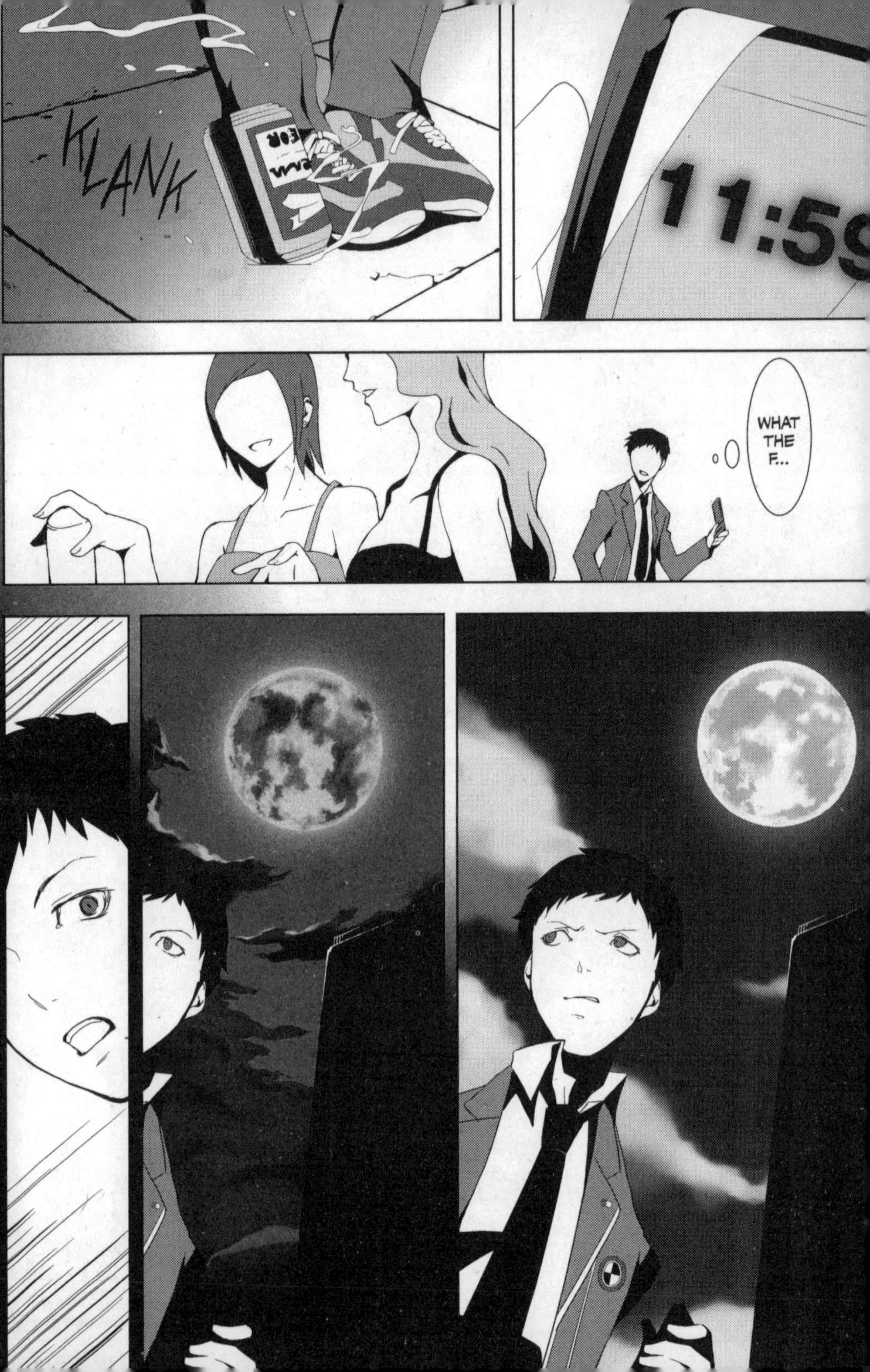
11:59
KLANK
WHAT THE F...

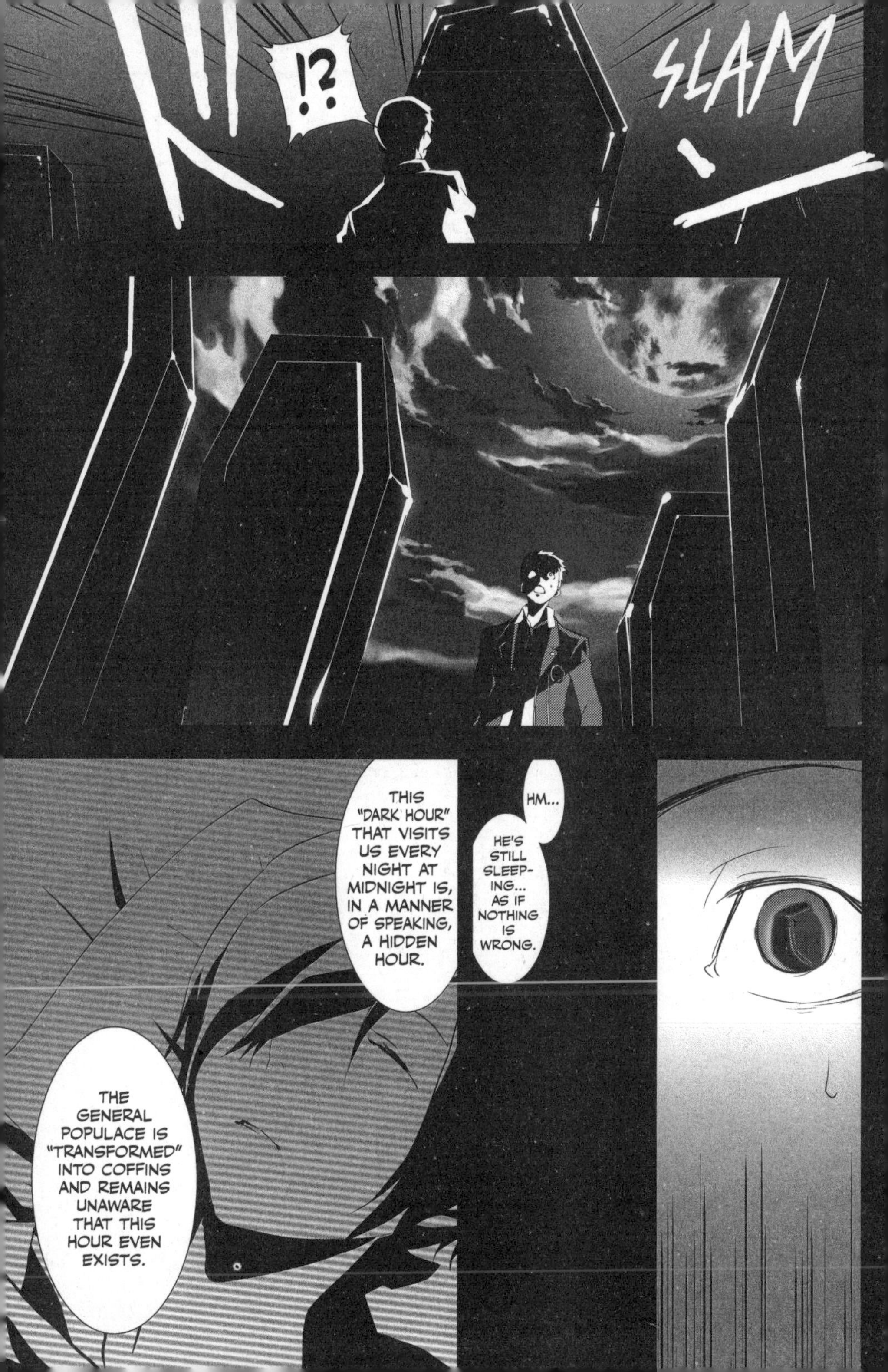
SLAM
!?
HM...
HE'S STILL SLEEPING... AS IF NOTHING IS WRONG.
THIS "DARK HOUR" THAT VISITS US EVERY NIGHT AT MIDNIGHT IS, IN A MANNER OF SPEAKING, A HIDDEN HOUR.
THE GENERAL POPULACE IS "TRANSFORMED" INTO COFFINS AND REMAINS UNAWARE THAT THIS HOUR EVEN EXISTS.

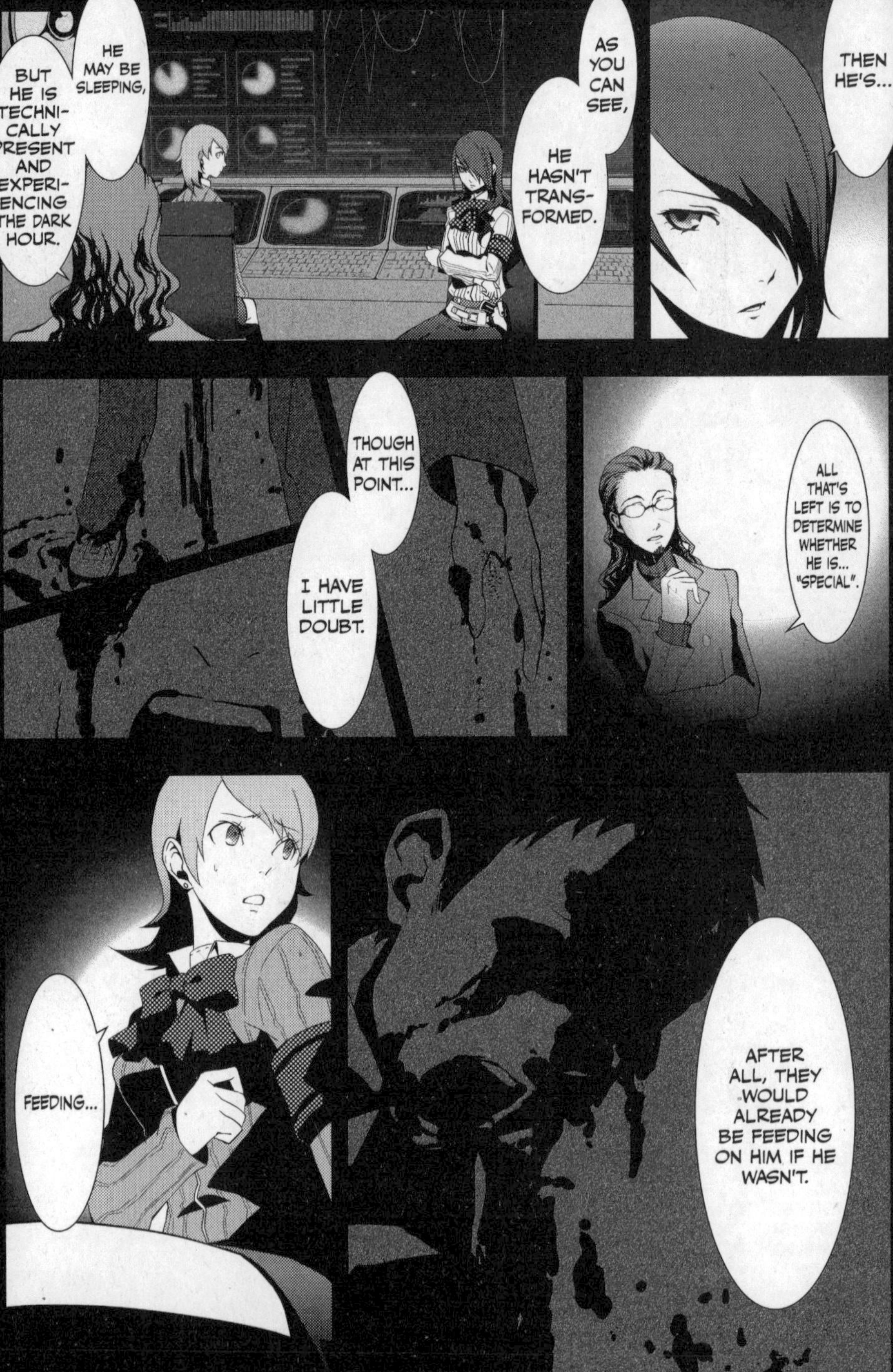
THEN HE'S...
AS YOU CAN SEE,
HE HASN'T TRANSFORMED.
HE MAY BE SLEEPING,
BUT HE IS TECHNICALLY PRESENT AND EXPERIENCING THE DARK HOUR.
ALL THAT'S LEFT IS TO DETERMINE WHETHER HE IS... "SPECIAL".
THOUGH AT THIS POINT...
I HAVE LITTLE DOUBT.
AFTER ALL, THEY WOULD ALREADY BE FEEDING ON HIM IF HE WASN'T.
FEEDING...

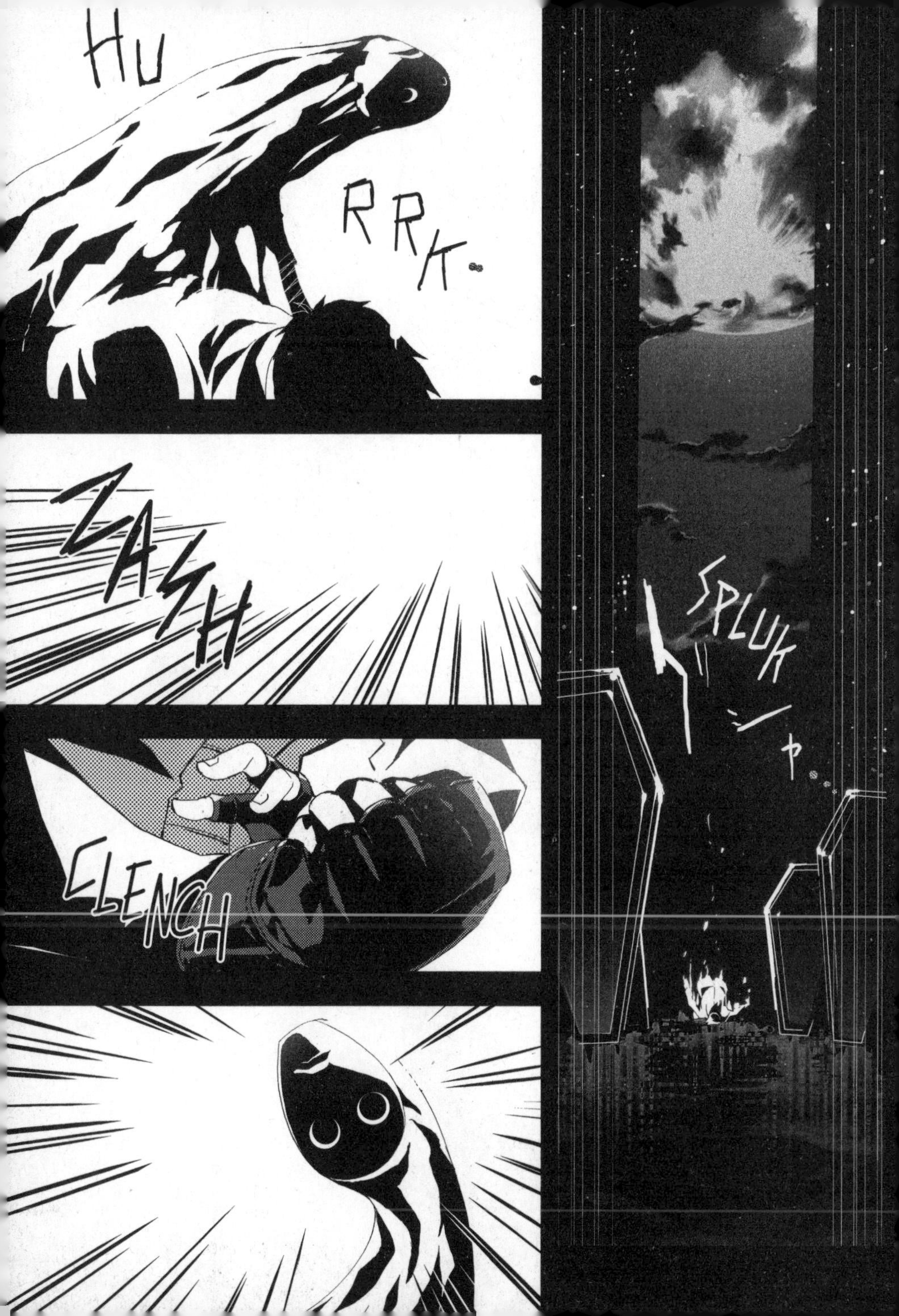
SPLUK
シャ
HU
RRRK
ZASH
CLENCH

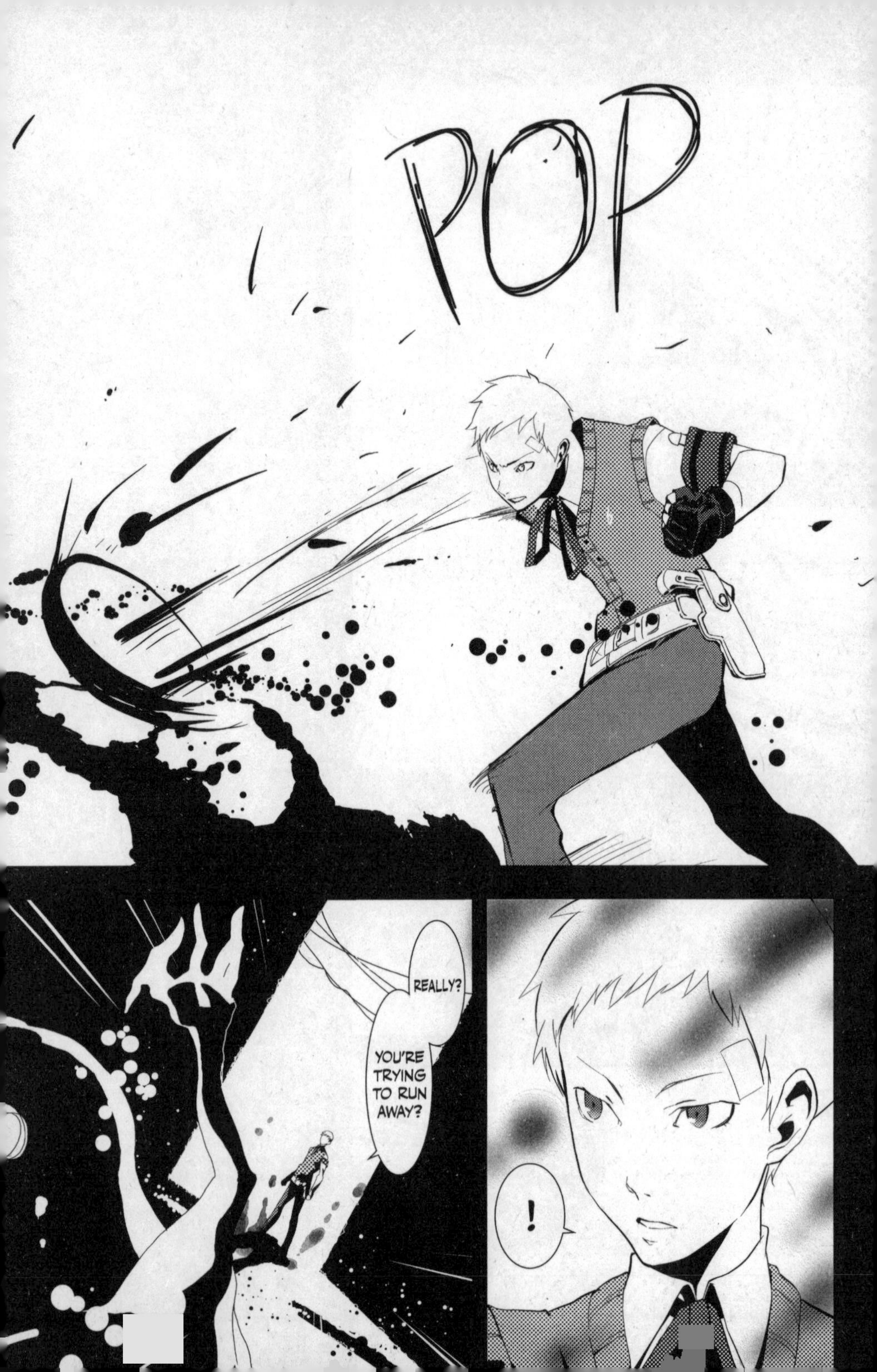
POP
!
REALLY?
YOU'RE TRYING TO RUN AWAY?

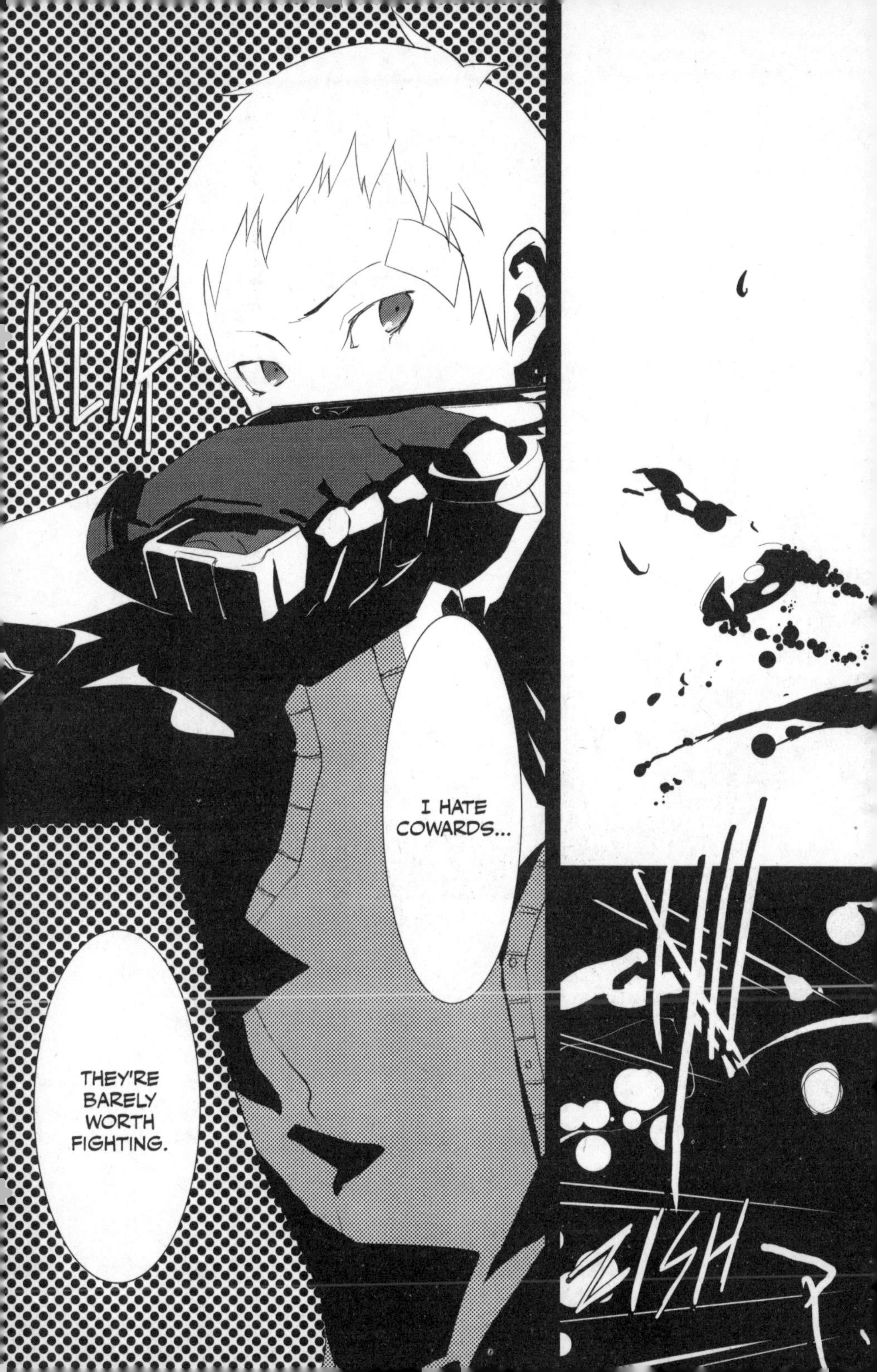
ZISH
KLIK
I HATE COWARDS...
THEY'RE BARELY WORTH FIGHTING.

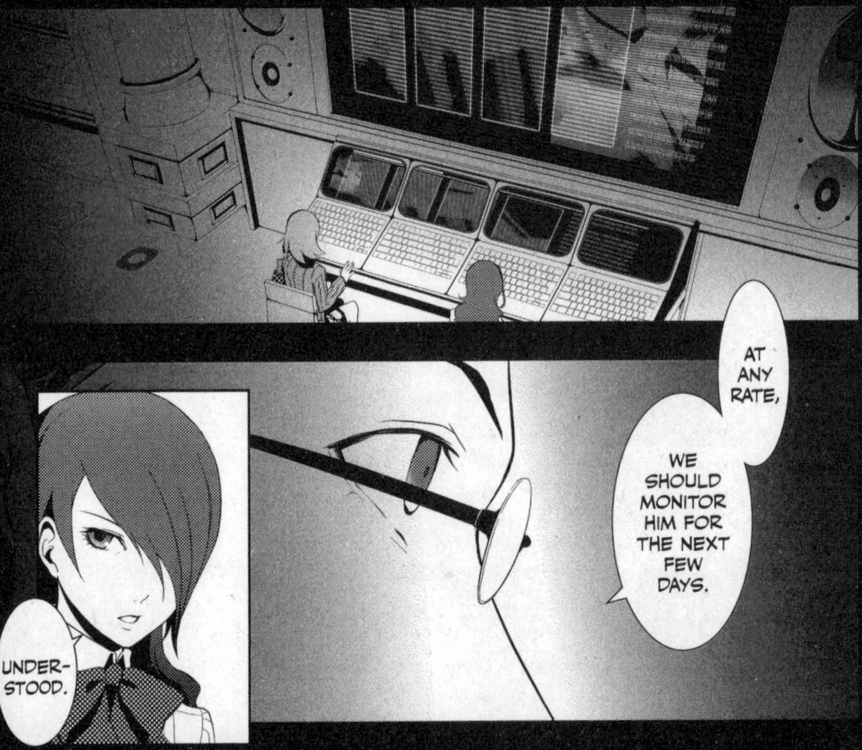
AT ANY RATE,
WE SHOULD MONITOR HIM FOR THE NEXT FEW DAYS.
UNDER-STOOD.

I suppose I had already stepped beyond the borders of a normal life by this point.

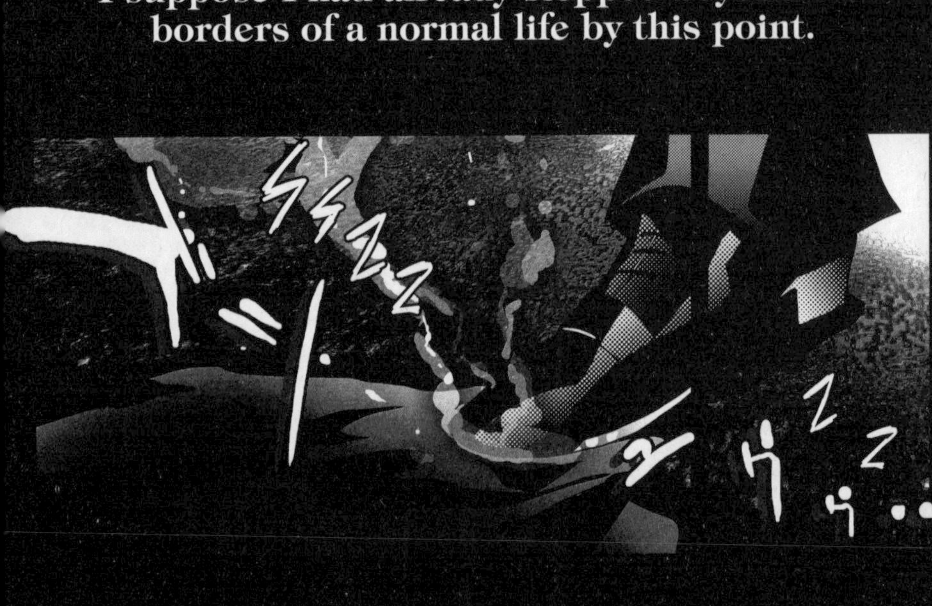

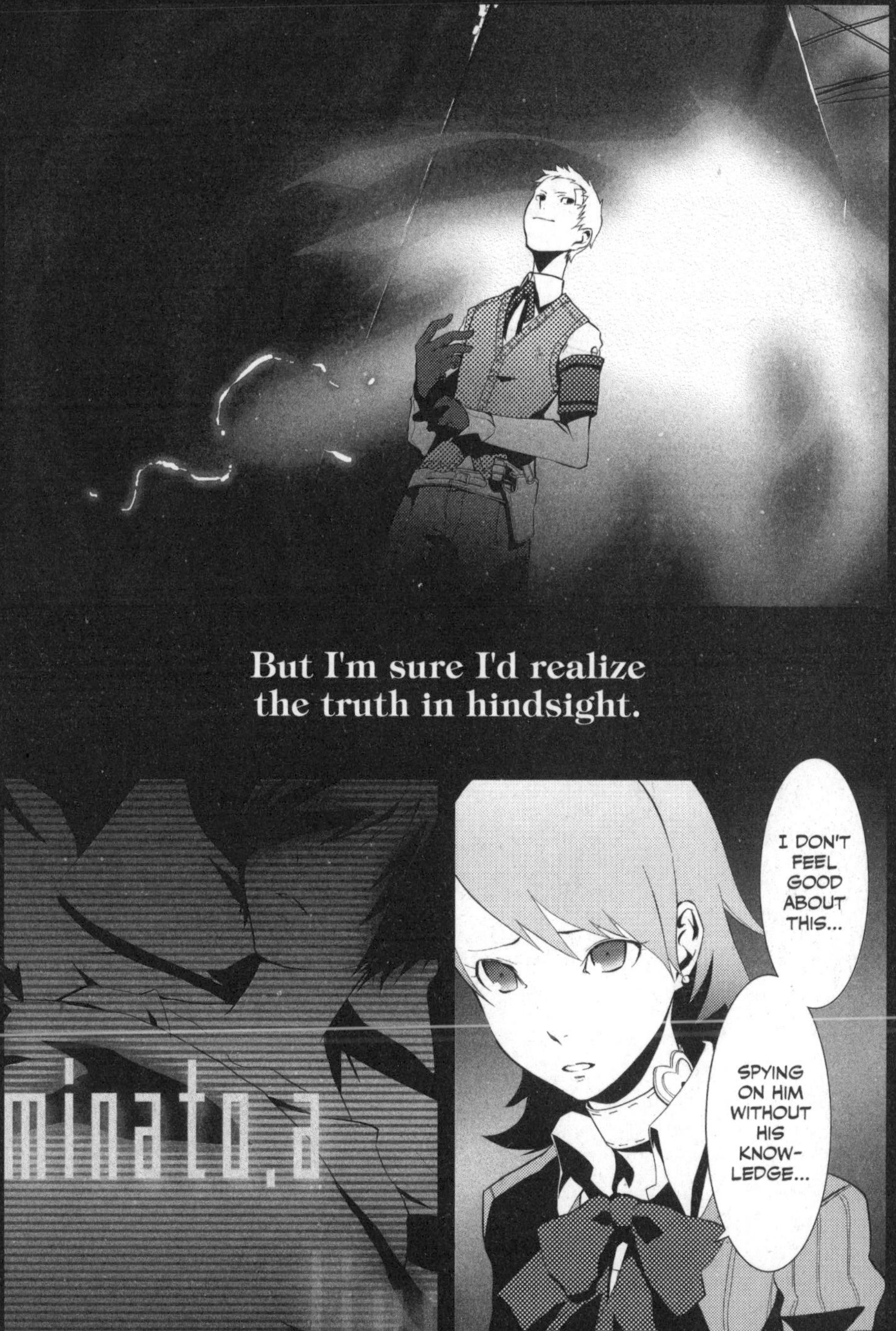
But I'm sure I'd realize the truth in hindsight.
I DON'T FEEL GOOD ABOUT THIS...
SPYING ON HIM WITHOUT HIS KNOW-LEDGE...
minato,a

That the
line between
dreams and
reality existed
within myself.

P3
PERSONA3

#03
Piece:02

TRIGGER OF INSTINCT

SHUJI SOGABE   ORIGINAL / ATLUS
Design&Finished : Studio Shortcake Screamer

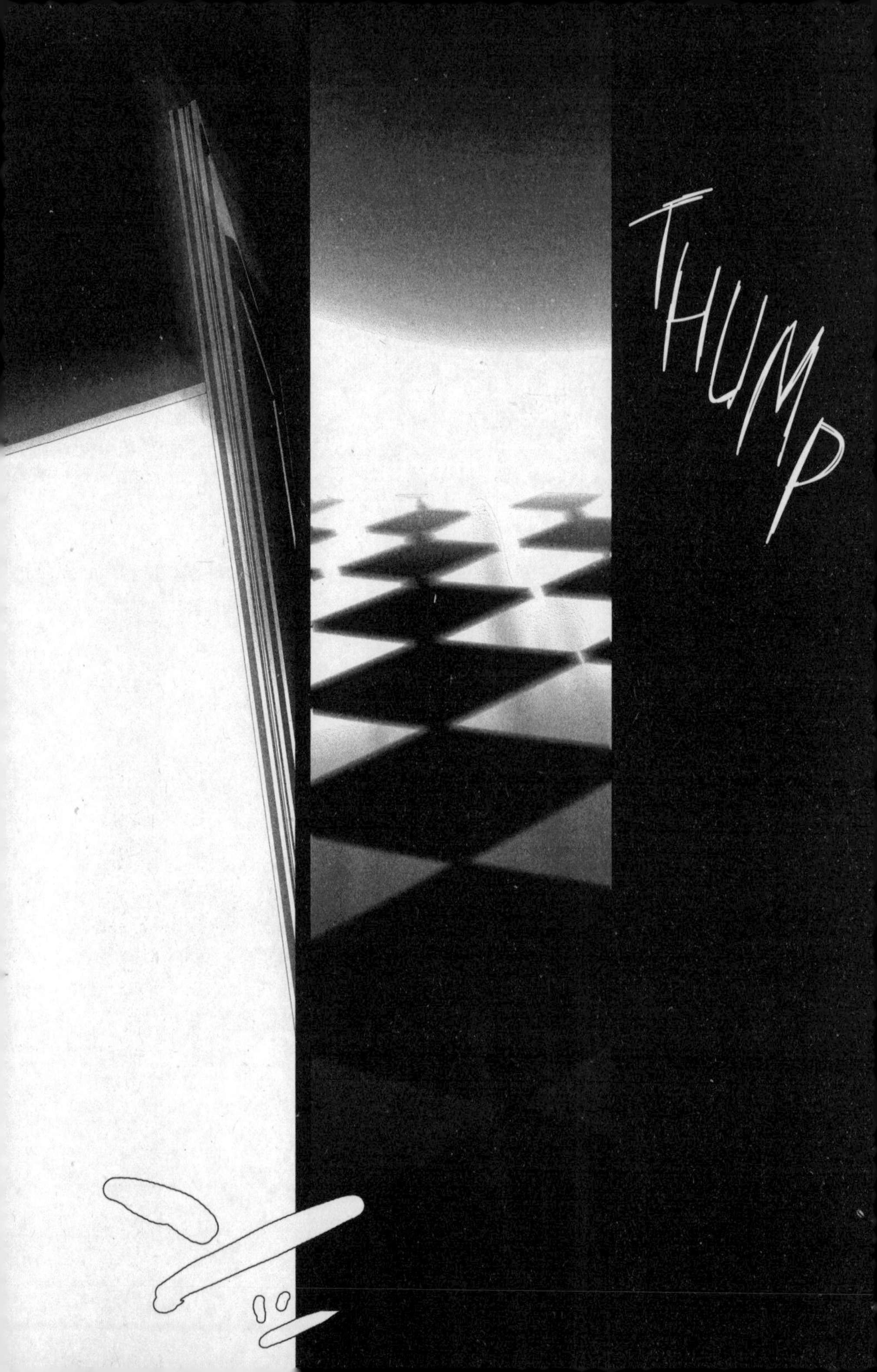
THUMP

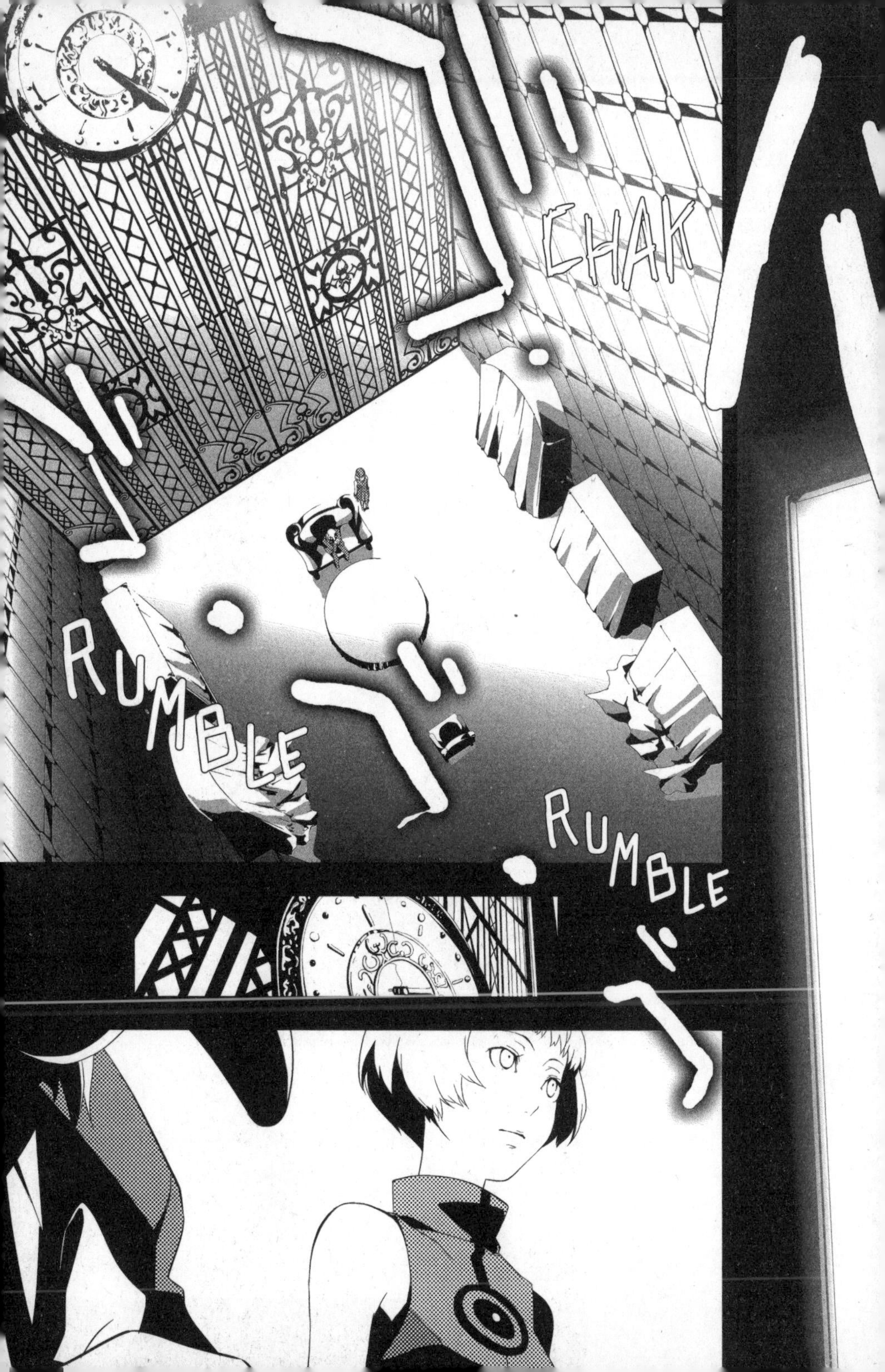
CHAK
RUMBLE
RUMBLE

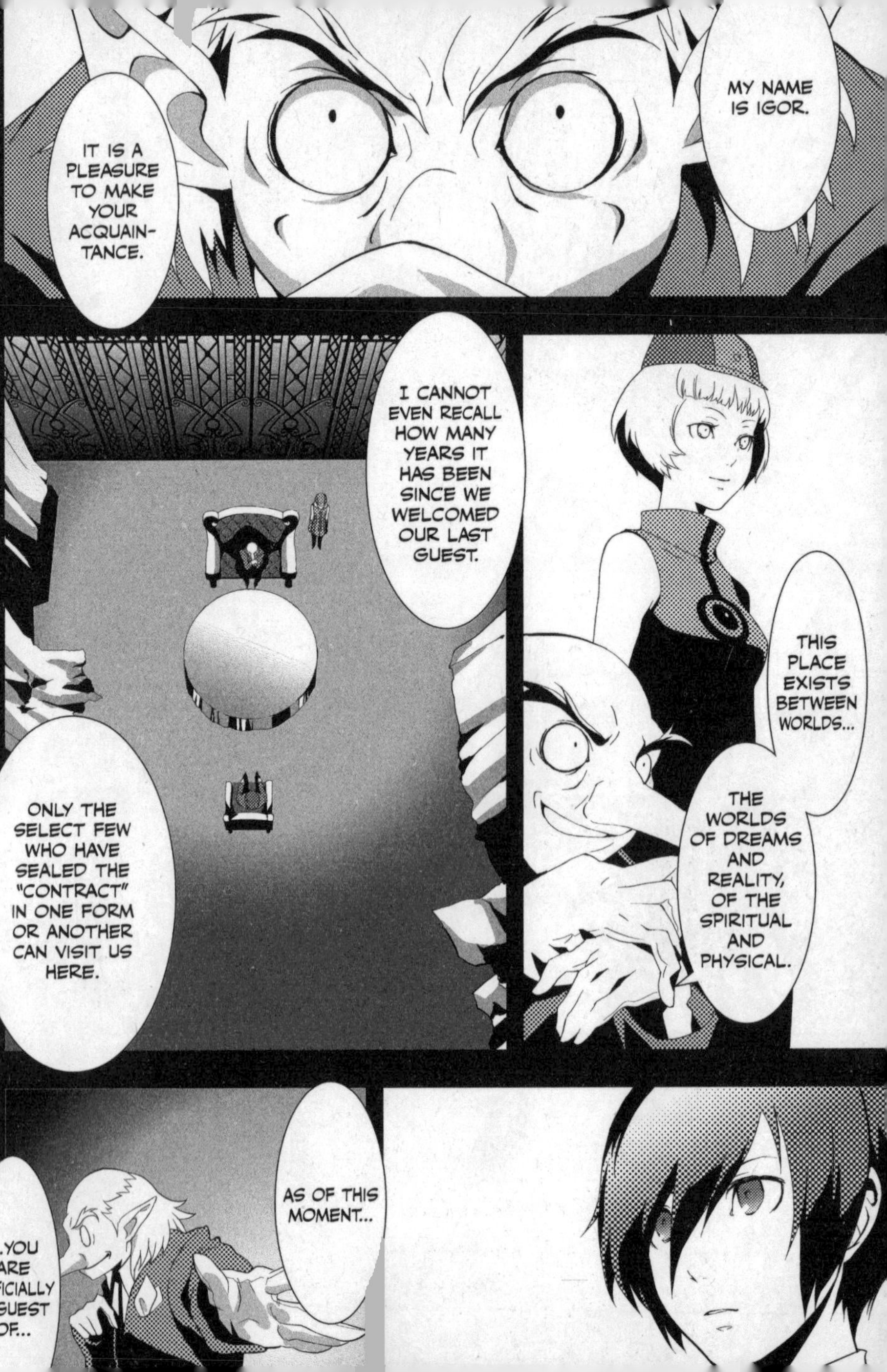
MY NAME IS IGOR.
IT IS A PLEASURE TO MAKE YOUR ACQUAIN-TANCE.
THIS PLACE EXISTS BETWEEN WORLDS...
THE WORLDS OF DREAMS AND REALITY, OF THE SPIRITUAL AND PHYSICAL.
I CANNOT EVEN RECALL HOW MANY YEARS IT HAS BEEN SINCE WE WELCOMED OUR LAST GUEST.
ONLY THE SELECT FEW WHO HAVE SEALED THE "CONTRACT" IN ONE FORM OR ANOTHER CAN VISIT US HERE.
AS OF THIS MOMENT...
...YOU ARE OFFICIALLY A GUEST OF...

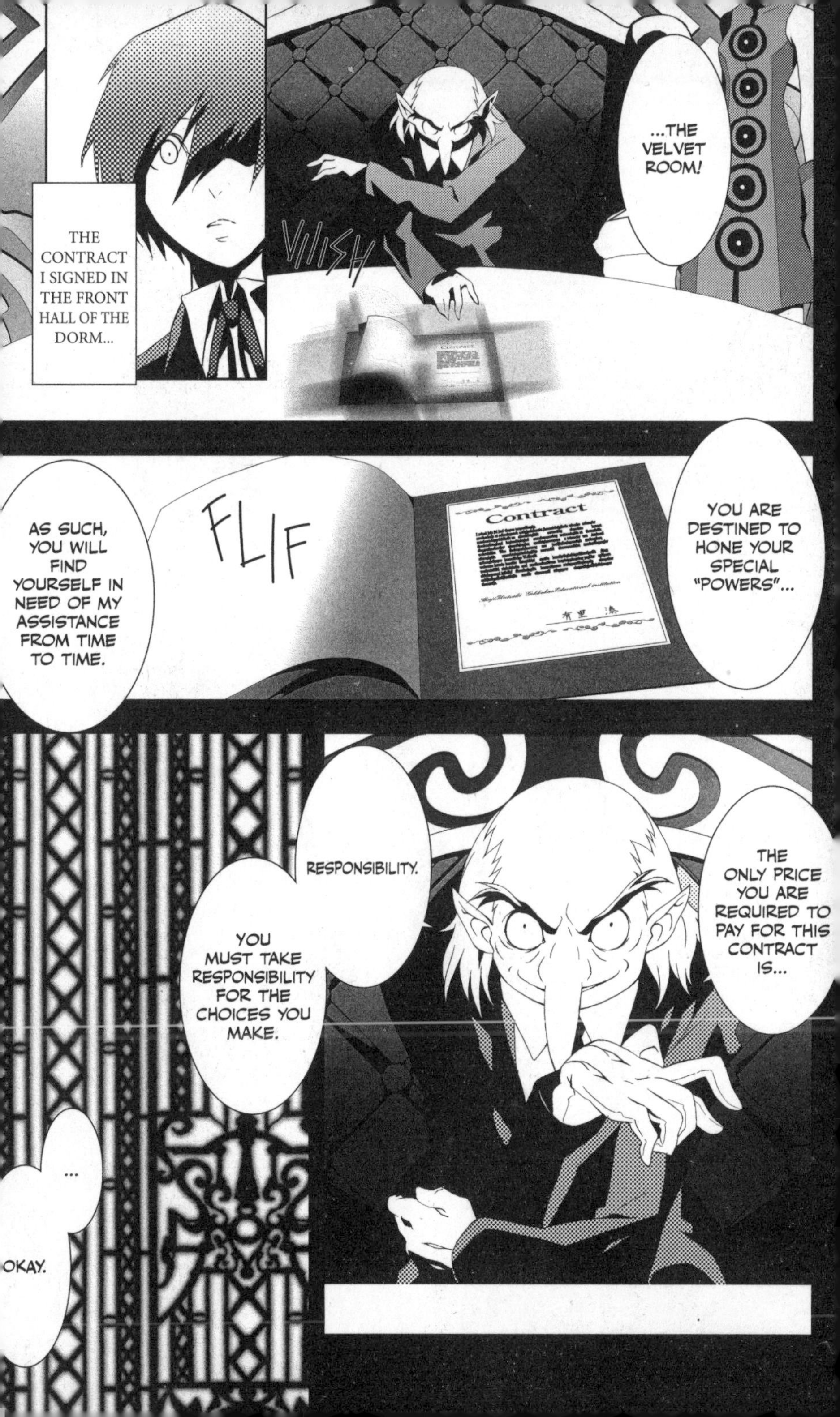
...THE VELVET ROOM!
THE CONTRACT I SIGNED IN THE FRONT HALL OF THE DORM...
VIISH
YOU ARE DESTINED TO HONE YOUR SPECIAL "POWERS"...
Contract
FLIP
AS SUCH, YOU WILL FIND YOURSELF IN NEED OF MY ASSISTANCE FROM TIME TO TIME.
THE ONLY PRICE YOU ARE REQUIRED TO PAY FOR THIS CONTRACT IS...
RESPONSIBILITY.
YOU MUST TAKE RESPONSIBILITY FOR THE CHOICES YOU MAKE.
...
OKAY.

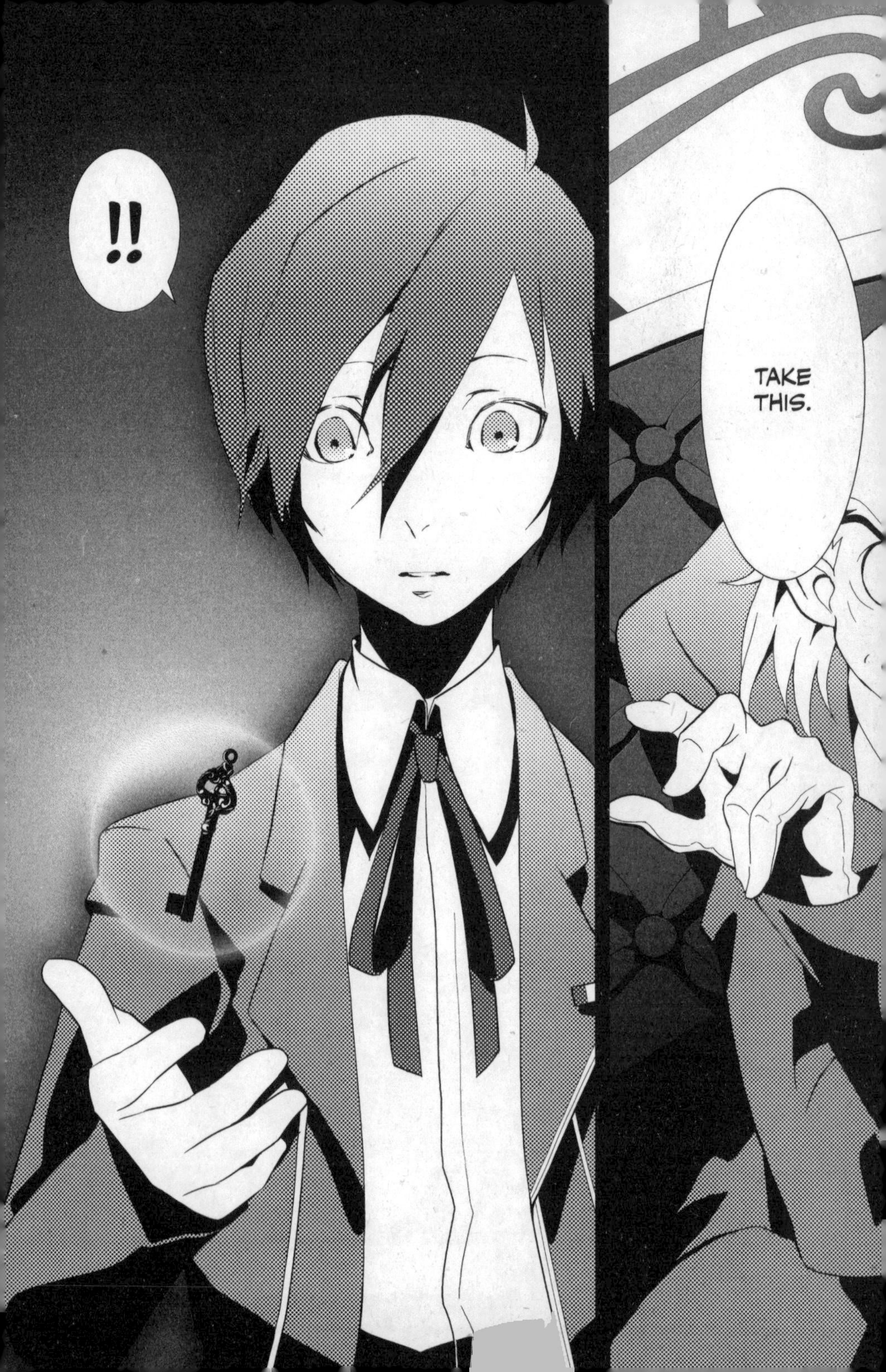
TAKE THIS.
!!

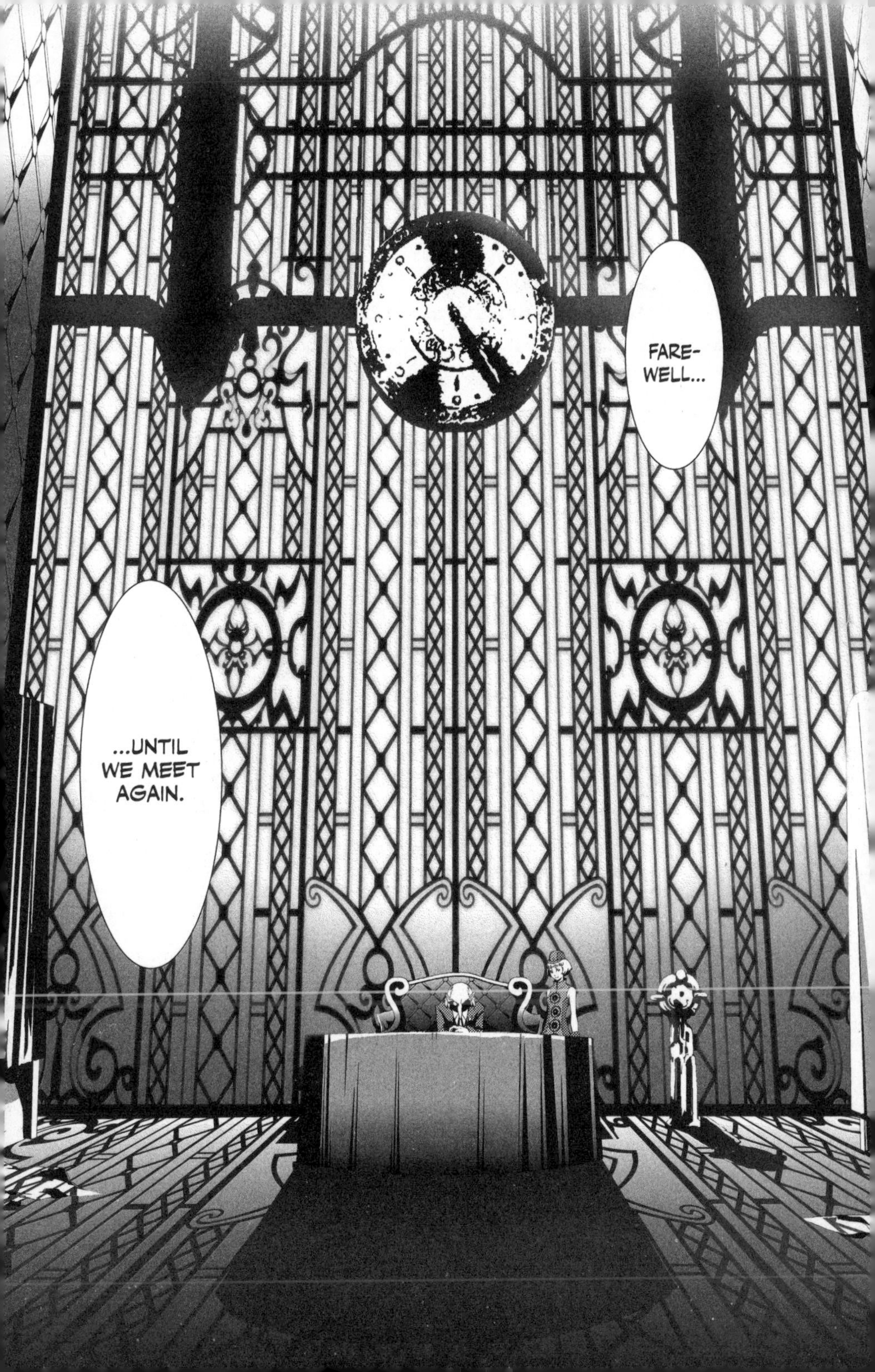
FARE-WELL...
...UNTIL WE MEET AGAIN.

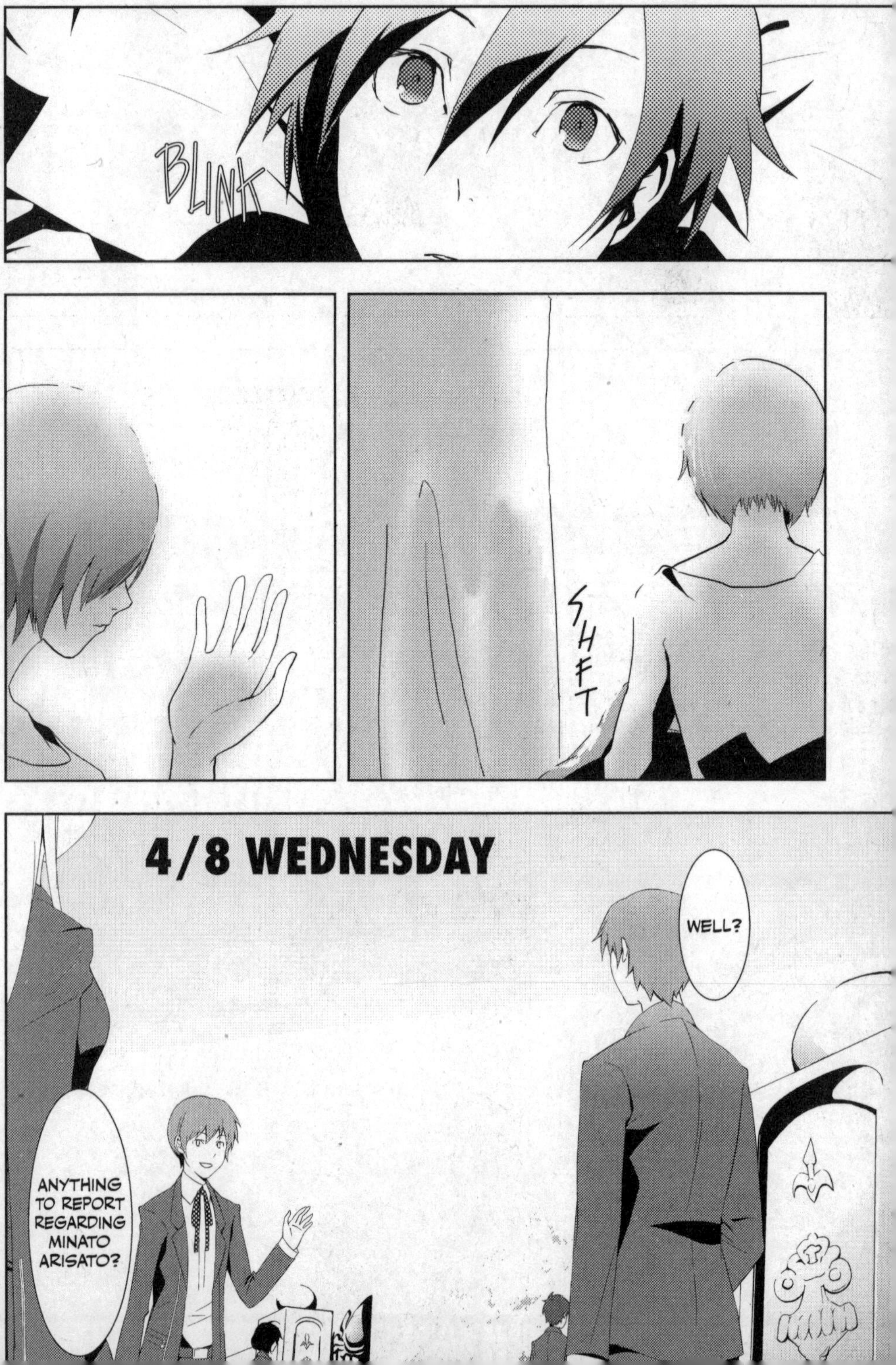
BLINK
SHFT
4/8 WEDNESDAY
WELL?
ANYTHING TO REPORT REGARDING MINATO ARISATO?

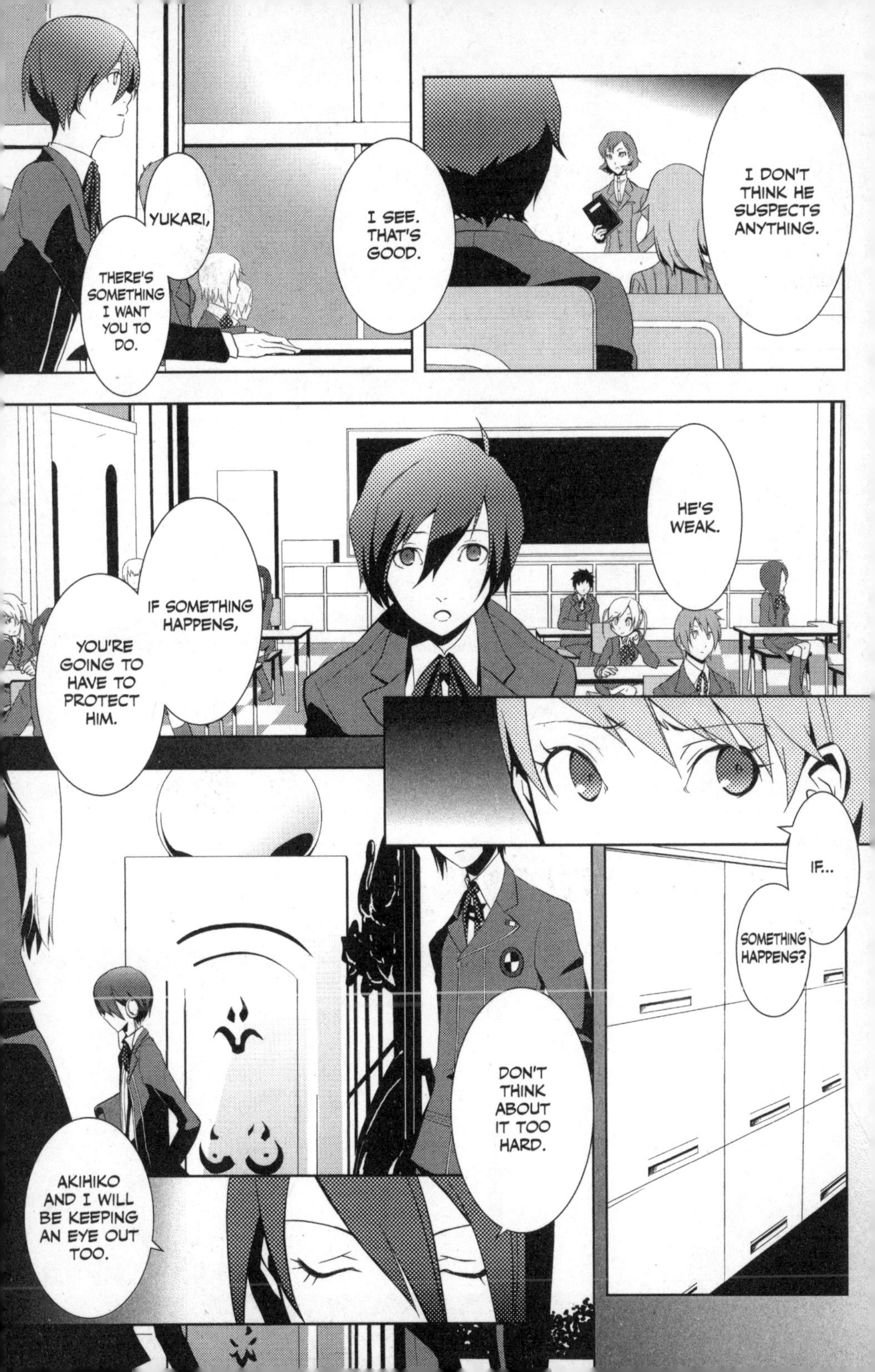
I DON'T THINK HE SUSPECTS ANYTHING.
I SEE. THAT'S GOOD.
YUKARI,
THERE'S SOMETHING I WANT YOU TO DO.
HE'S WEAK.
IF SOMETHING HAPPENS,
YOU'RE GOING TO HAVE TO PROTECT HIM.
IF...
SOMETHING HAPPENS?
DON'T THINK ABOUT IT TOO HARD.
AKIHIKO AND I WILL BE KEEPING AN EYE OUT TOO.

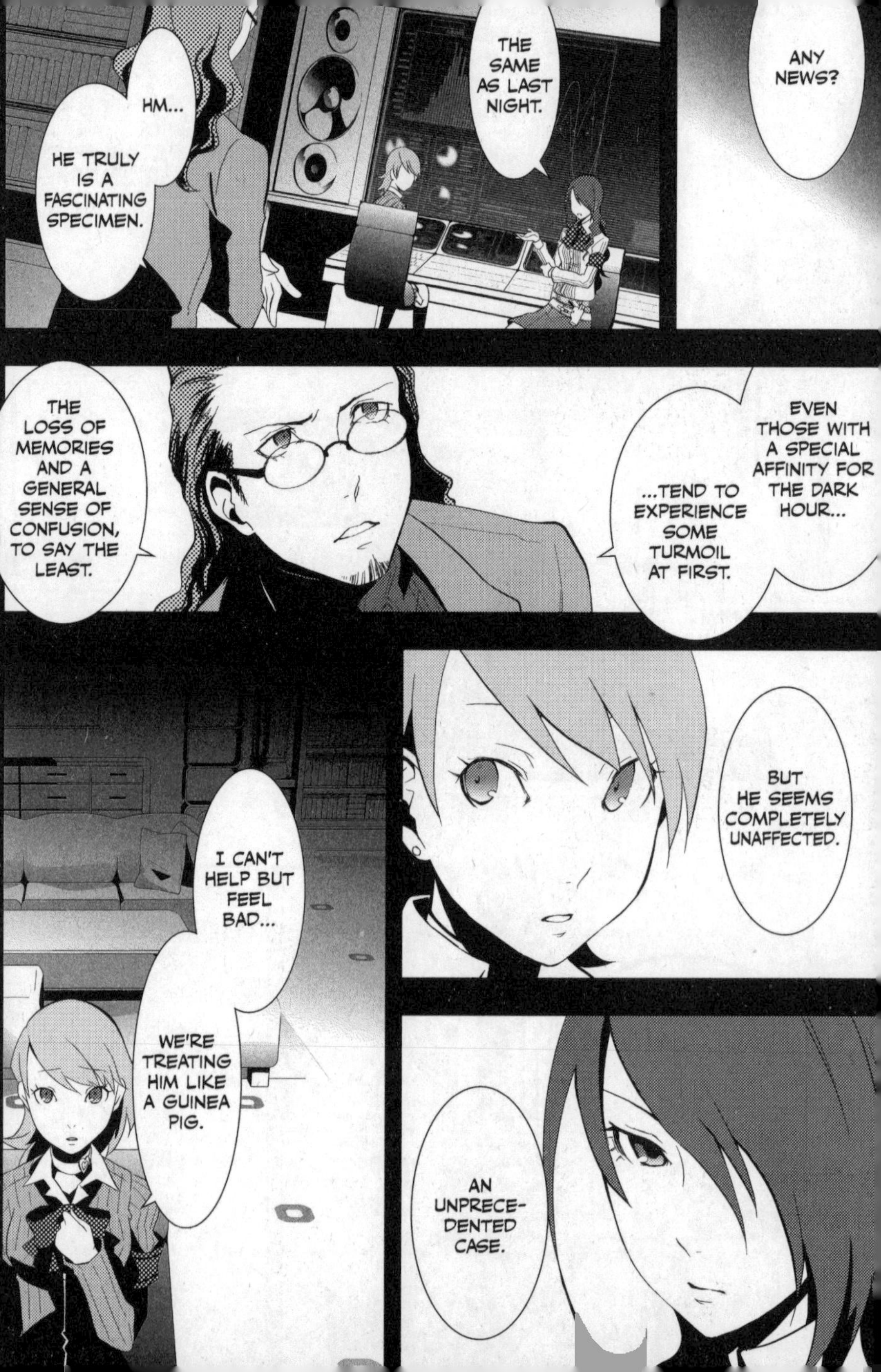
ANY NEWS?
THE SAME AS LAST NIGHT.
HM...
HE TRULY IS A FASCINATING SPECIMEN.
EVEN THOSE WITH A SPECIAL AFFINITY FOR THE DARK HOUR...
...TEND TO EXPERIENCE SOME TURMOIL AT FIRST.
THE LOSS OF MEMORIES AND A GENERAL SENSE OF CONFUSION, TO SAY THE LEAST.
BUT HE SEEMS COMPLETELY UNAFFECTED.
AN UNPRECE-DENTED CASE.
I CAN'T HELP BUT FEEL BAD...
WE'RE TREATING HIM LIKE A GUINEA PIG.

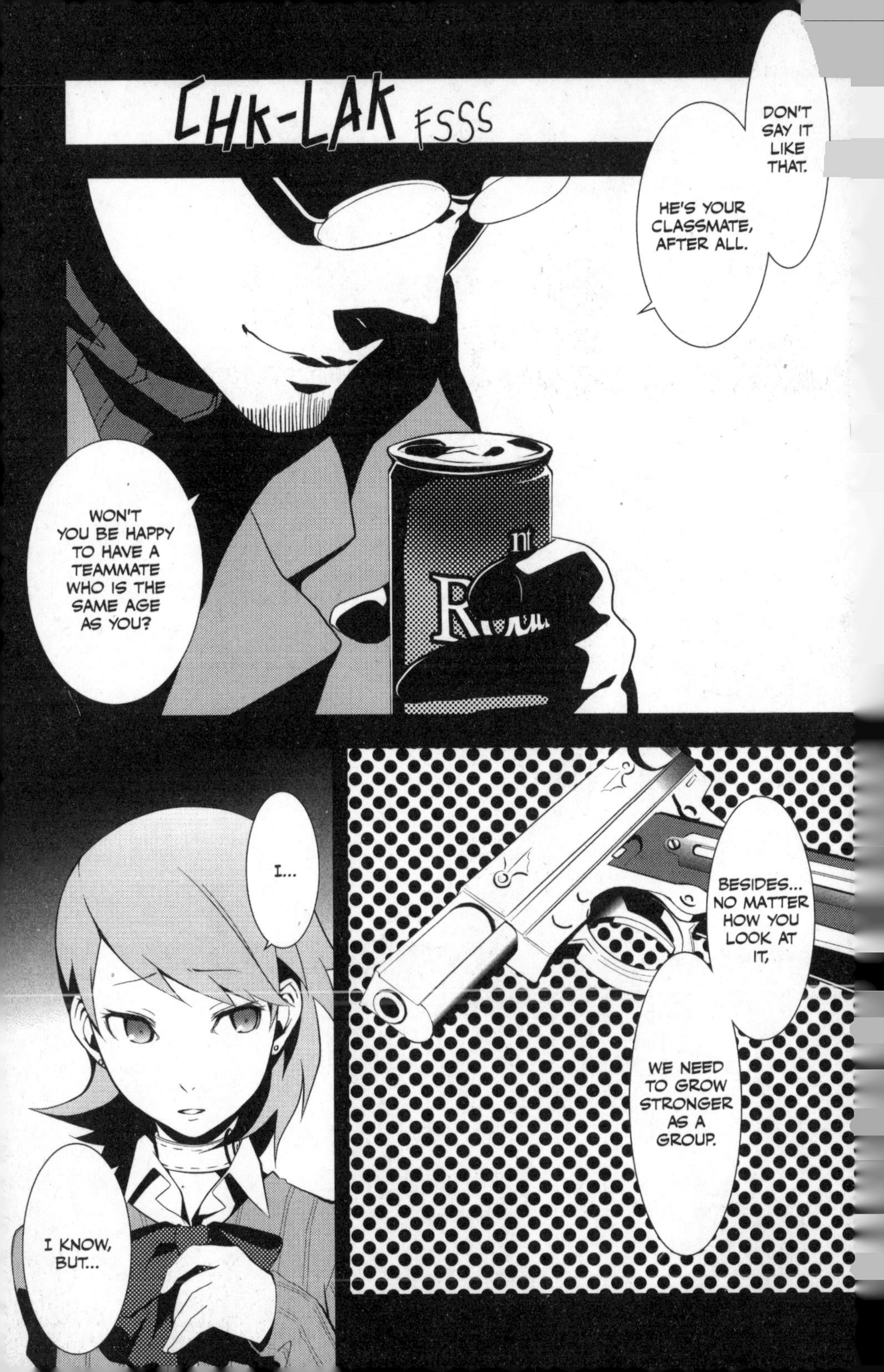
DON'T SAY IT LIKE THAT.
HE'S YOUR CLASSMATE, AFTER ALL.
CHK-LAK
FSSS
WON'T YOU BE HAPPY TO HAVE A TEAMMATE WHO IS THE SAME AGE AS YOU?
BESIDES... NO MATTER HOW YOU LOOK AT IT,
WE NEED TO GROW STRONGER AS A GROUP.
I...
I KNOW, BUT...

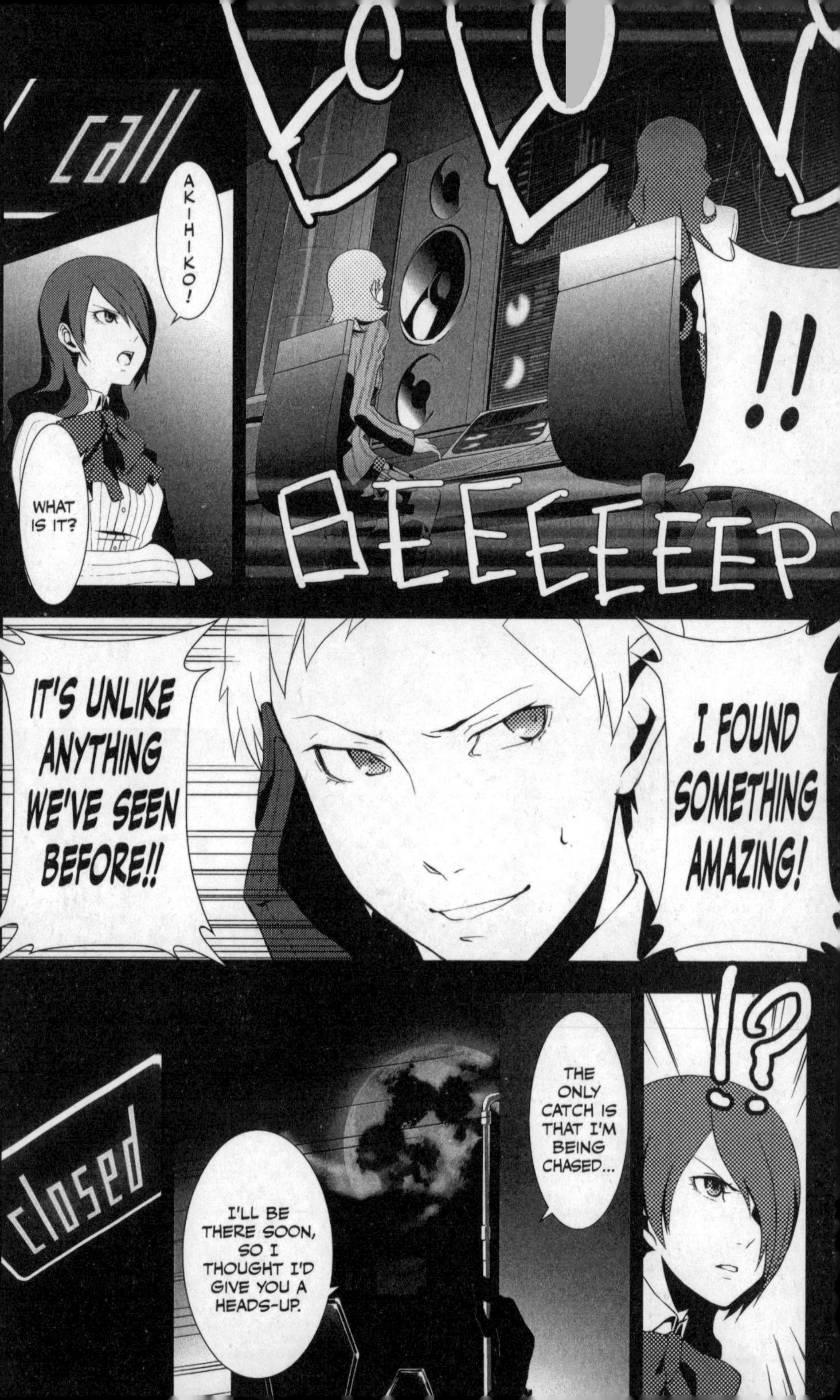
!!
BEEEEEEP
call
AKIHIKO!
WHAT IS IT?
I FOUND SOMETHING AMAZING!
IT'S UNLIKE ANYTHING WE'VE SEEN BEFORE!!
!?
THE ONLY CATCH IS THAT I'M BEING CHASED...
I'LL BE THERE SOON, SO I THOUGHT I'D GIVE YOU A HEADS-UP.
closed

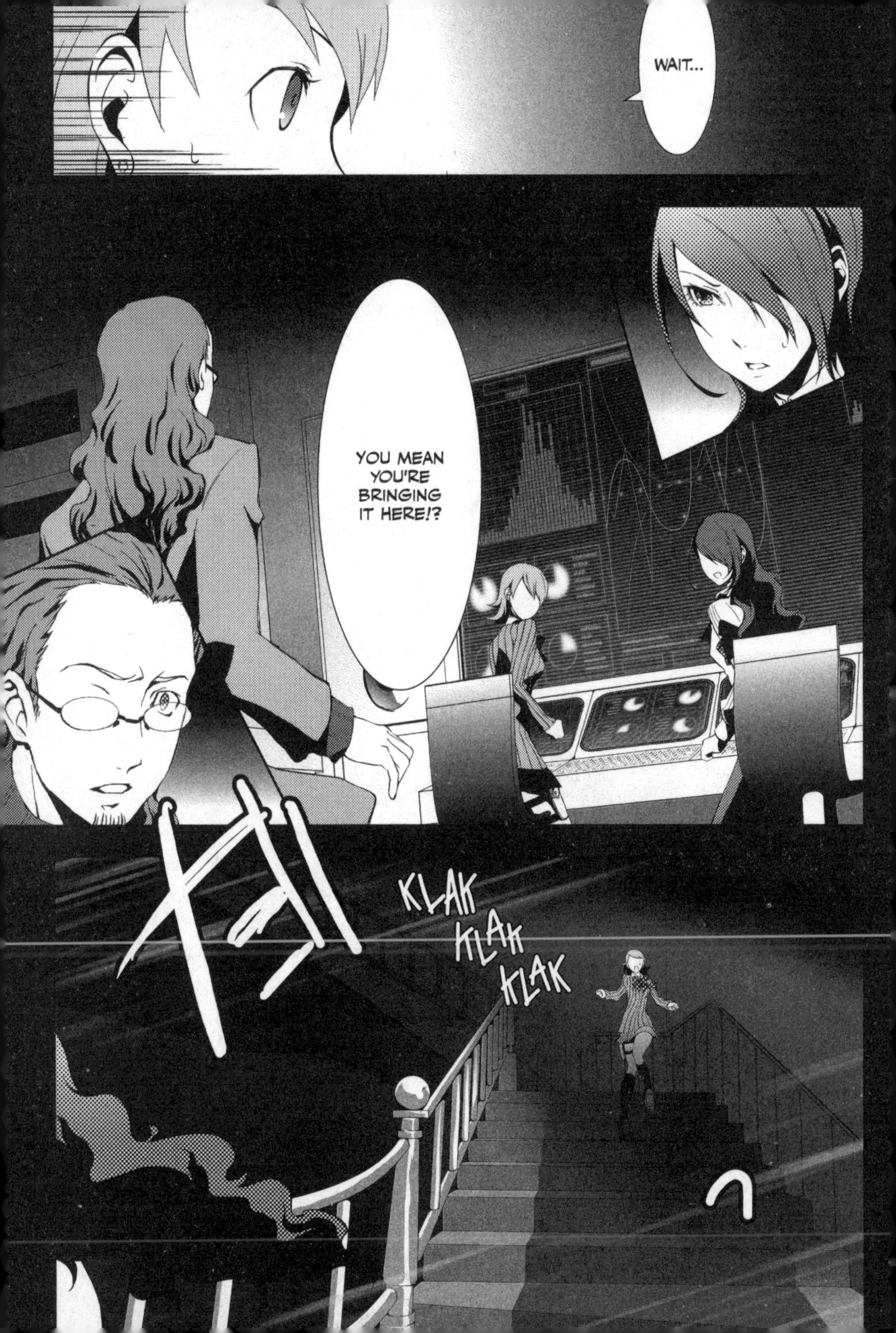
WAIT...
YOU MEAN YOU'RE BRINGING IT HERE!?
KLAK
KLAK
KLAK

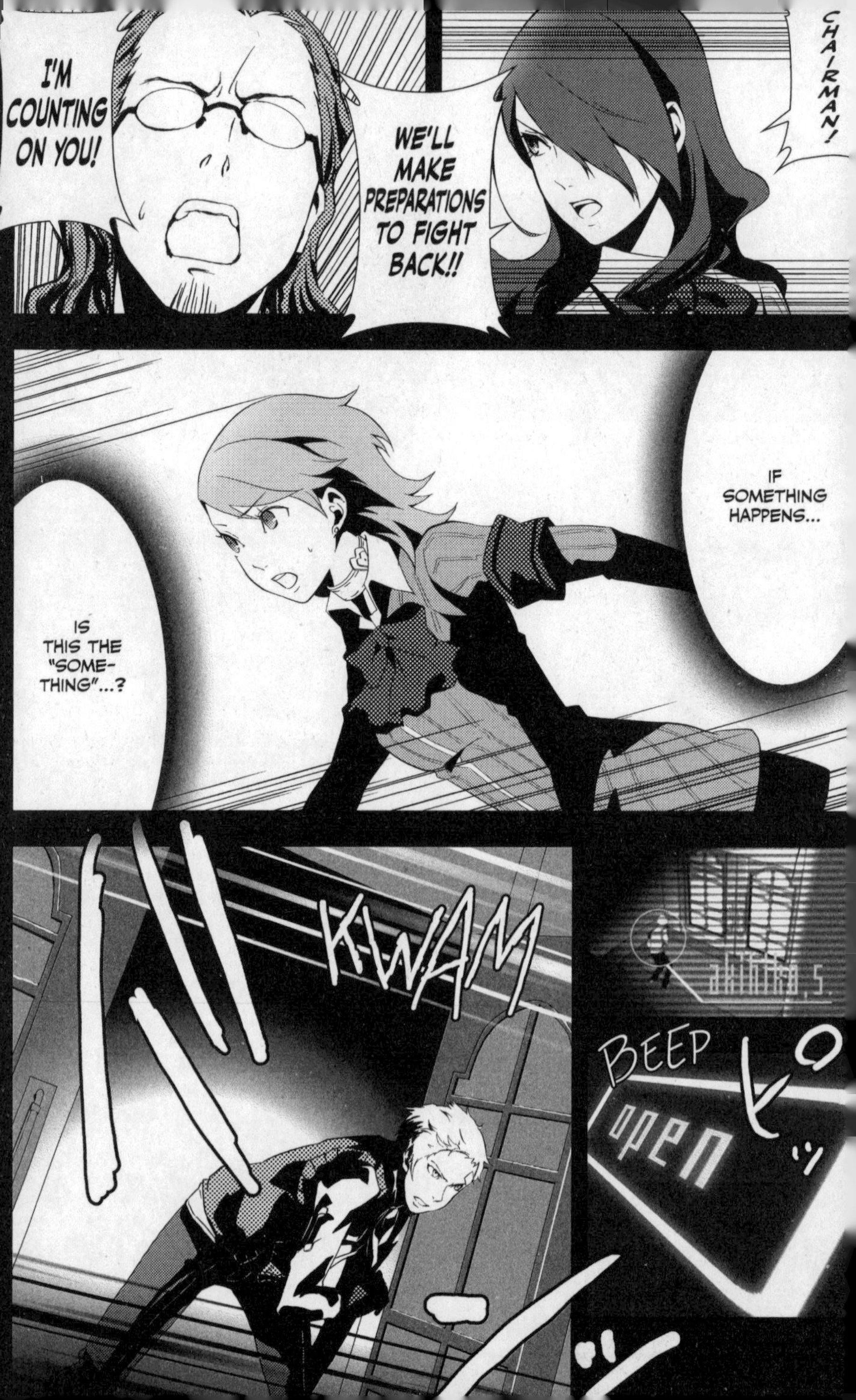
CHAIRMAN!
WE'LL MAKE PREPARATIONS TO FIGHT BACK!!
I'M COUNTING ON YOU!
IF SOMETHING HAPPENS...
IS THIS THE "SOME-THING"...?
akihiko.s.
BEEP
open
ピッ
KWAM

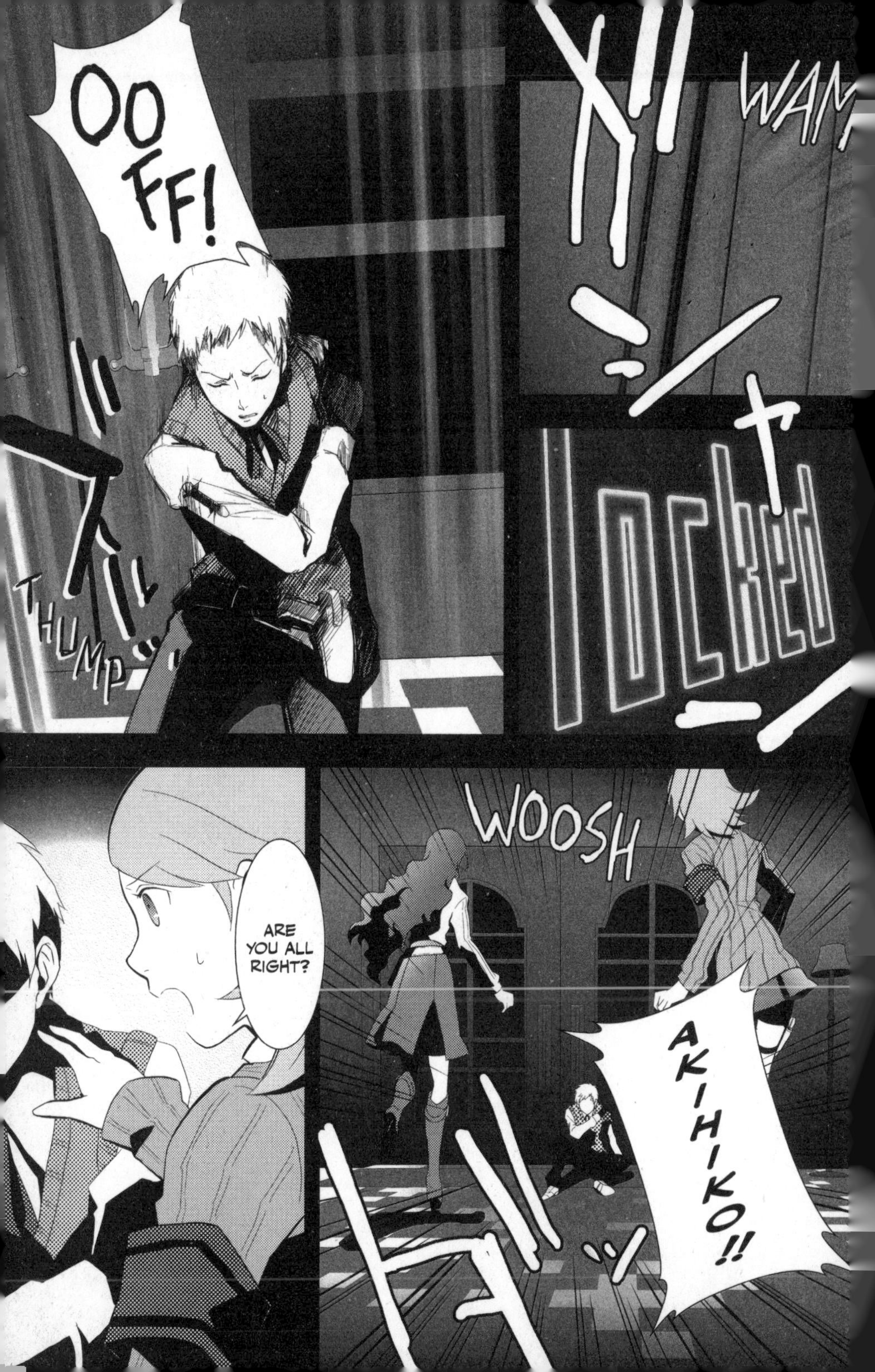
WAM
locked
OOFF!
THUMP
WOOSH
AKIHIKO!!
ARE YOU ALL RIGHT?

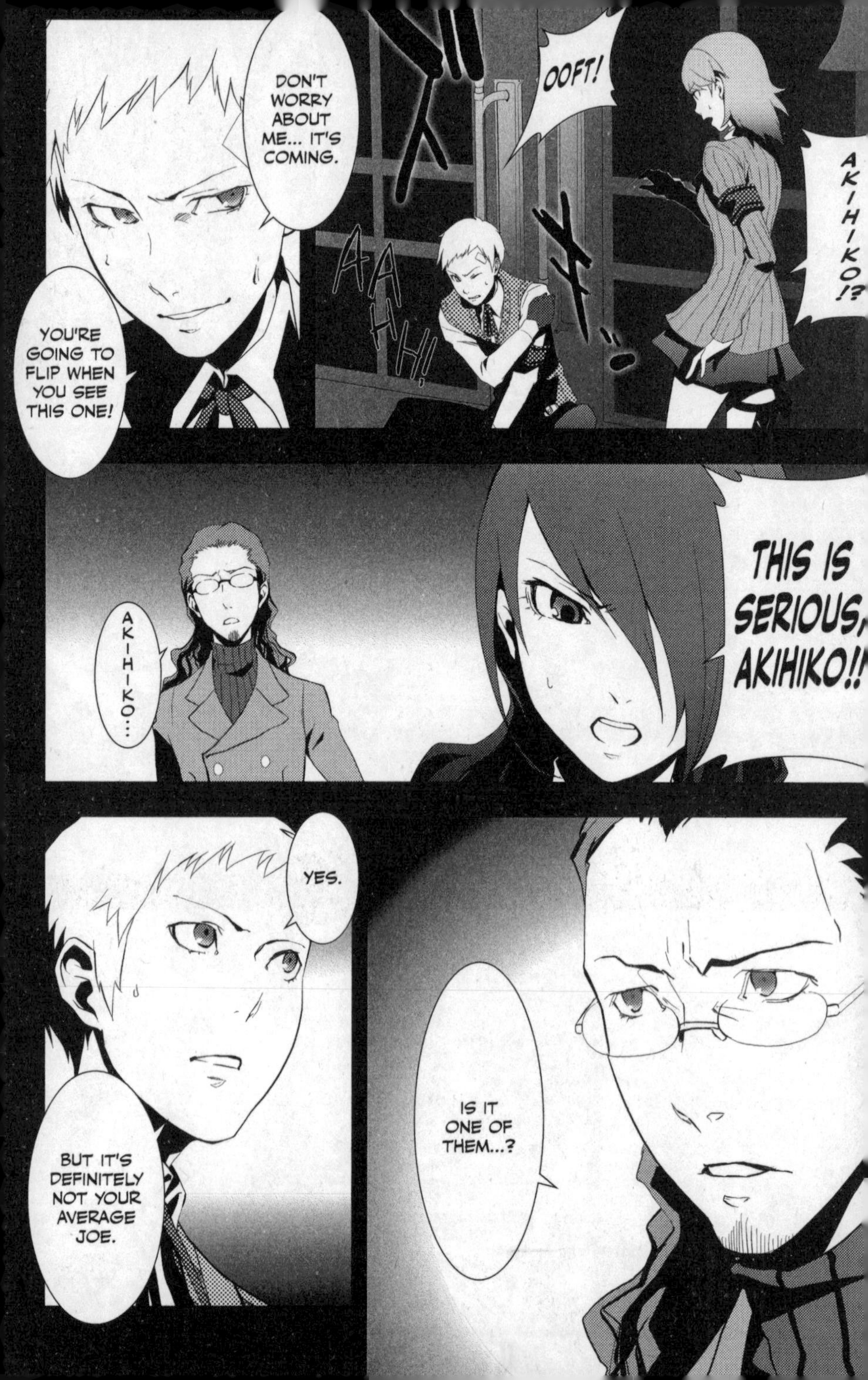
AKIHIKO!?
OOFT!
AAHH!
DON'T WORRY ABOUT ME... IT'S COMING.
YOU'RE GOING TO FLIP WHEN YOU SEE THIS ONE!
THIS IS SERIOUS, AKIHIKO!!
AKIHIKO...
IS IT ONE OF THEM...?
YES.
BUT IT'S DEFINITELY NOT YOUR AVERAGE JOE.

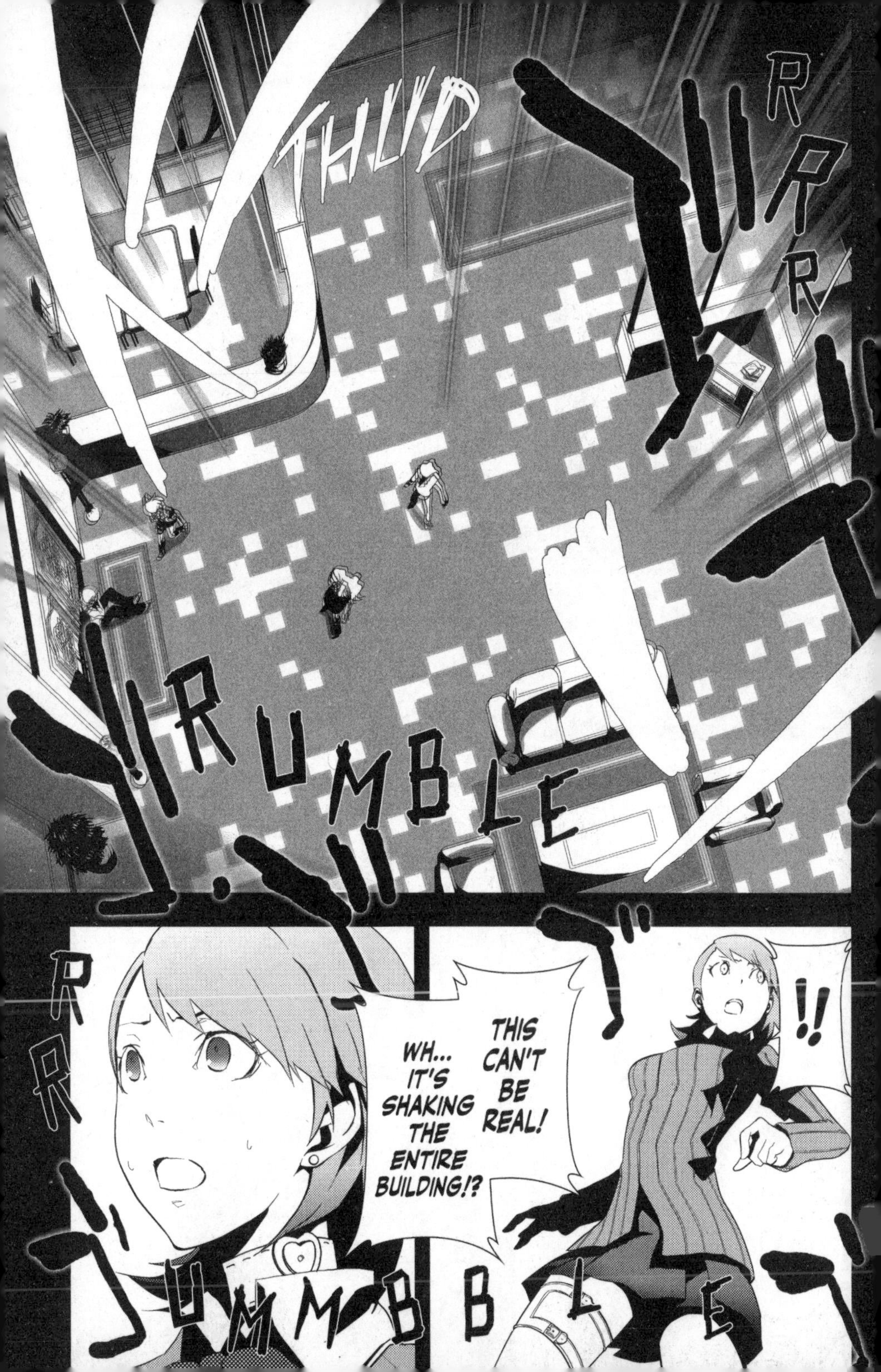
THUD
RRR
RUMBLE
!!
THIS CAN'T BE REAL!
WH... IT'S SHAKING THE ENTIRE BUILDING!?
RR
UMMBBLE

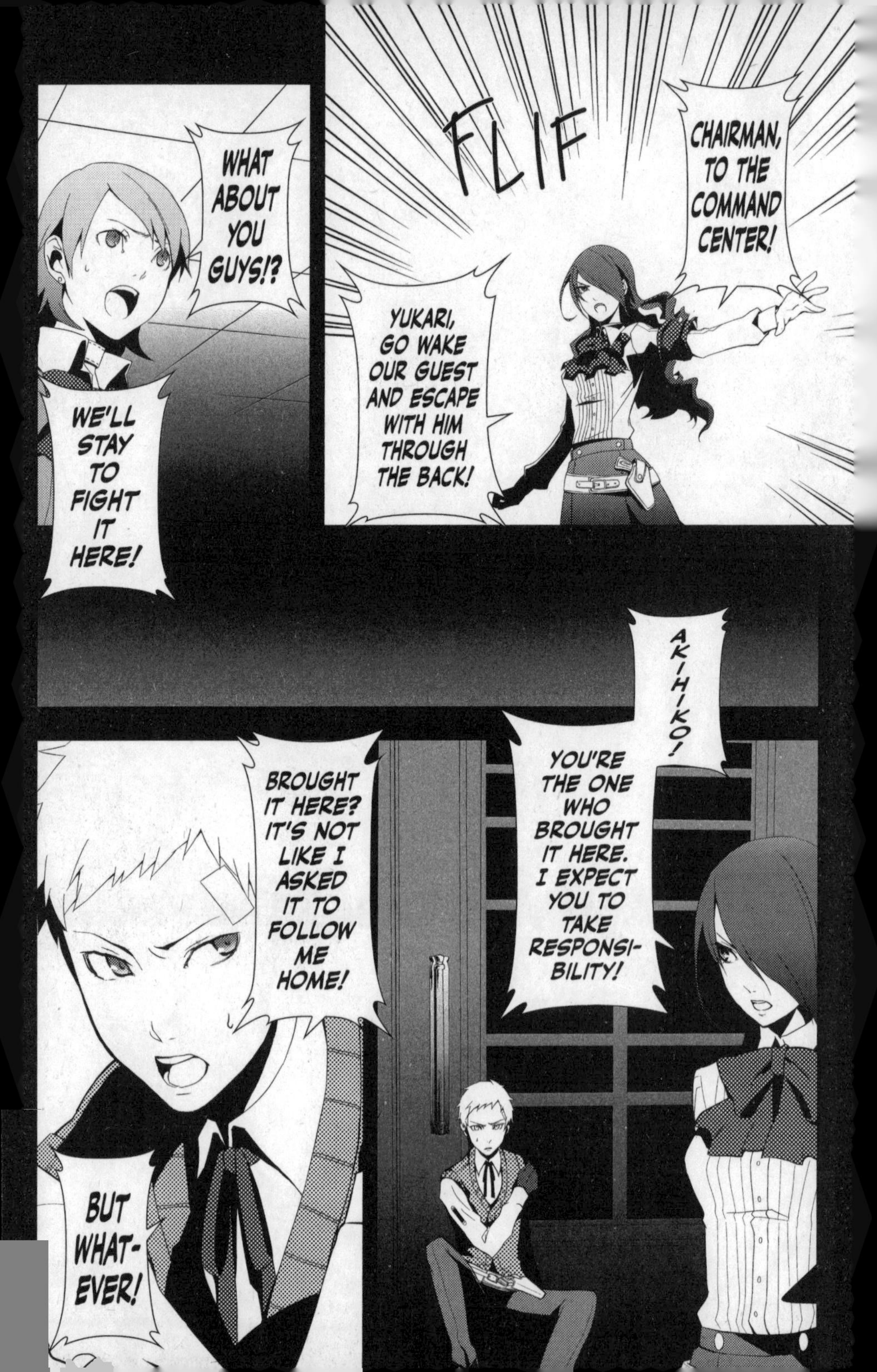
CHAIRMAN, TO THE COMMAND CENTER!
FLIF
YUKARI, GO WAKE OUR GUEST AND ESCAPE WITH HIM THROUGH THE BACK!
WHAT ABOUT YOU GUYS!?
WE'LL STAY TO FIGHT IT HERE!
AKIHIKO!
YOU'RE THE ONE WHO BROUGHT IT HERE. I EXPECT YOU TO TAKE RESPONSI-BILITY!
BROUGHT IT HERE? IT'S NOT LIKE I ASKED IT TO FOLLOW ME HOME!
BUT WHAT-EVER!

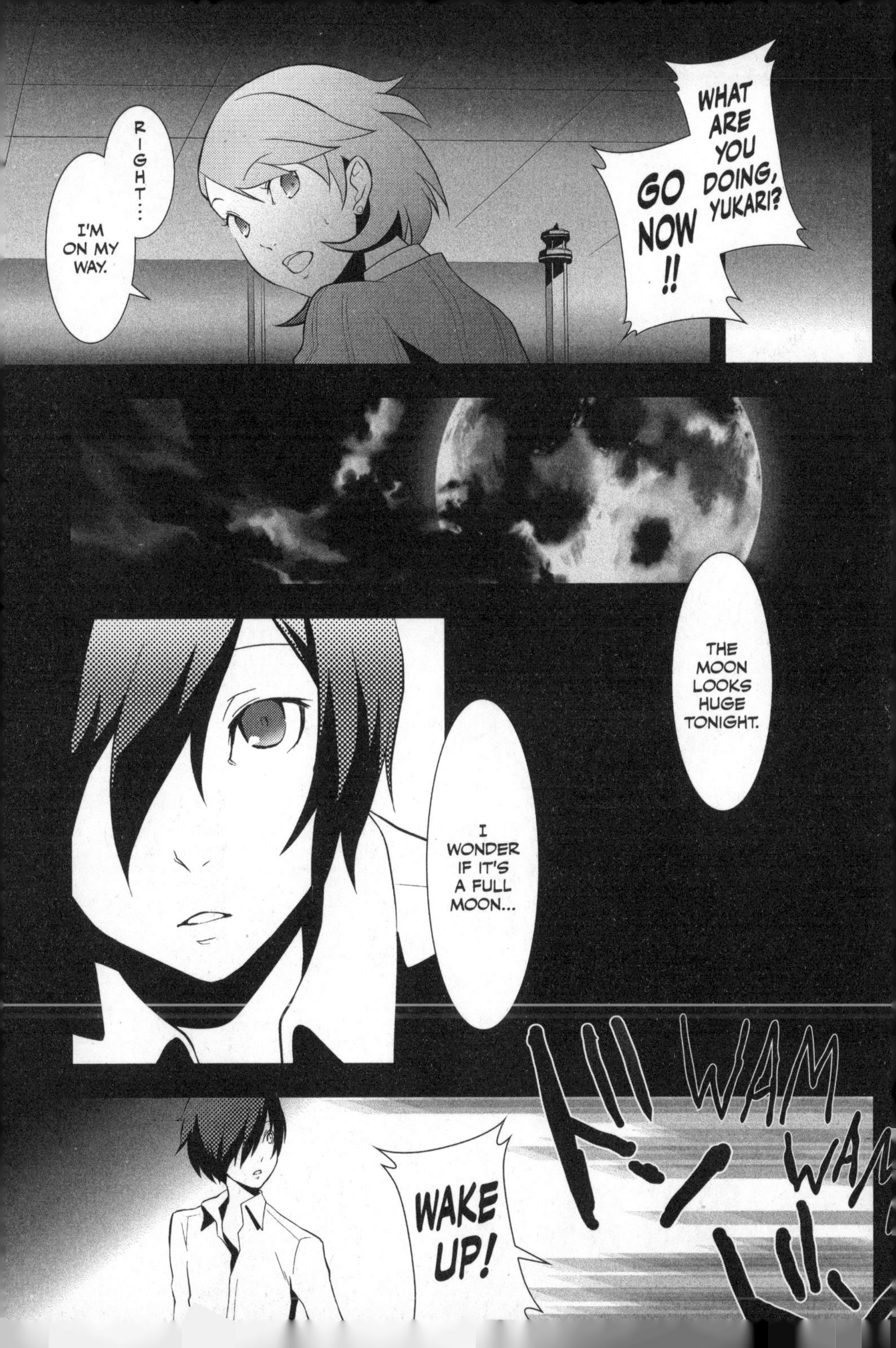
WHAT ARE YOU DOING, YUKARI?
GO NOW!!
RIGHT...
I'M ON MY WAY.
THE MOON LOOKS HUGE TONIGHT.
I WONDER IF IT'S A FULL MOON...
WAM
WAM
WAKE UP!

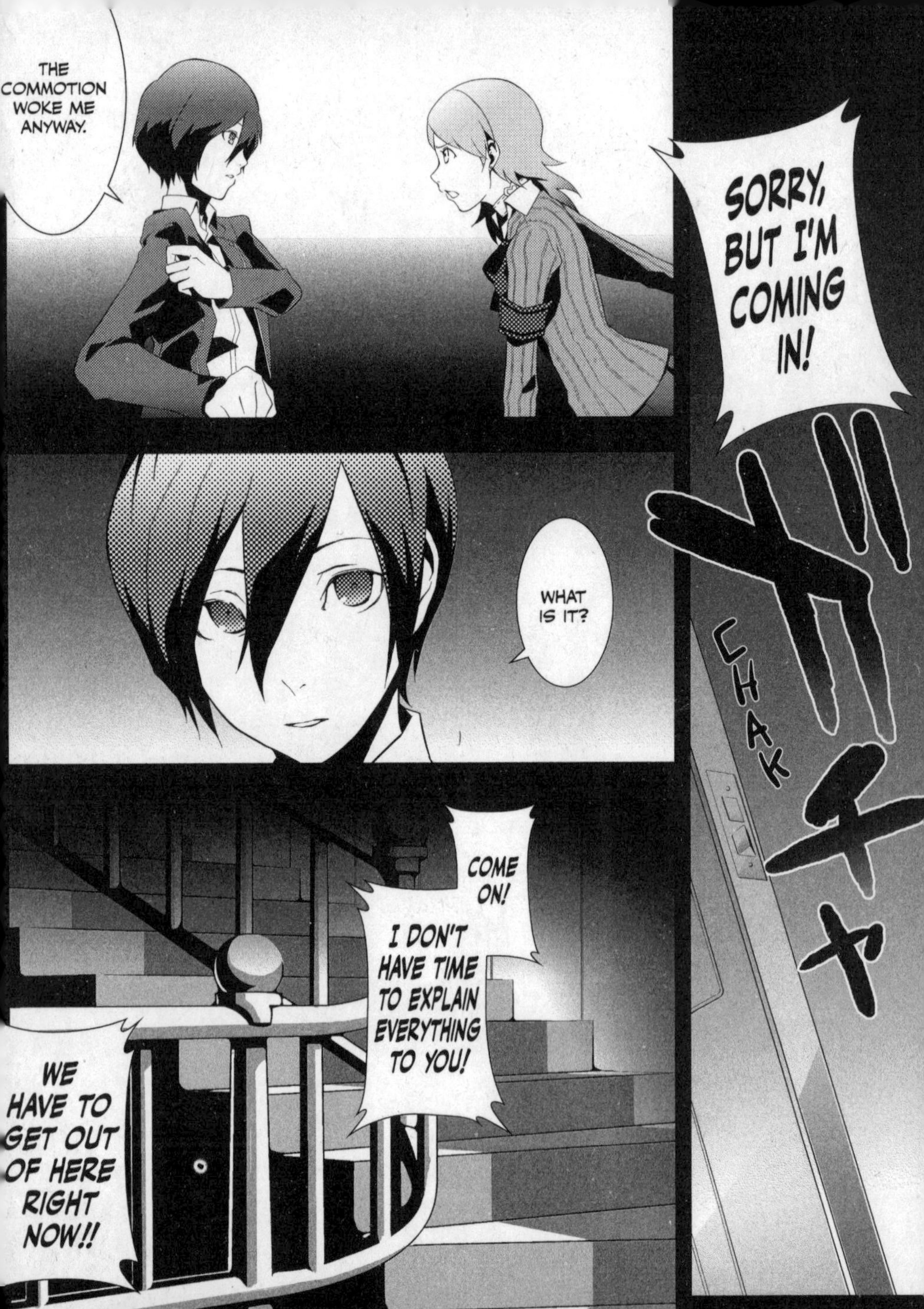
SORRY, BUT I'M COMING IN!
CHAK
ガチャ
THE COMMOTION WOKE ME ANYWAY.
WHAT IS IT?
COME ON!
I DON'T HAVE TIME TO EXPLAIN EVERYTHING TO YOU!
WE HAVE TO GET OUT OF HERE RIGHT NOW!!

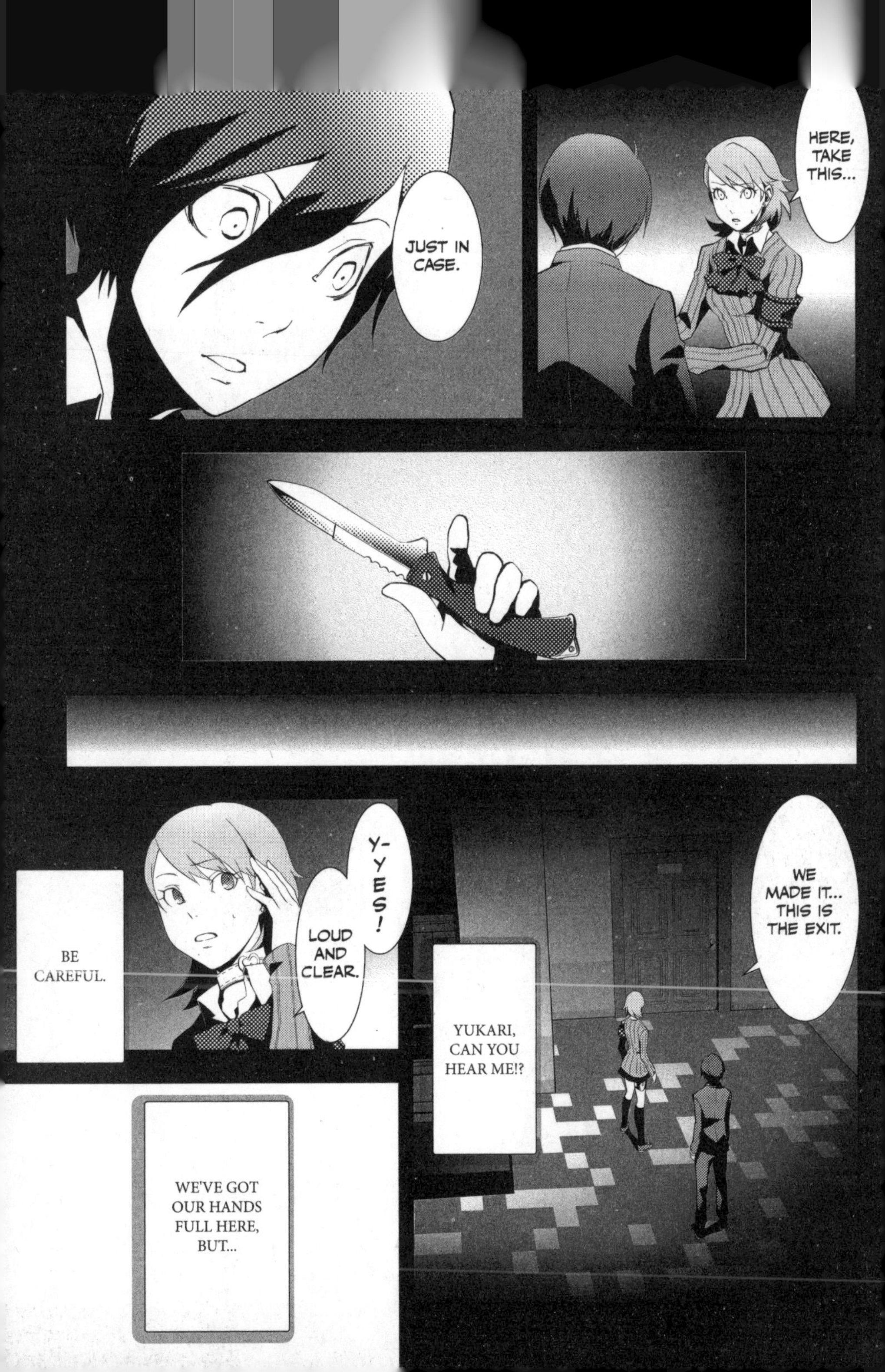
HERE, TAKE THIS...
JUST IN CASE.
WE MADE IT... THIS IS THE EXIT.
YUKARI, CAN YOU HEAR ME!?
Y-YES!
LOUD AND CLEAR.
BE CAREFUL.
WE'VE GOT OUR HANDS FULL HERE, BUT...

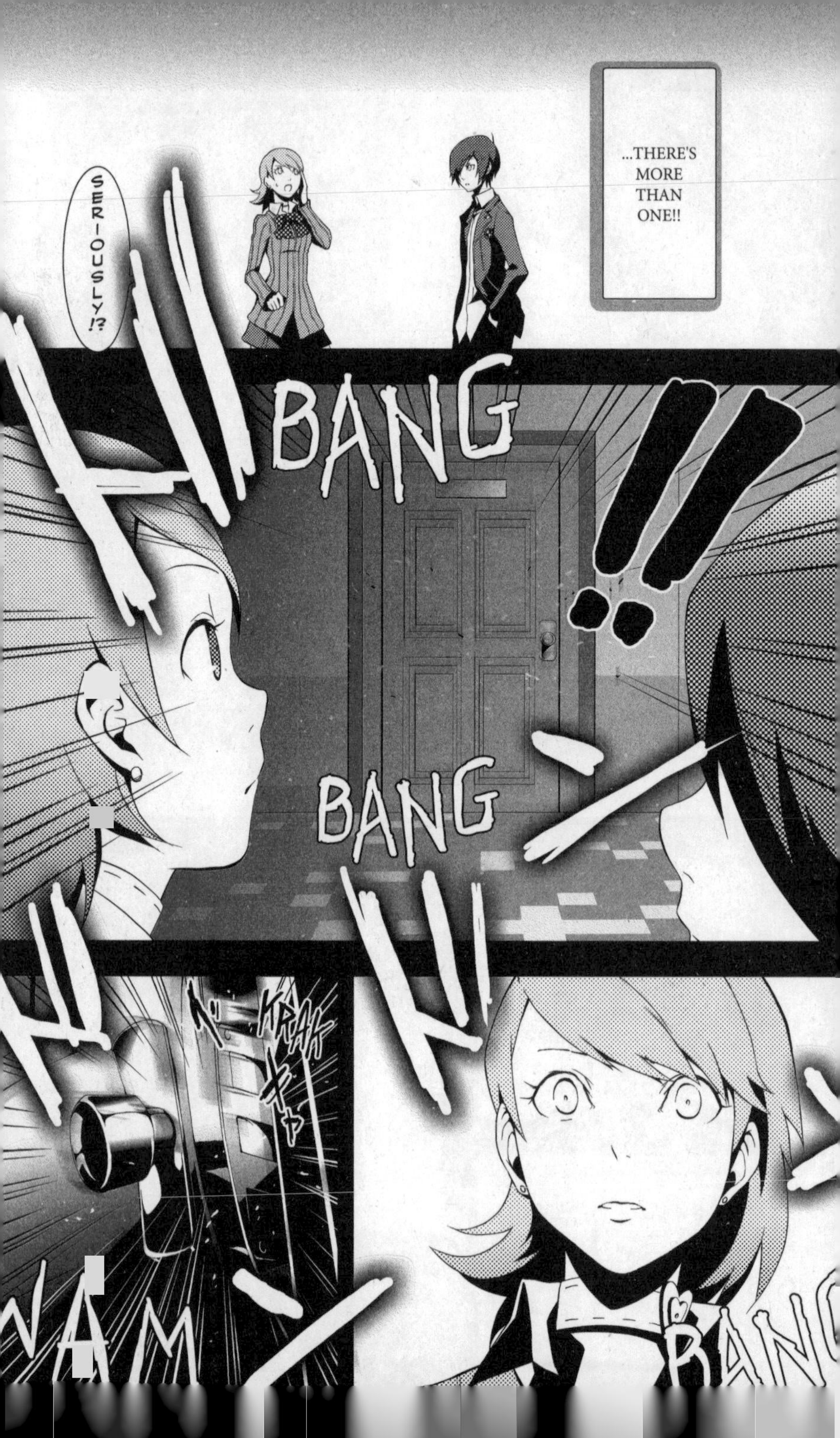
...THERE'S MORE THAN ONE!!
SERIOUSLY!?
BANG
BANG
KRAK

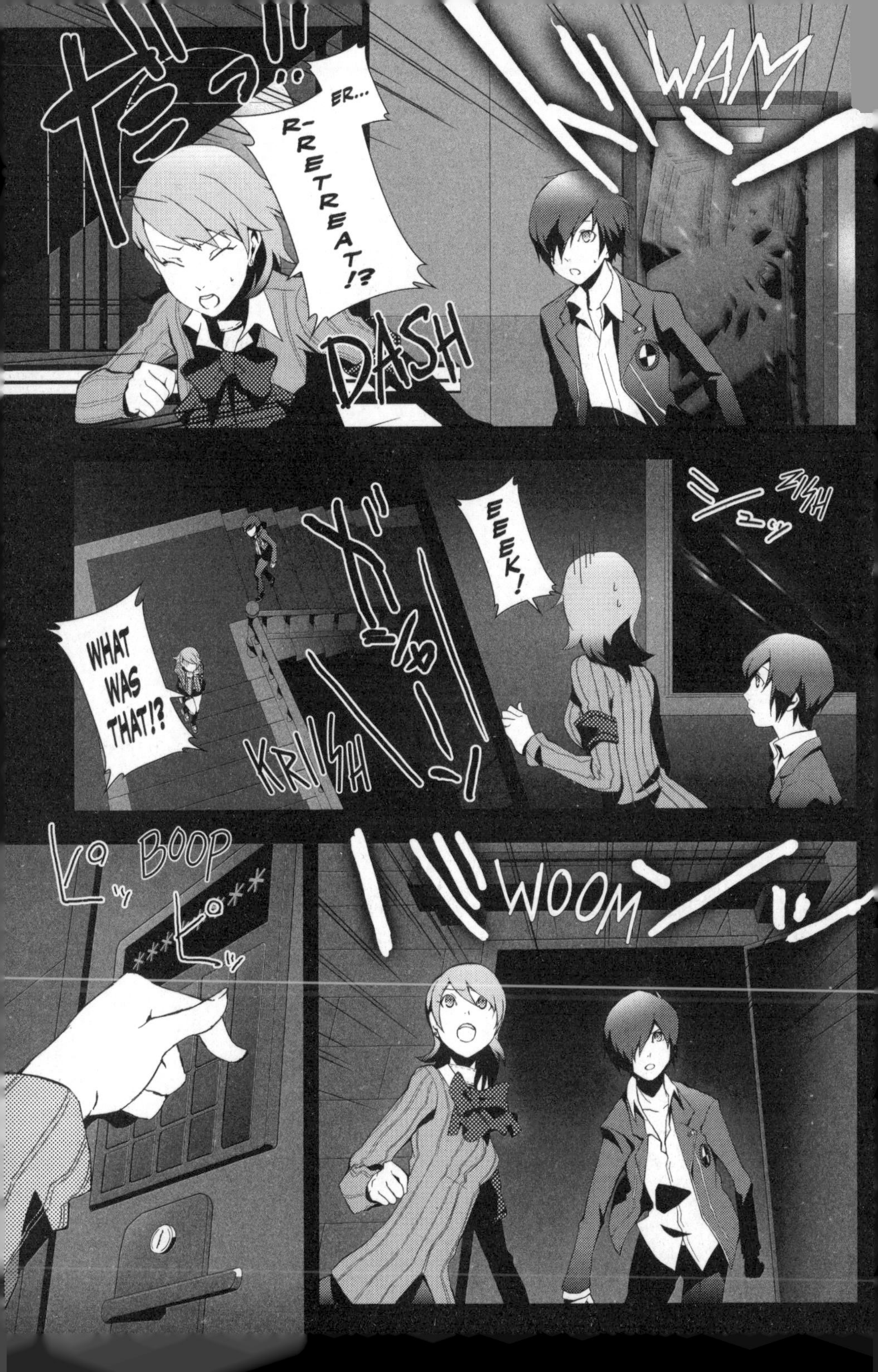
WAM
ER... R-RETREAT!?
DASH
KRISH
EEEK!
KRISH
WHAT WAS THAT!?
WOOM
BOOP

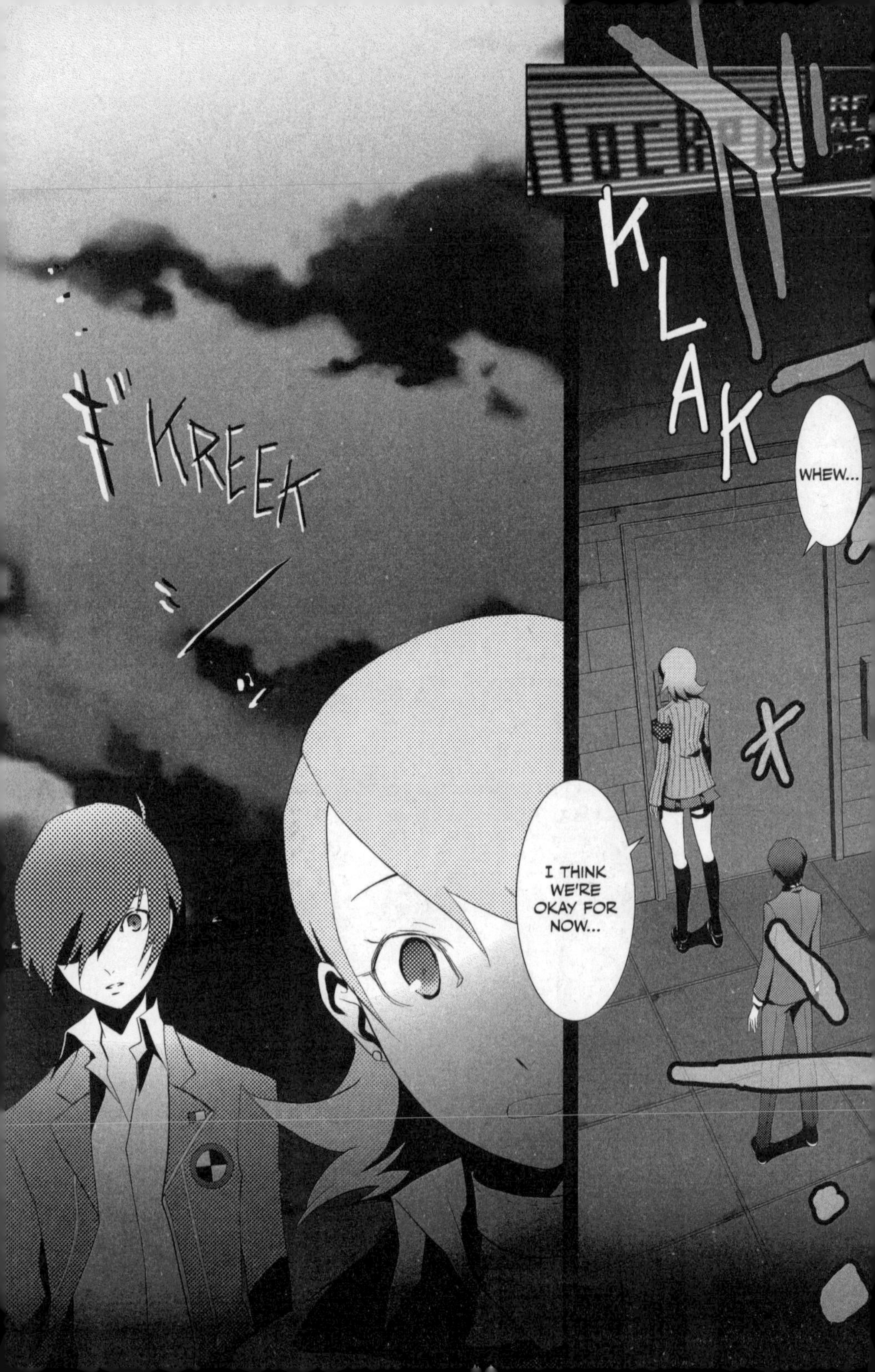
KLAK
WHEW...
I THINK WE'RE OKAY FOR NOW...
KREEK

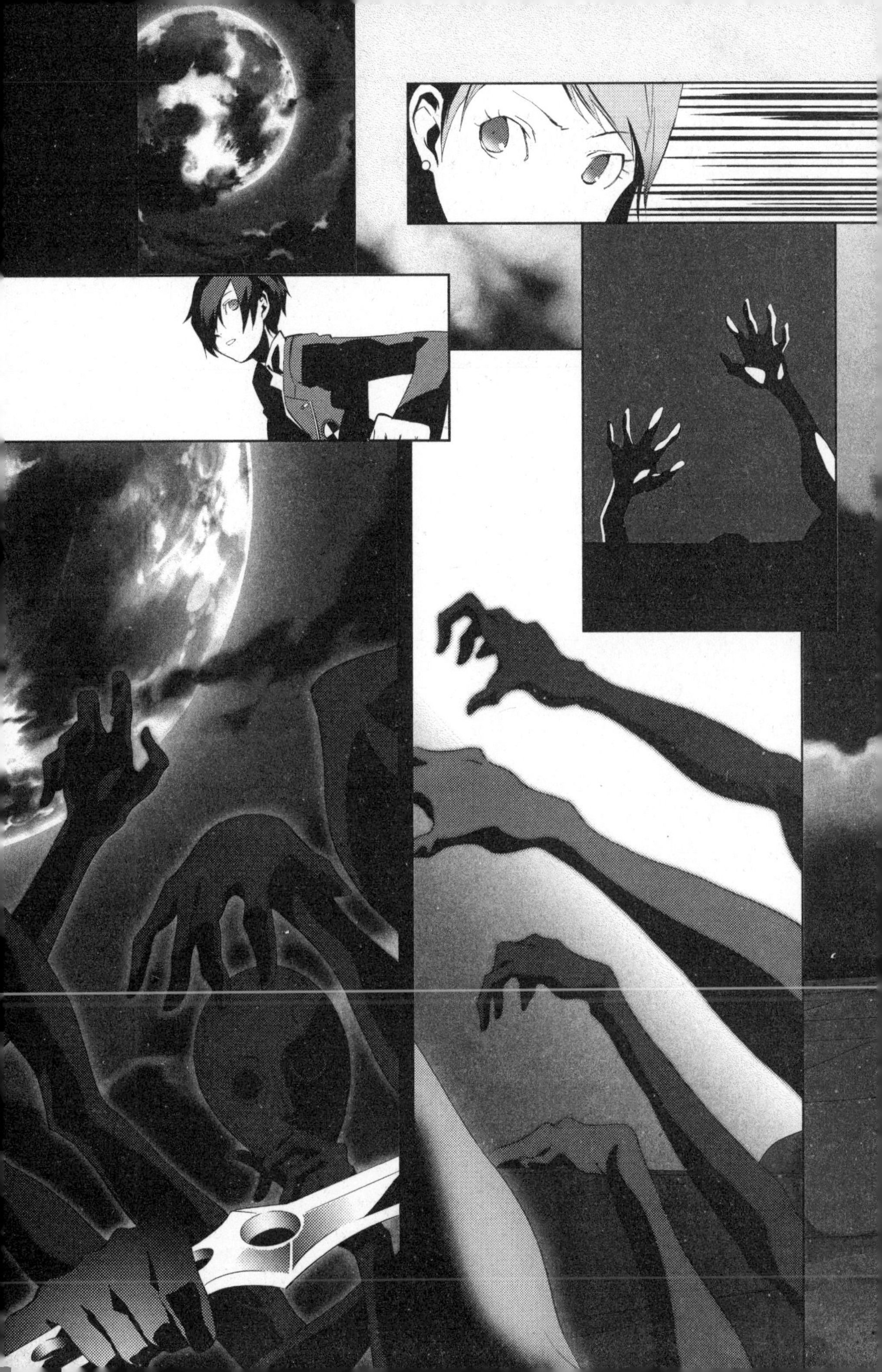

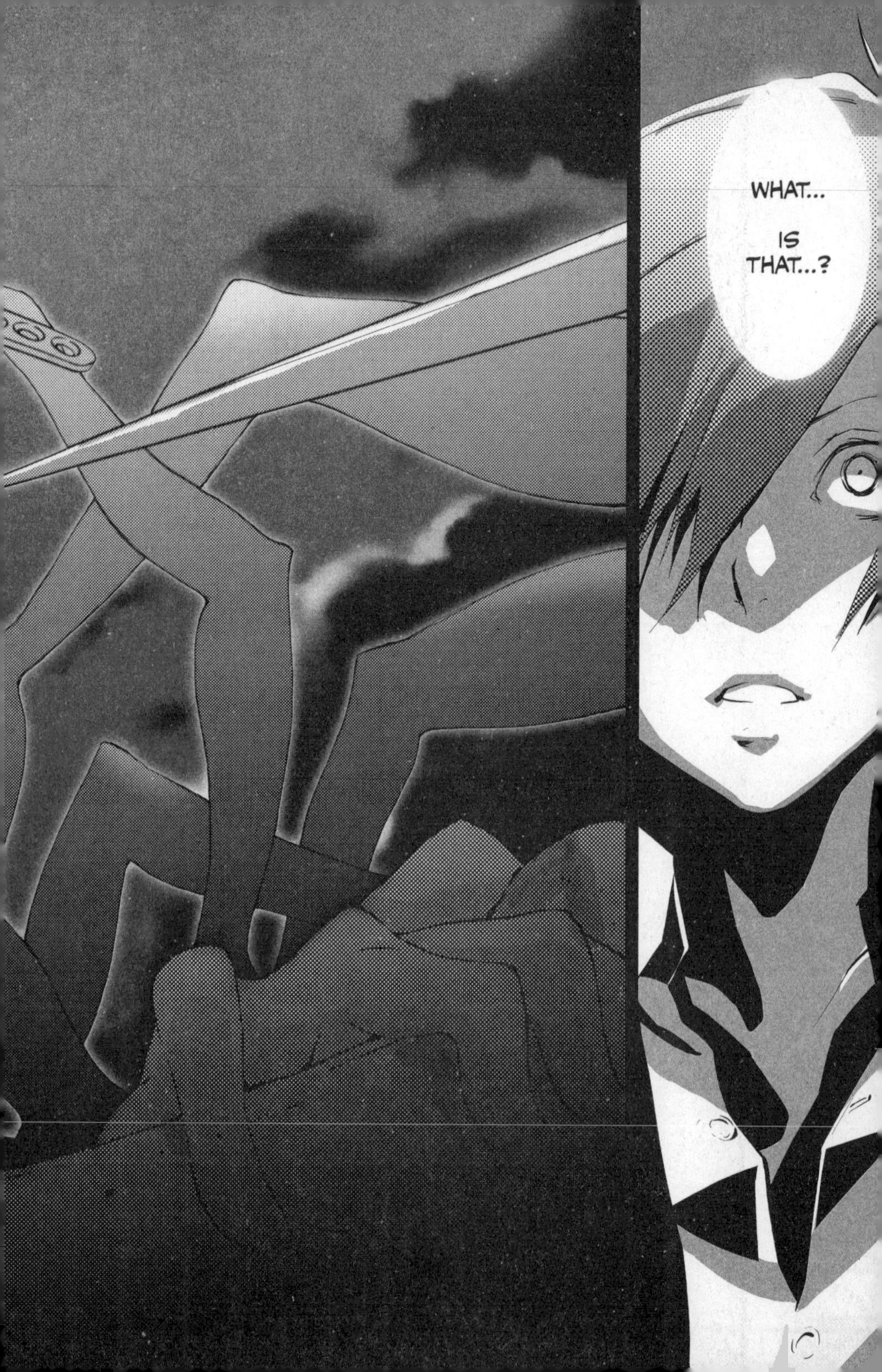
WHAT... IS THAT...?

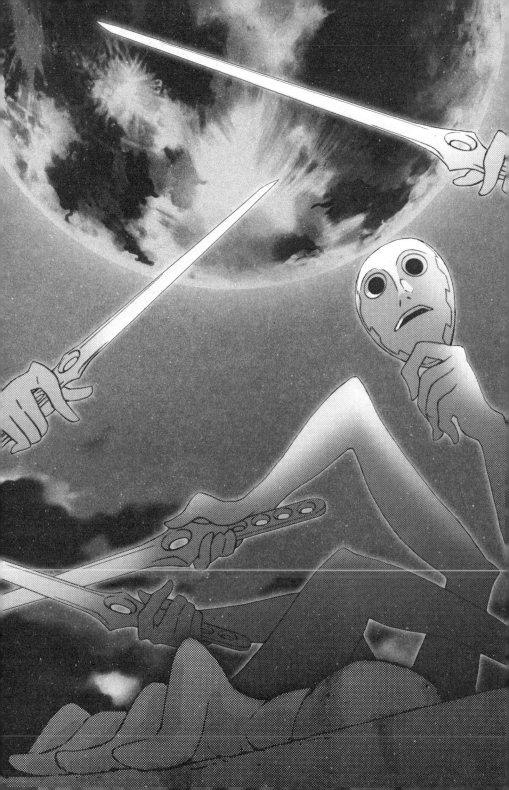

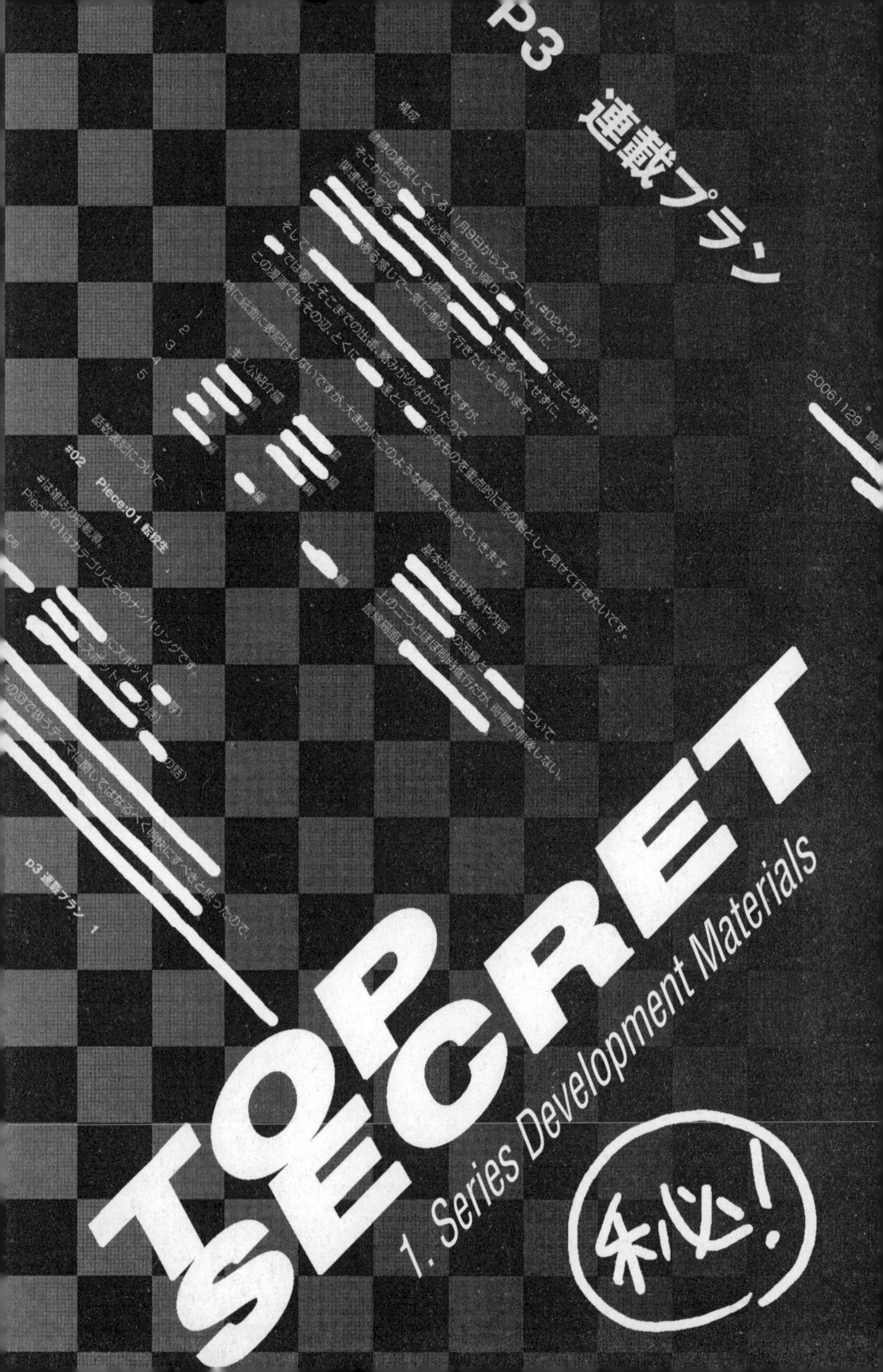
P3 連載プラン
TOP SECRET
1. Series Development Materials
秘!

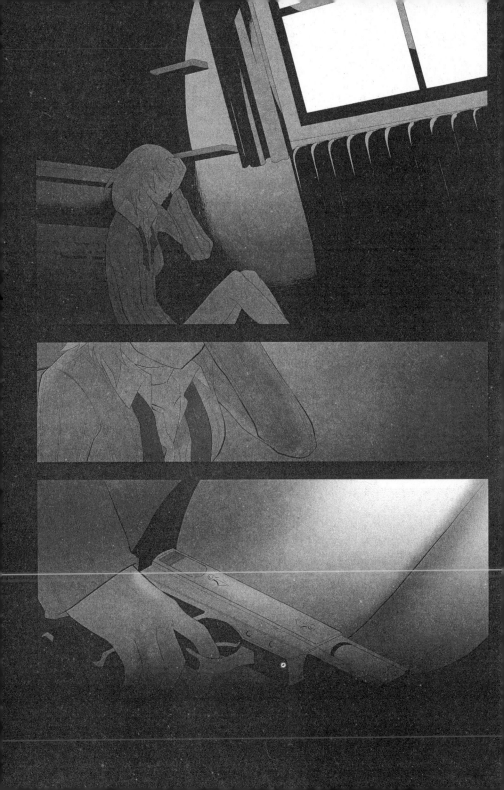

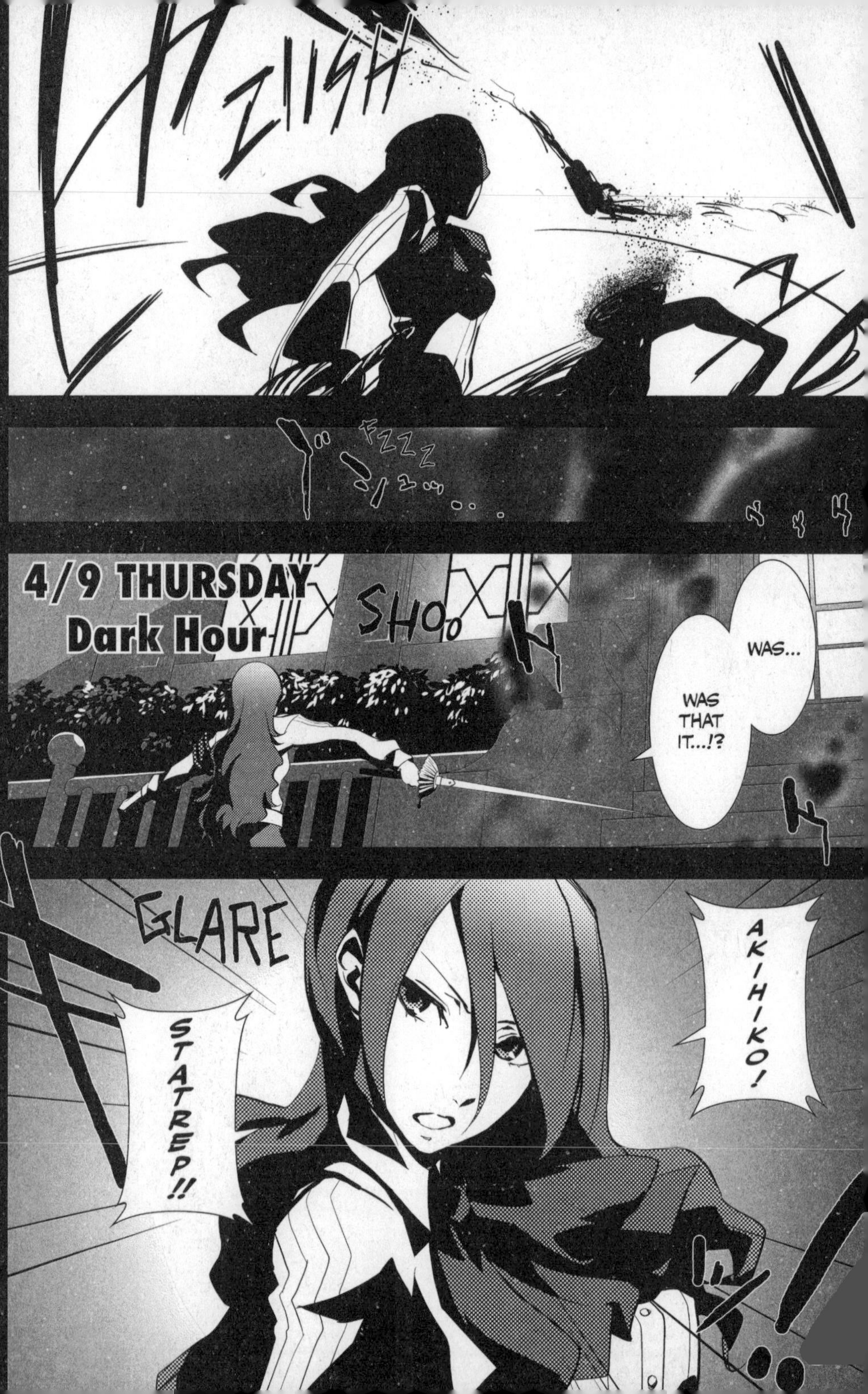
ZIISH
FZZZ
WAS...
WAS THAT IT...!?
SHOoN
4/9 THURSDAY
Dark Hour
AKIHIKO!
GLARE
STATREP!!

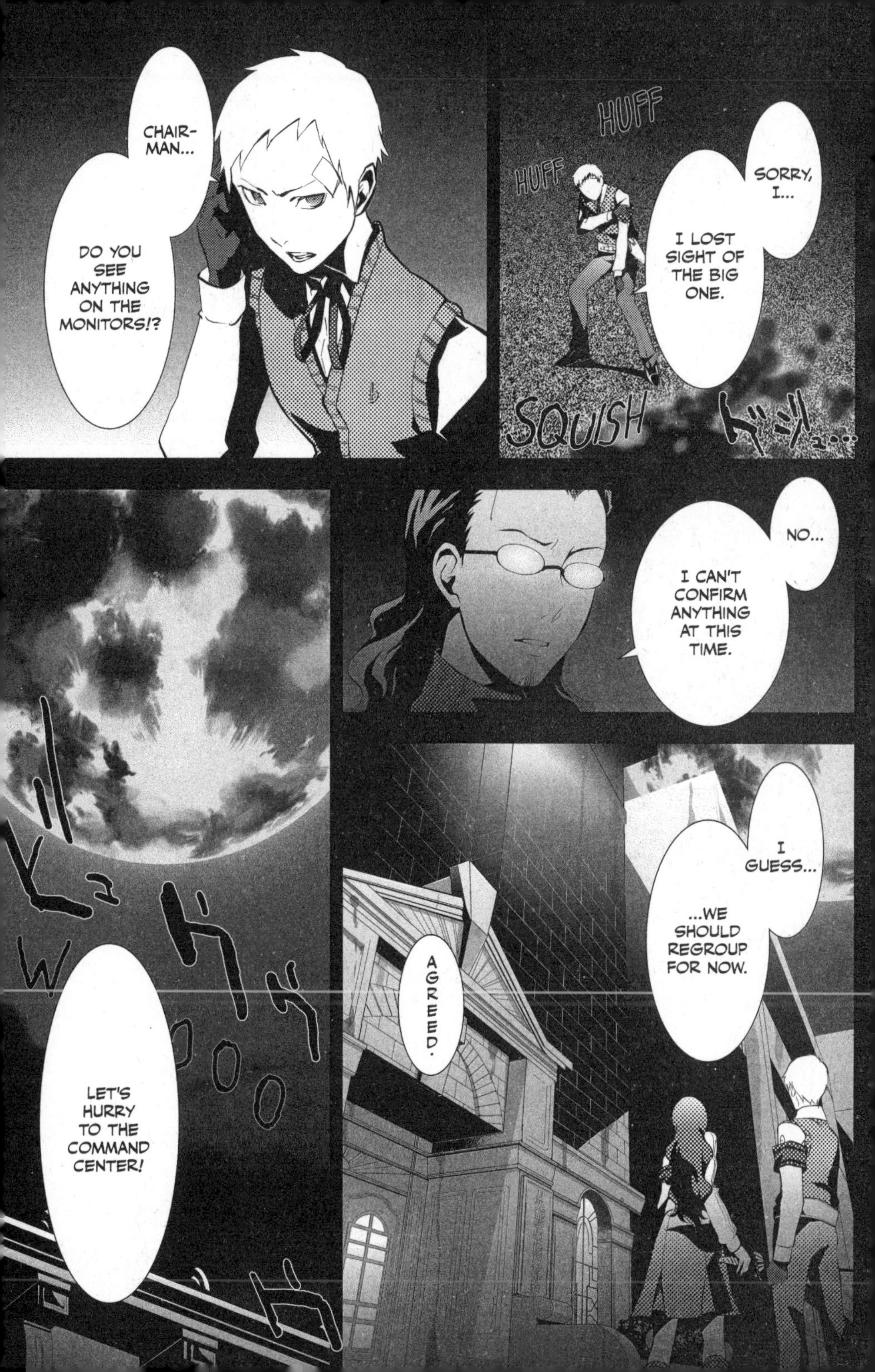
HUFF
HUFF
SORRY, I...
I LOST SIGHT OF THE BIG ONE.
SQUISH
CHAIR-MAN...
DO YOU SEE ANYTHING ON THE MONITORS!?
NO...
I CAN'T CONFIRM ANYTHING AT THIS TIME.
I GUESS...
...WE SHOULD REGROUP FOR NOW.
AGREED.
LET'S HURRY TO THE COMMAND CENTER!

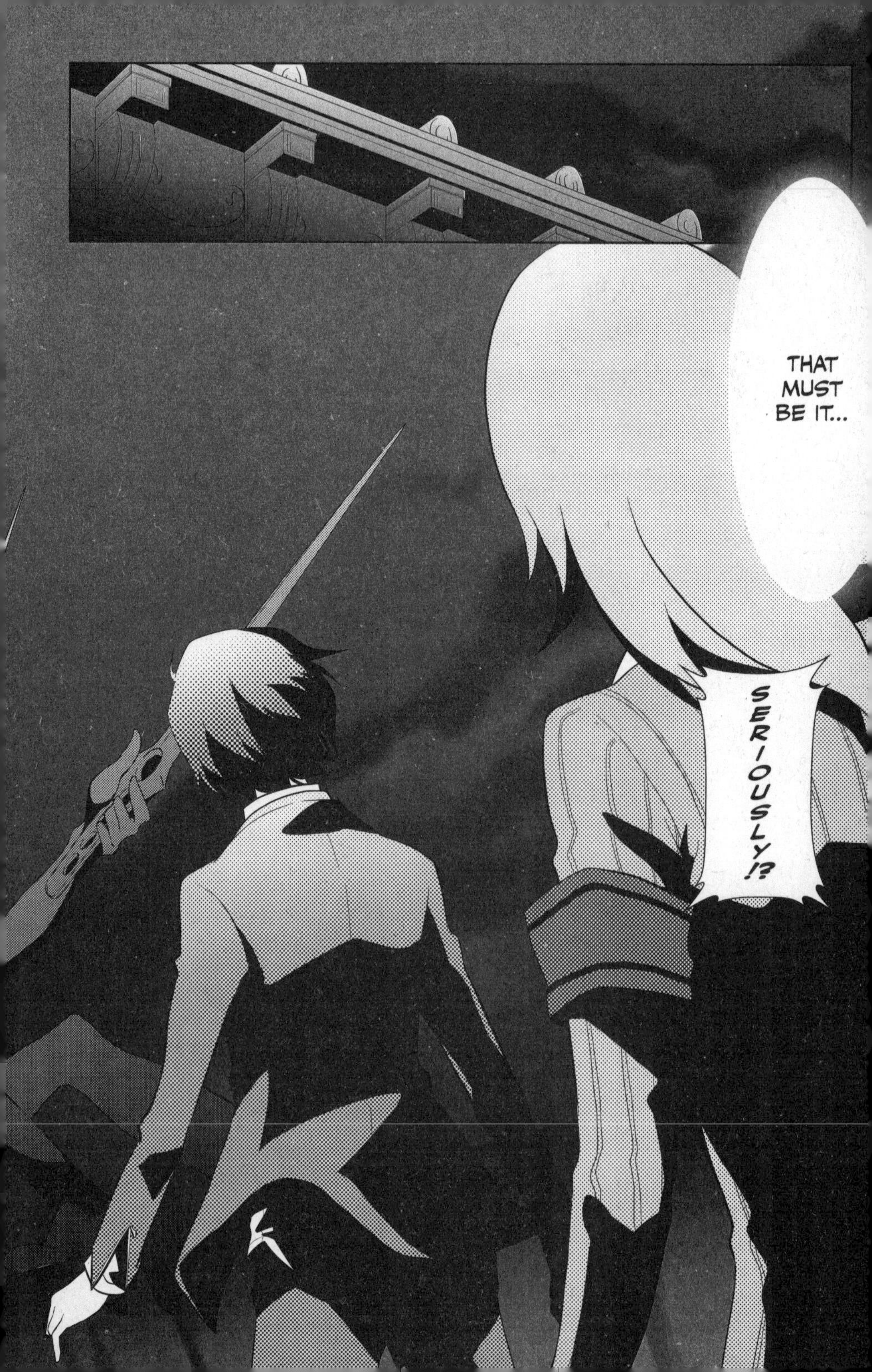
THAT MUST BE IT...
SERIOUSLY!?

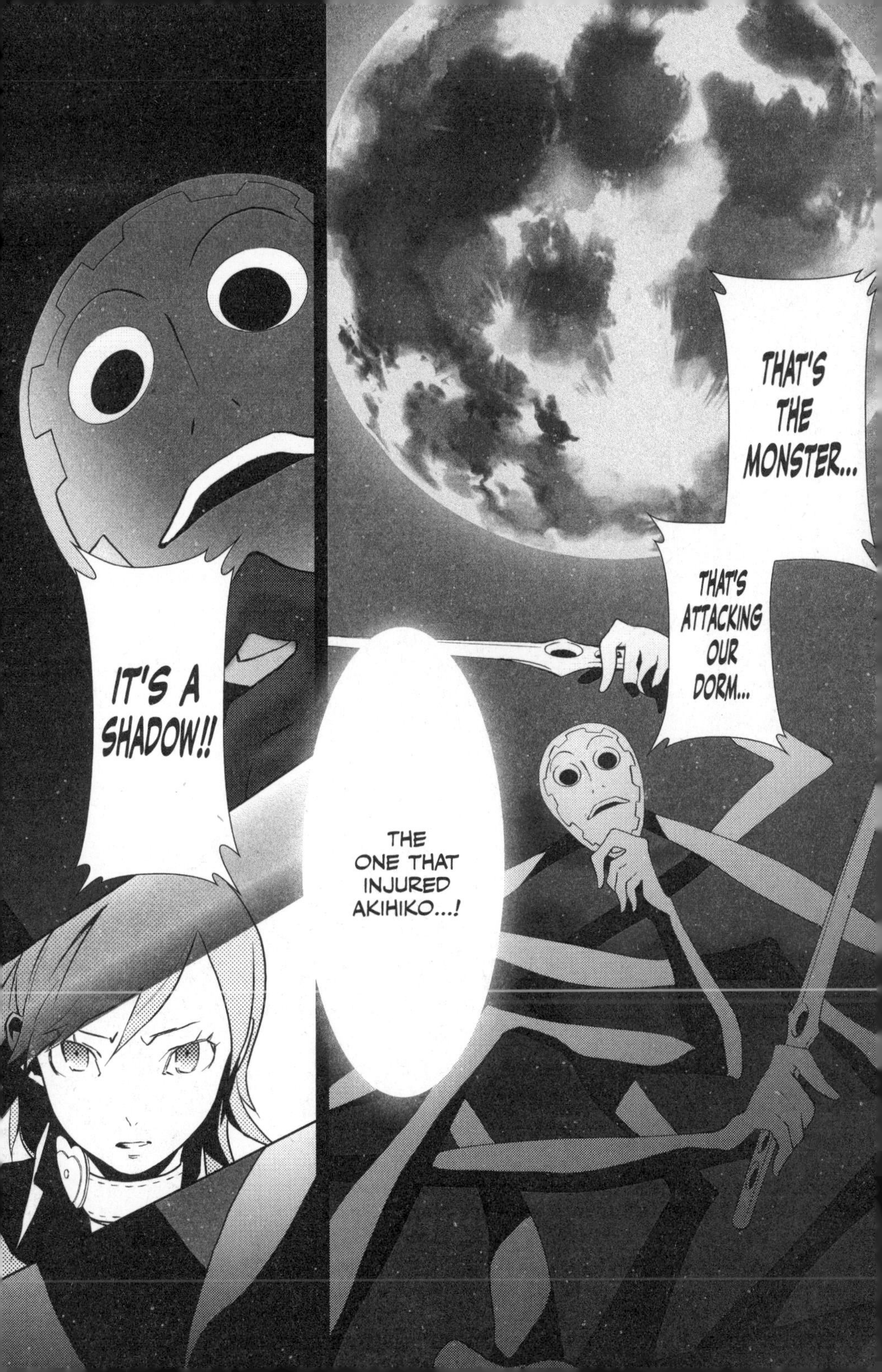
THAT'S THE MONSTER...
THAT'S ATTACKING OUR DORM...
THE ONE THAT INJURED AKIHIKO...!
IT'S A SHADOW!!

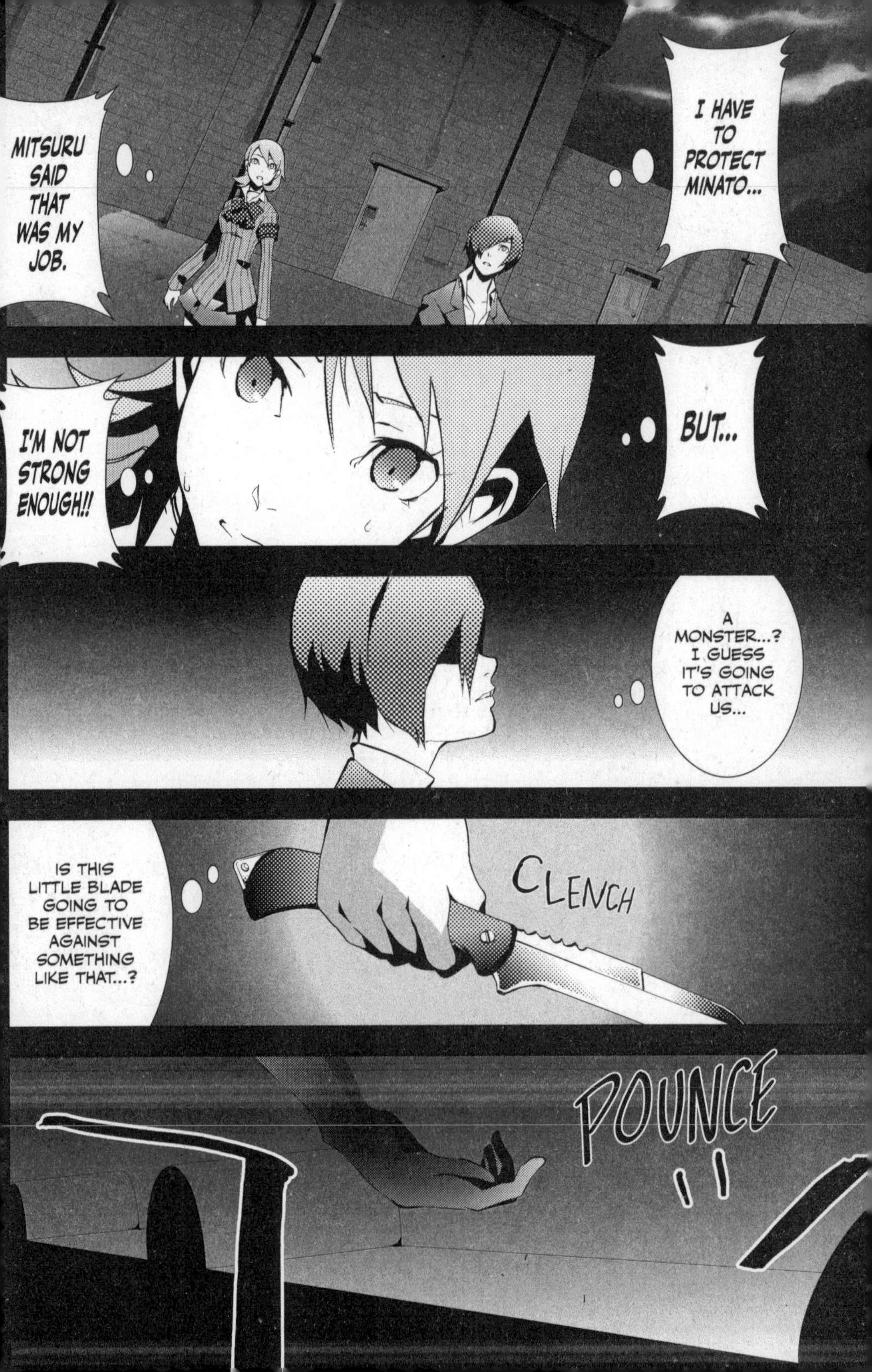
I HAVE TO PROTECT MINATO...
MITSURU SAID THAT WAS MY JOB.
BUT...
I'M NOT STRONG ENOUGH!!
A MONSTER...? I GUESS IT'S GOING TO ATTACK US...
CLENCH
IS THIS LITTLE BLADE GOING TO BE EFFECTIVE AGAINST SOMETHING LIKE THAT...?
POUNCE

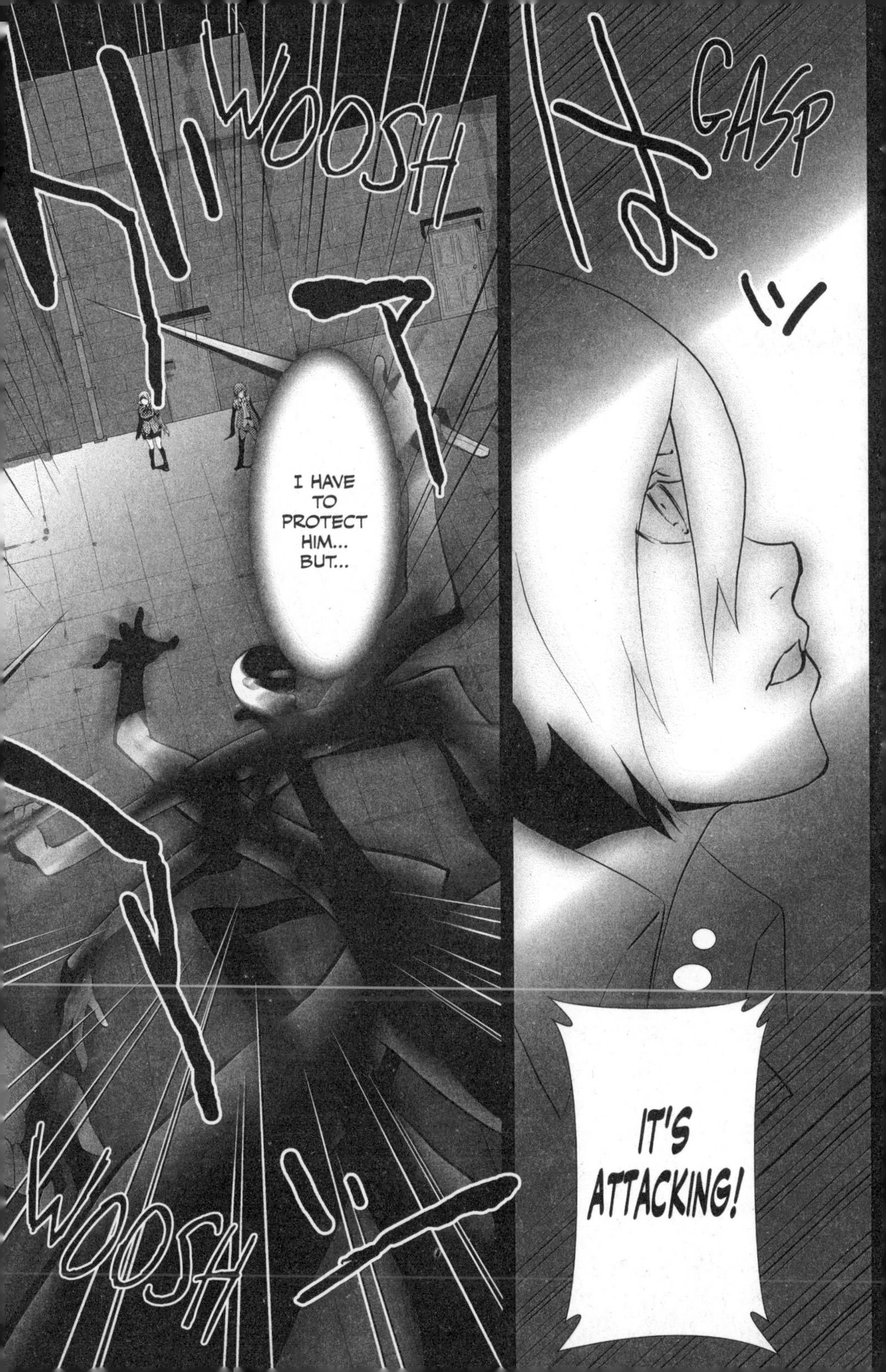
GASP
IT'S ATTACKING!
WOOSH
I HAVE TO PROTECT HIM... BUT...
WOOSH

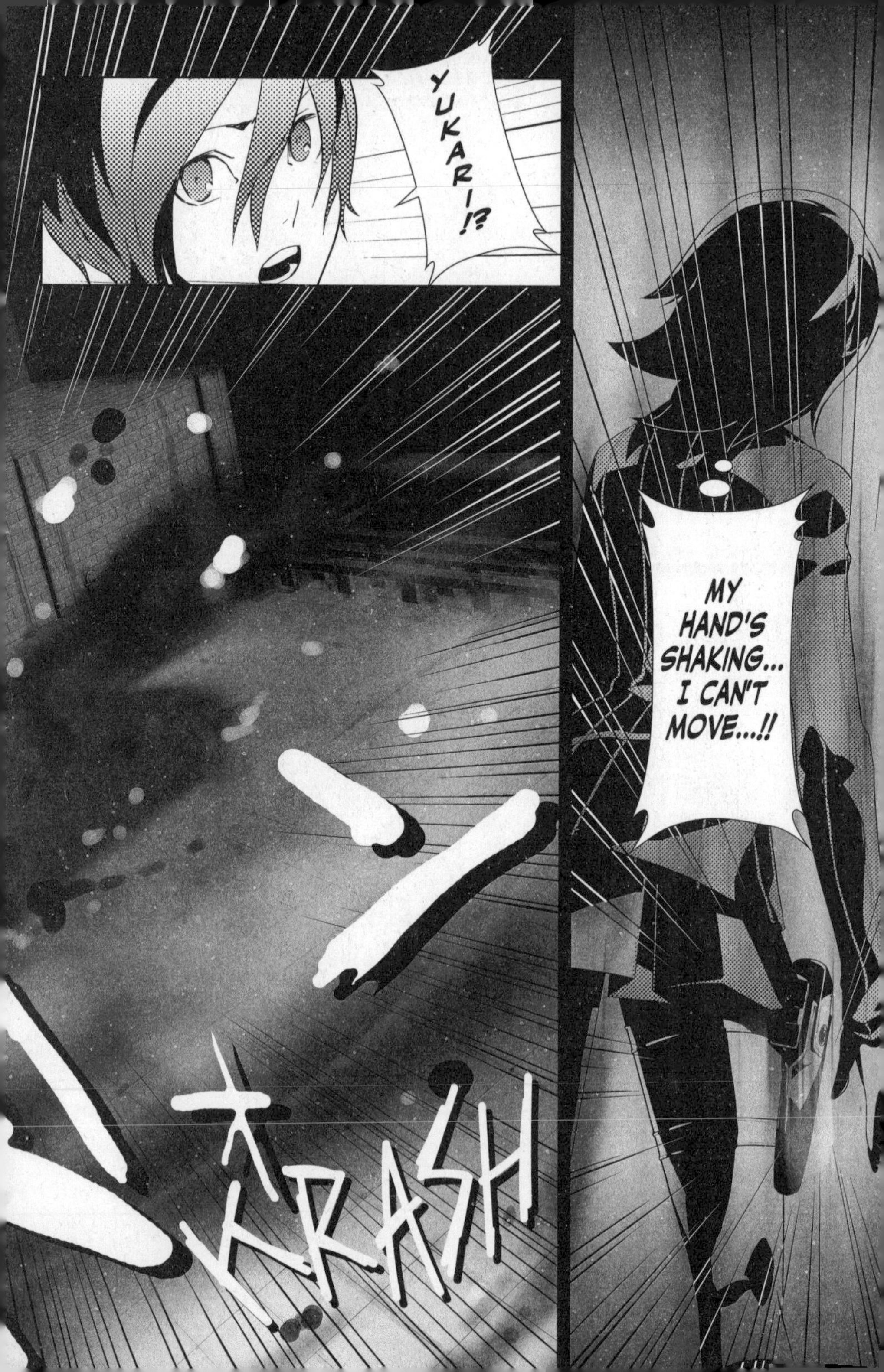
MY HAND'S SHAKING... I CAN'T MOVE...!!
YUKARI!?
KRASH

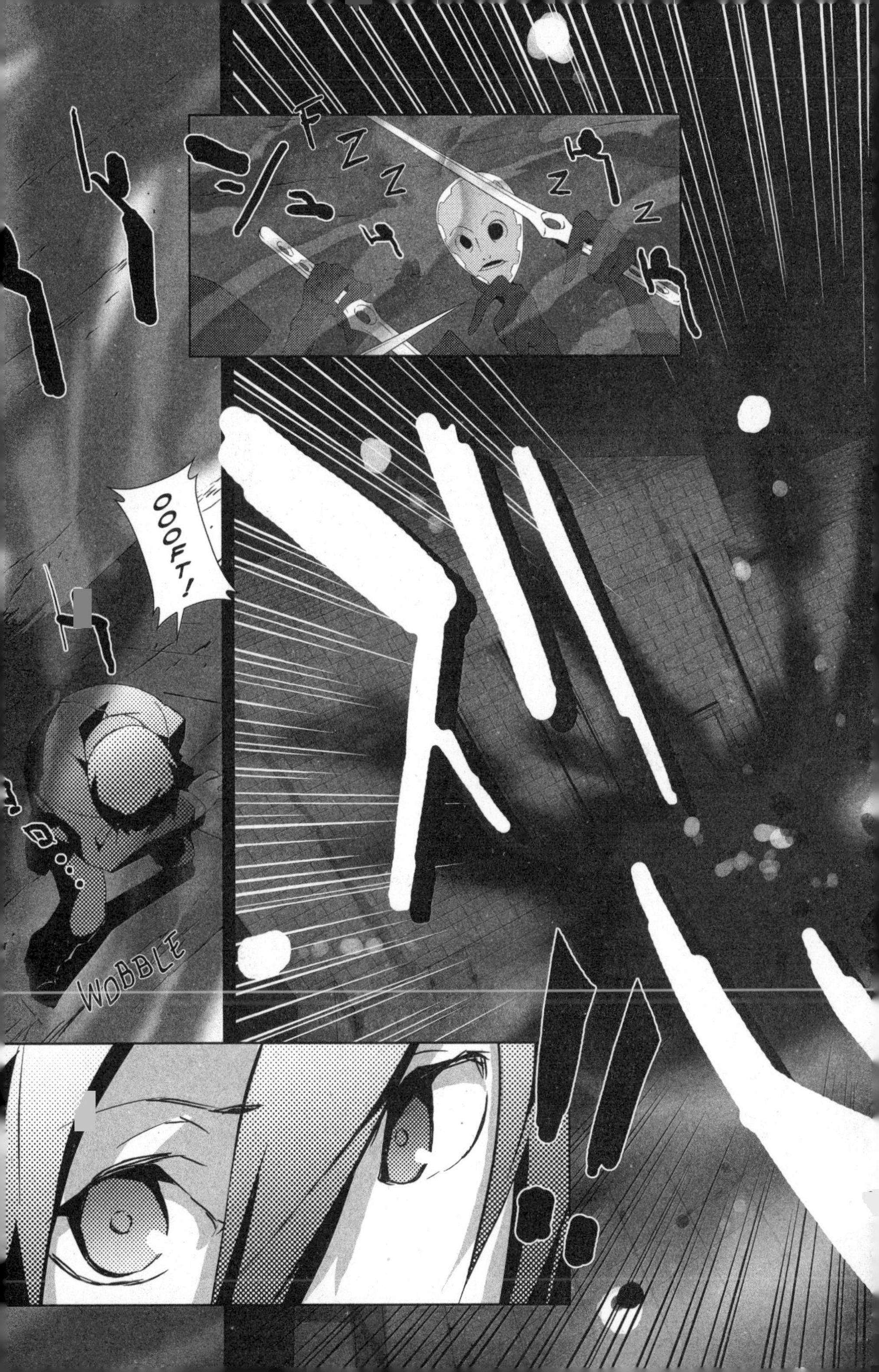
FZZZZ
OOOFT!
WOBBLE

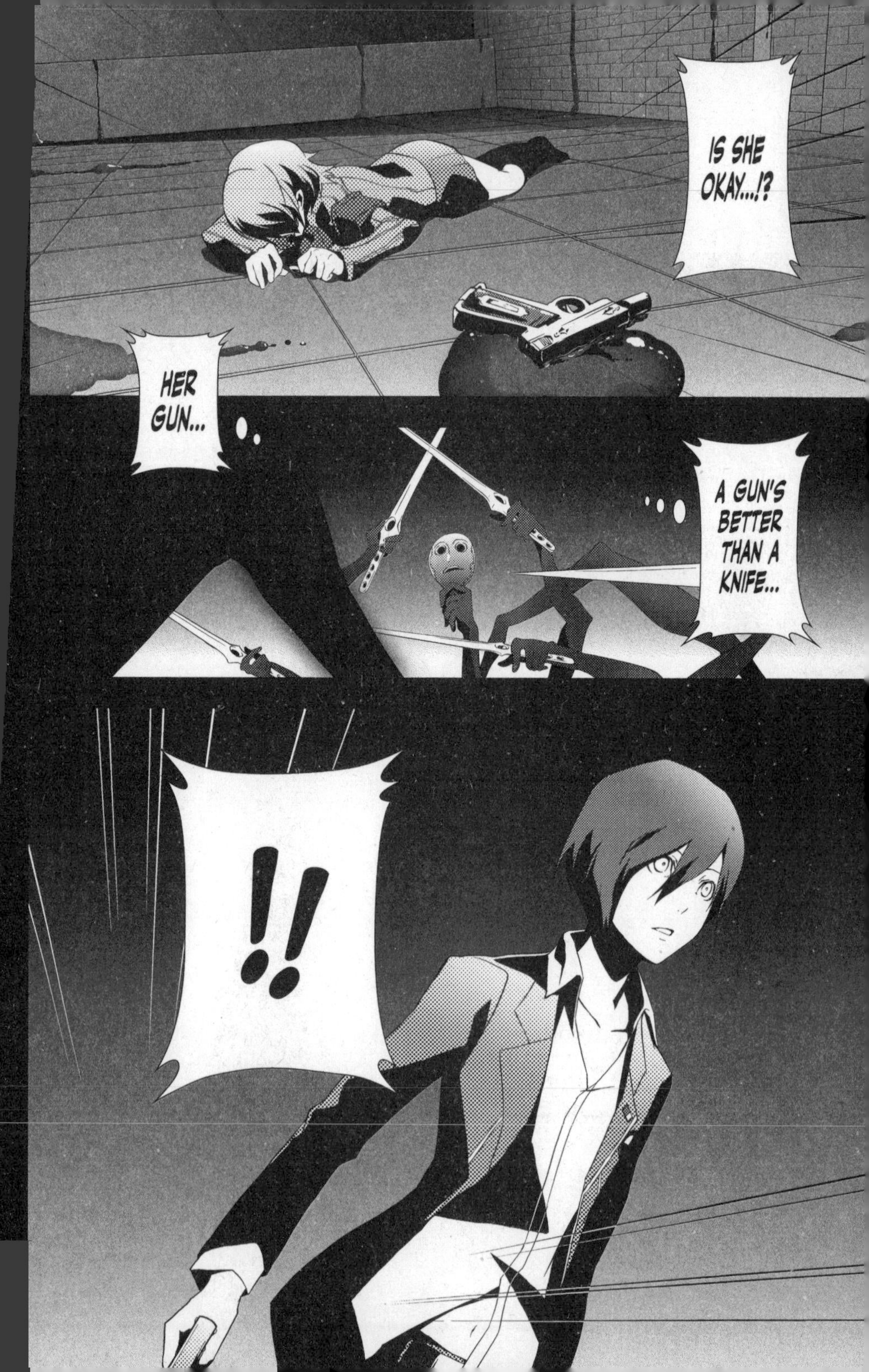
IS SHE OKAY...!?
HER GUN...
A GUN'S BETTER THAN A KNIFE...
!!

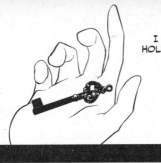

I WAS
HOLDING...

A KEY...?

HE SAID...

CAN
YOU...

...DO
WHAT
IT
TAKES?

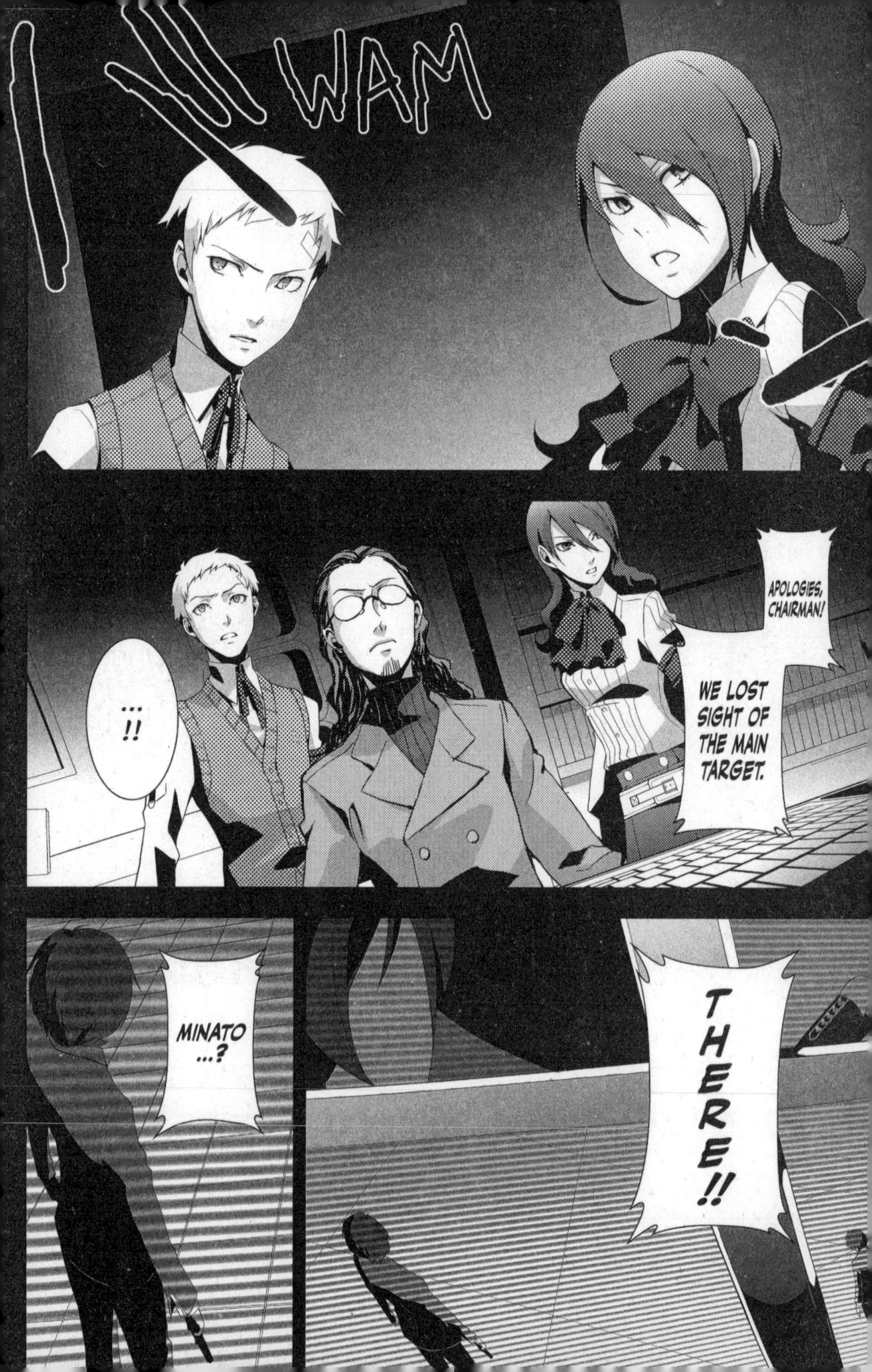
WAM
APOLOGIES, CHAIRMAN!
WE LOST SIGHT OF THE MAIN TARGET.
...!!
THERE!!
MINATO...?

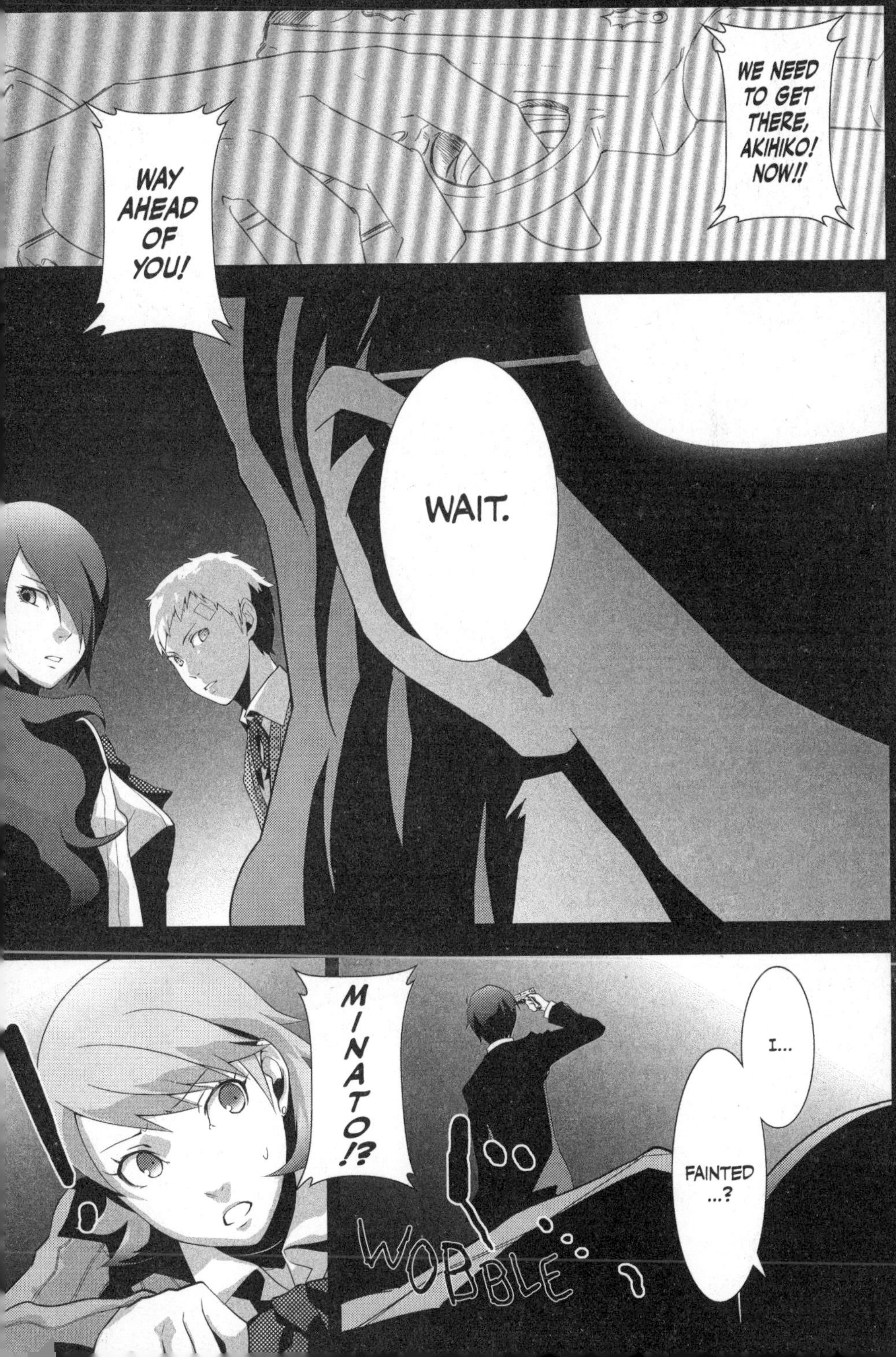
WE NEED TO GET THERE, AKIHIKO! NOW!!
WAY AHEAD OF YOU!
WAIT.
I...
FAINTED ...?
WOBBLE
MINATO!?

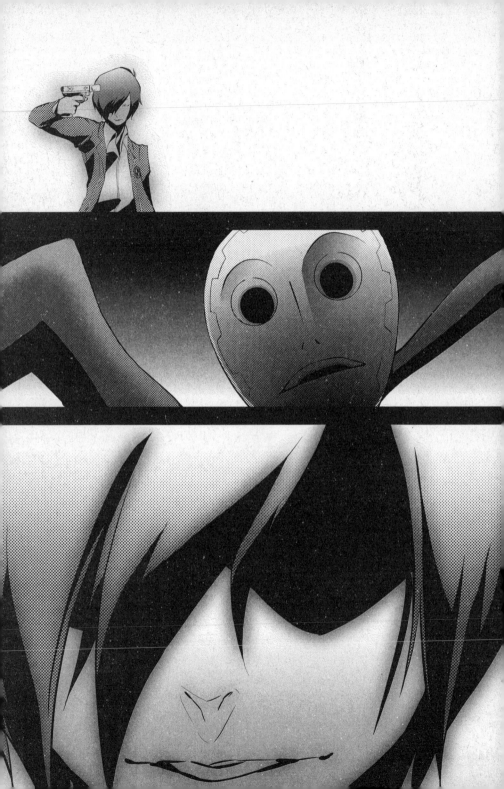

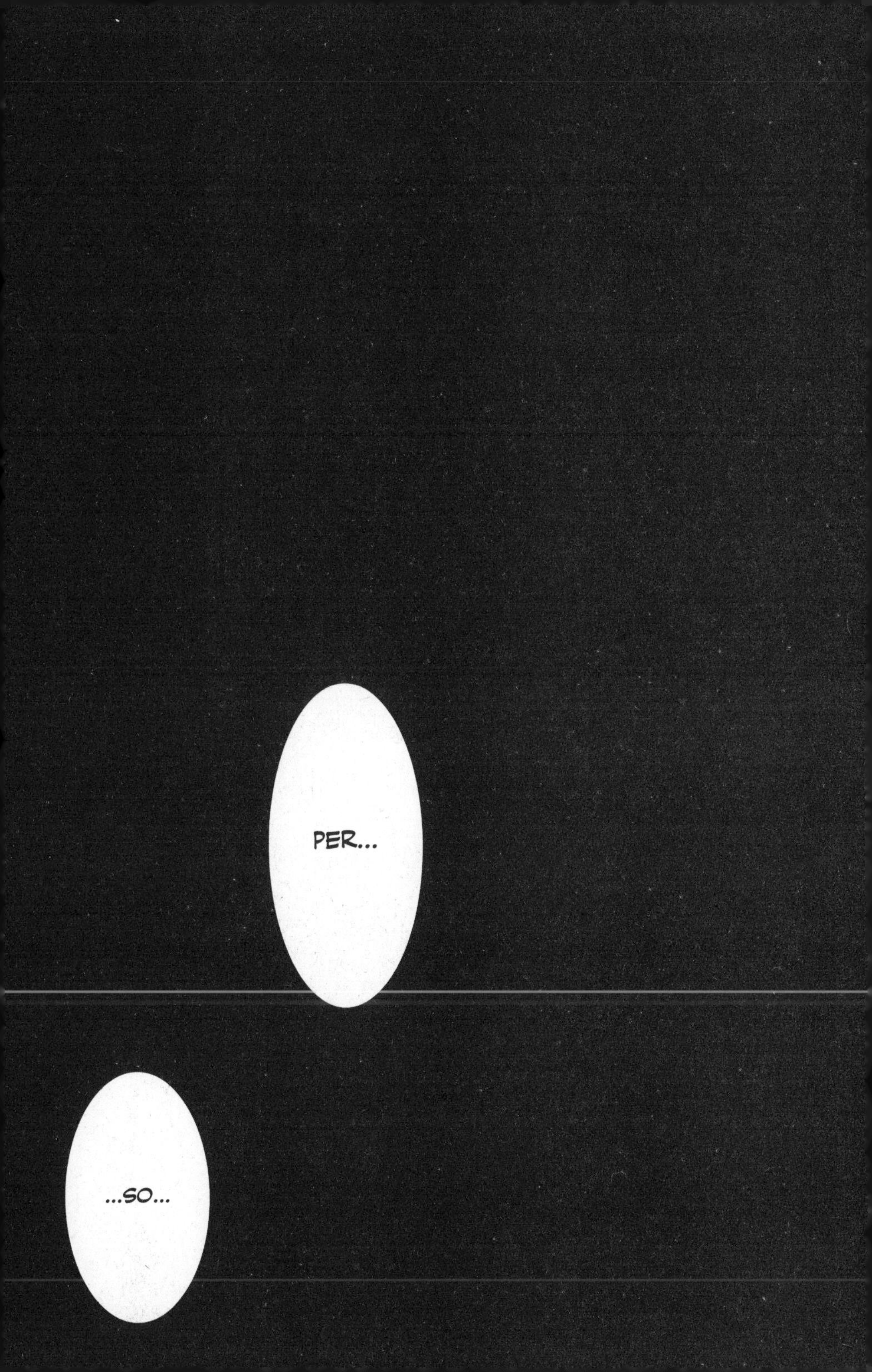
PER...
...SO...

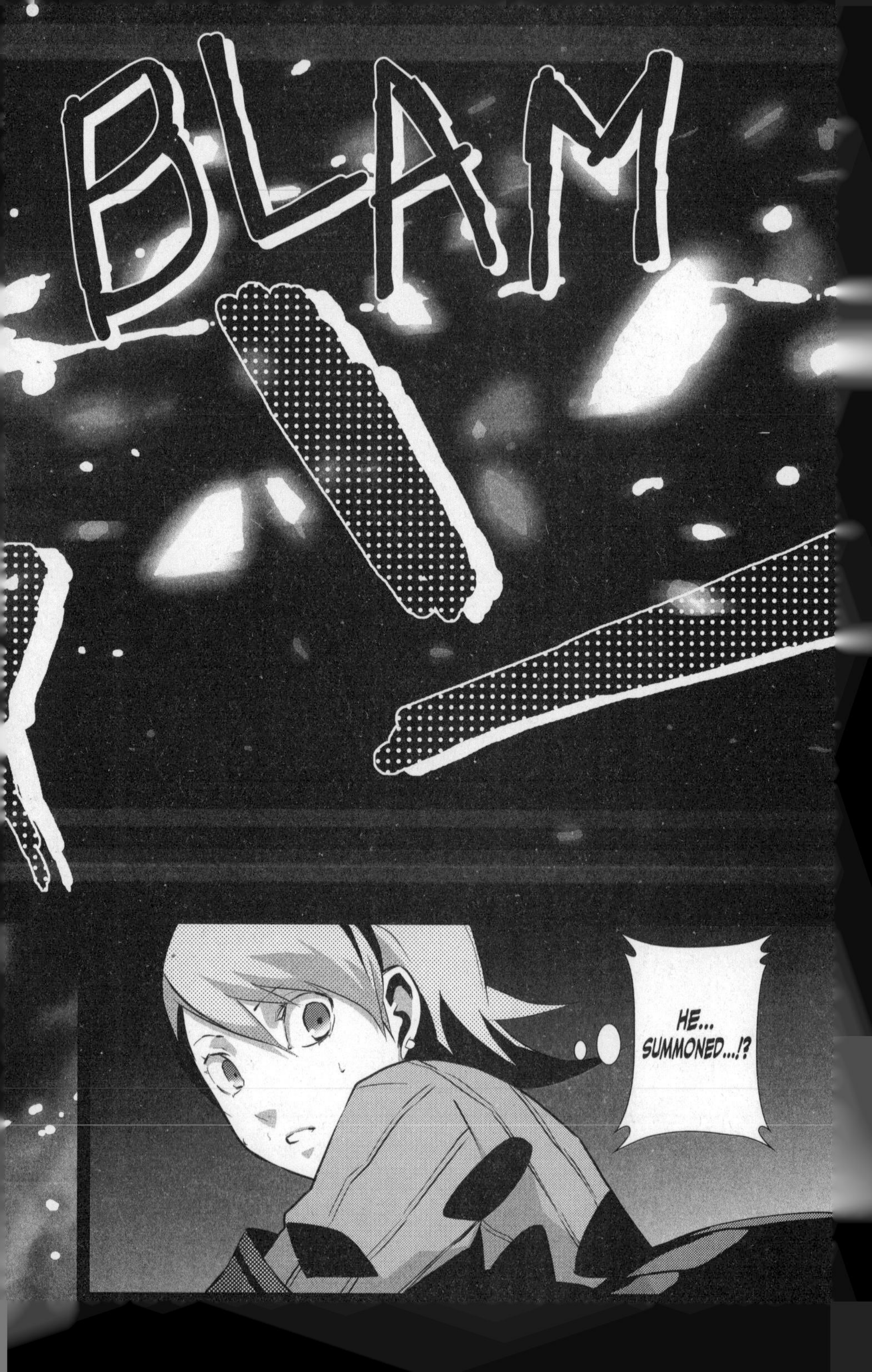
BLAM
HE... SUMMONED...!?

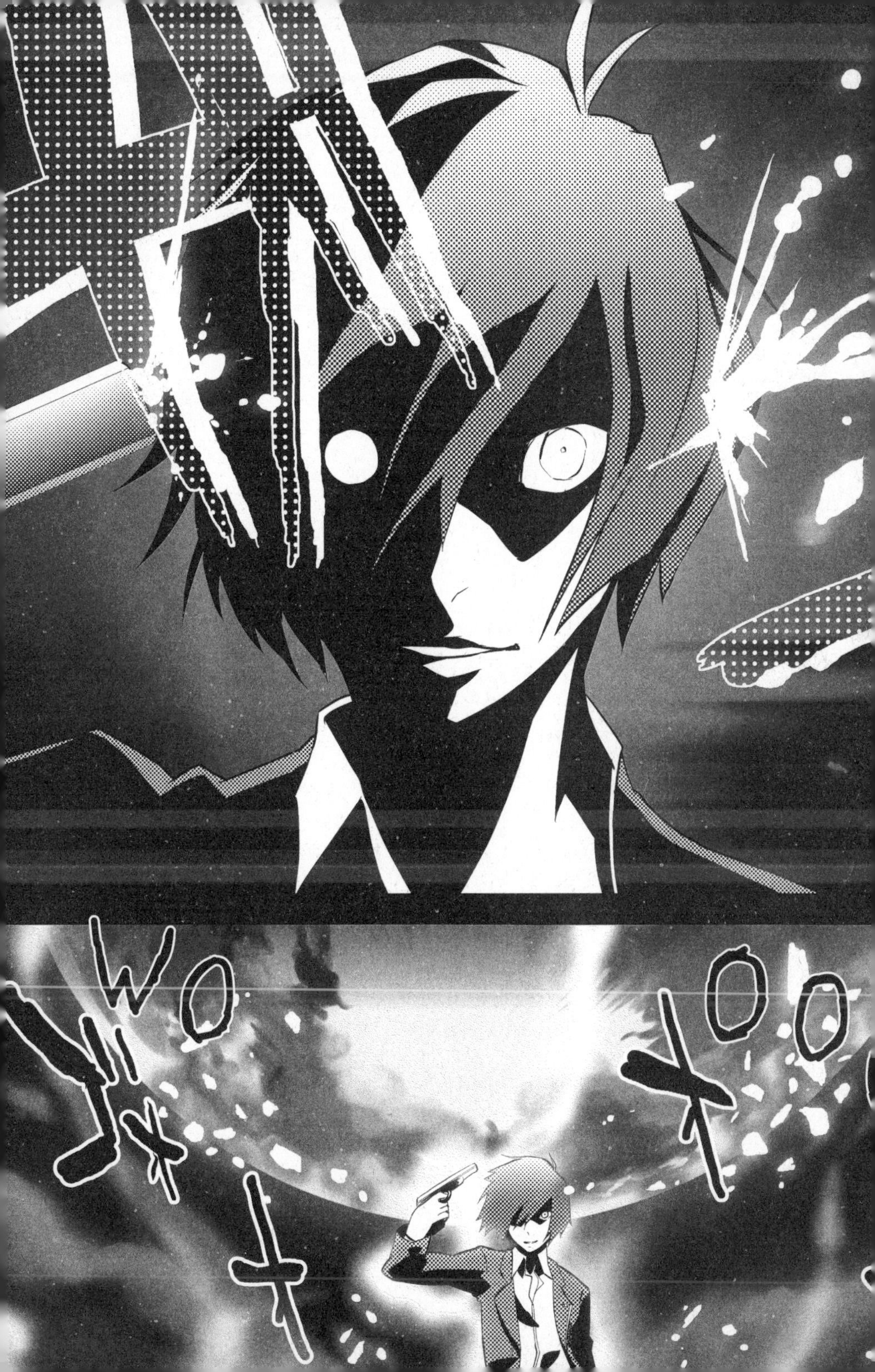

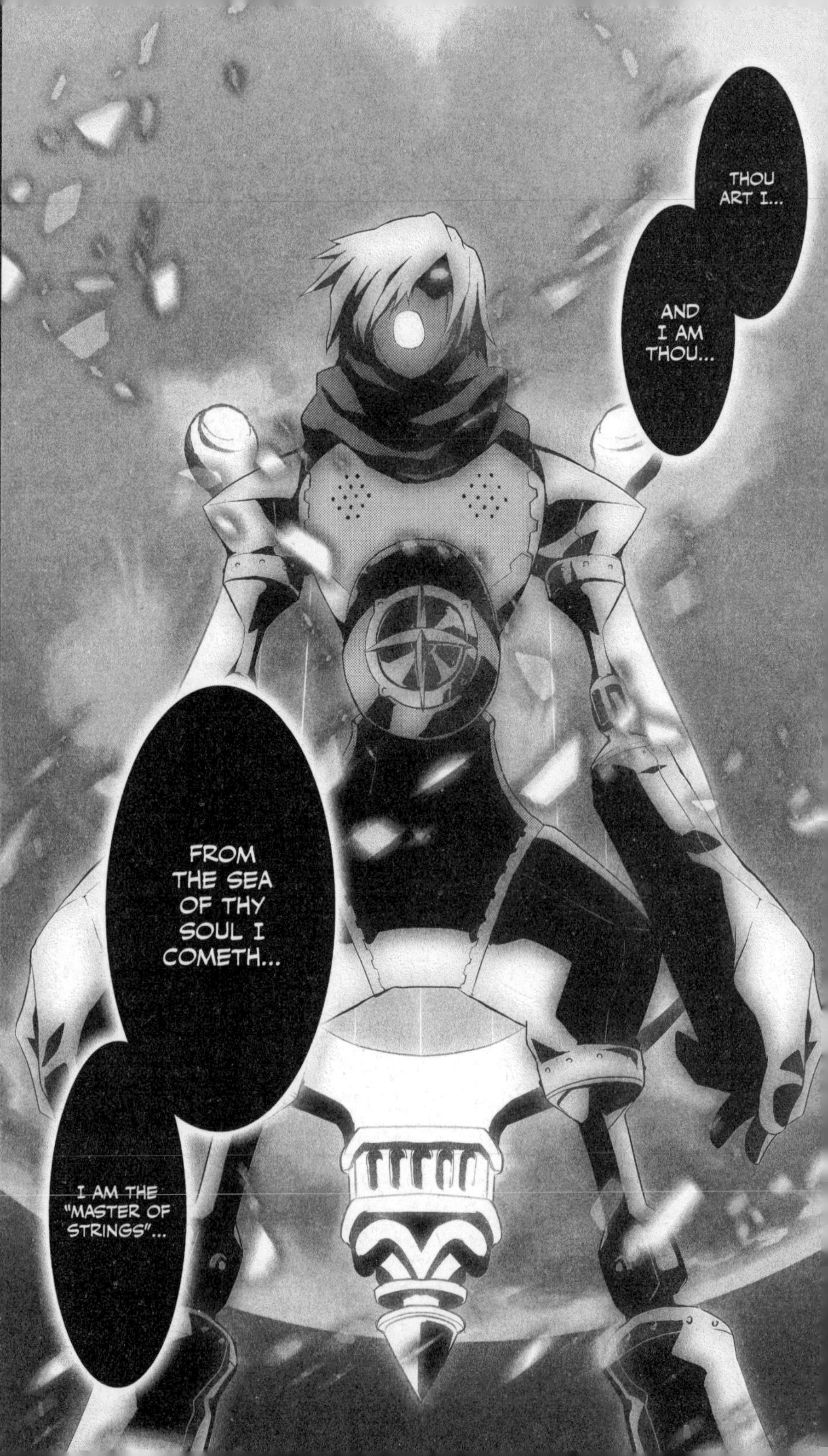
THOU ART I...
AND I AM THOU...
FROM THE SEA OF THY SOUL I COMETH...
I AM THE "MASTER OF STRINGS"...

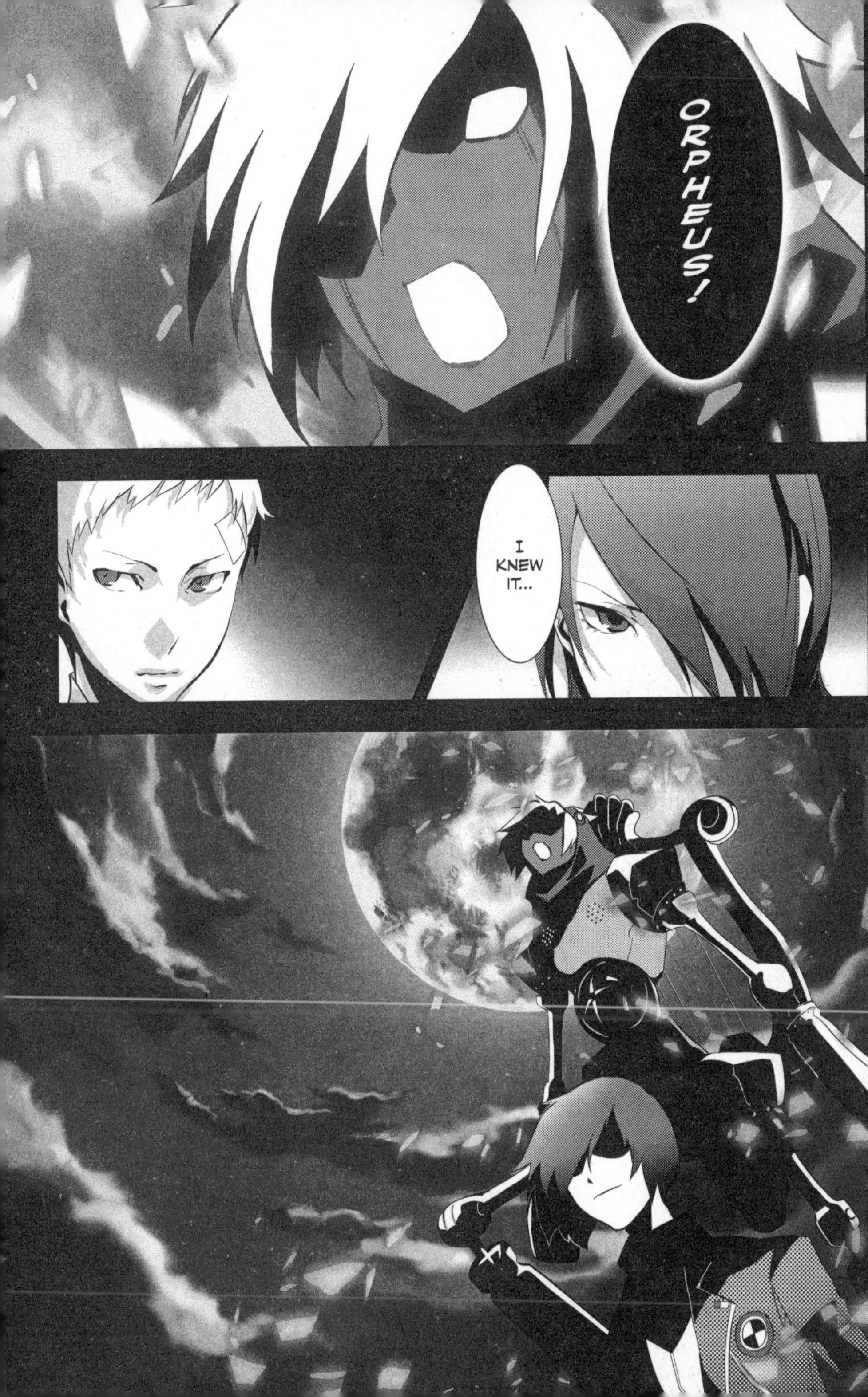
ORPHEUS!
I KNEW IT...

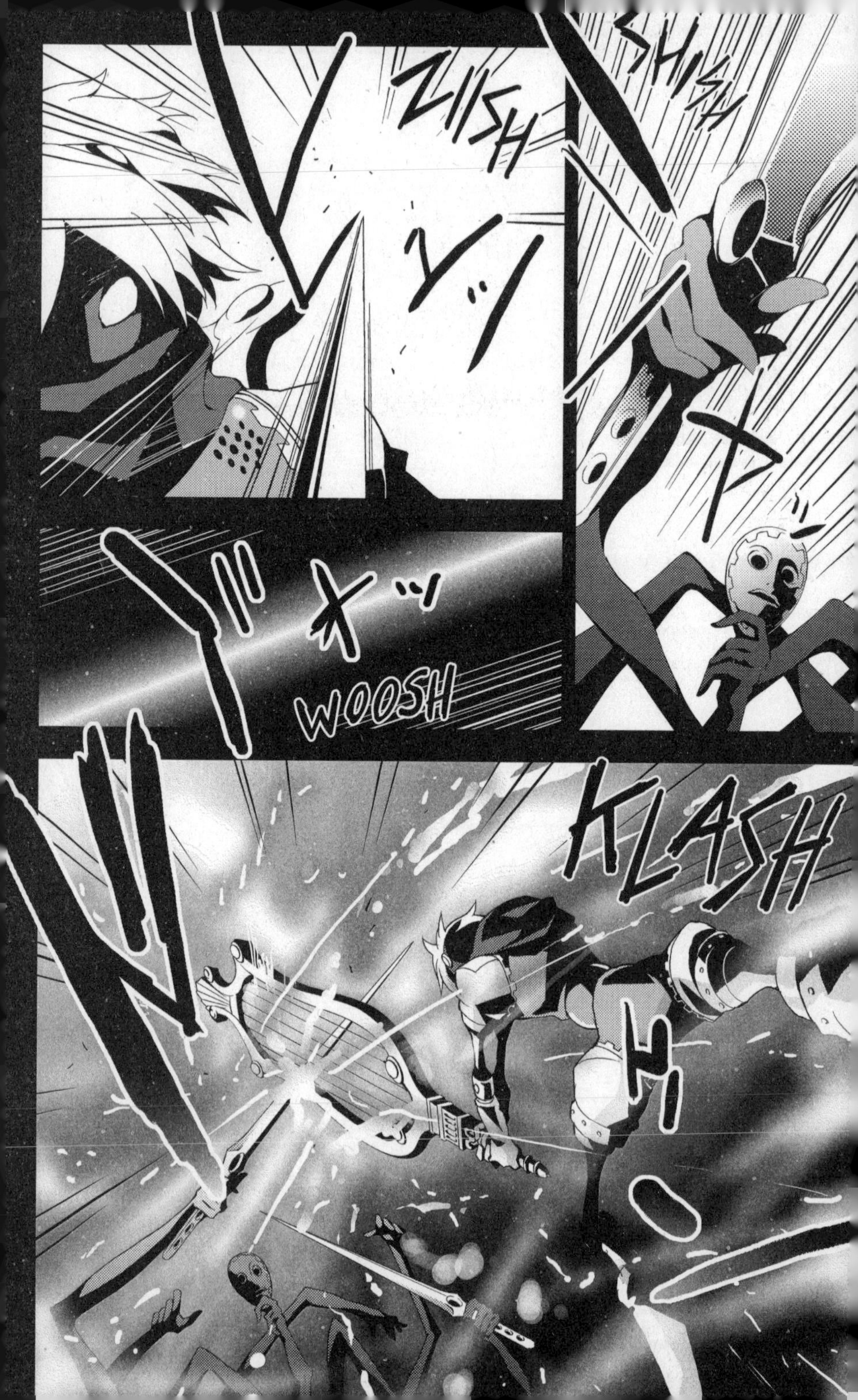
SHISH
ZIISH
WOOSH
KLASH

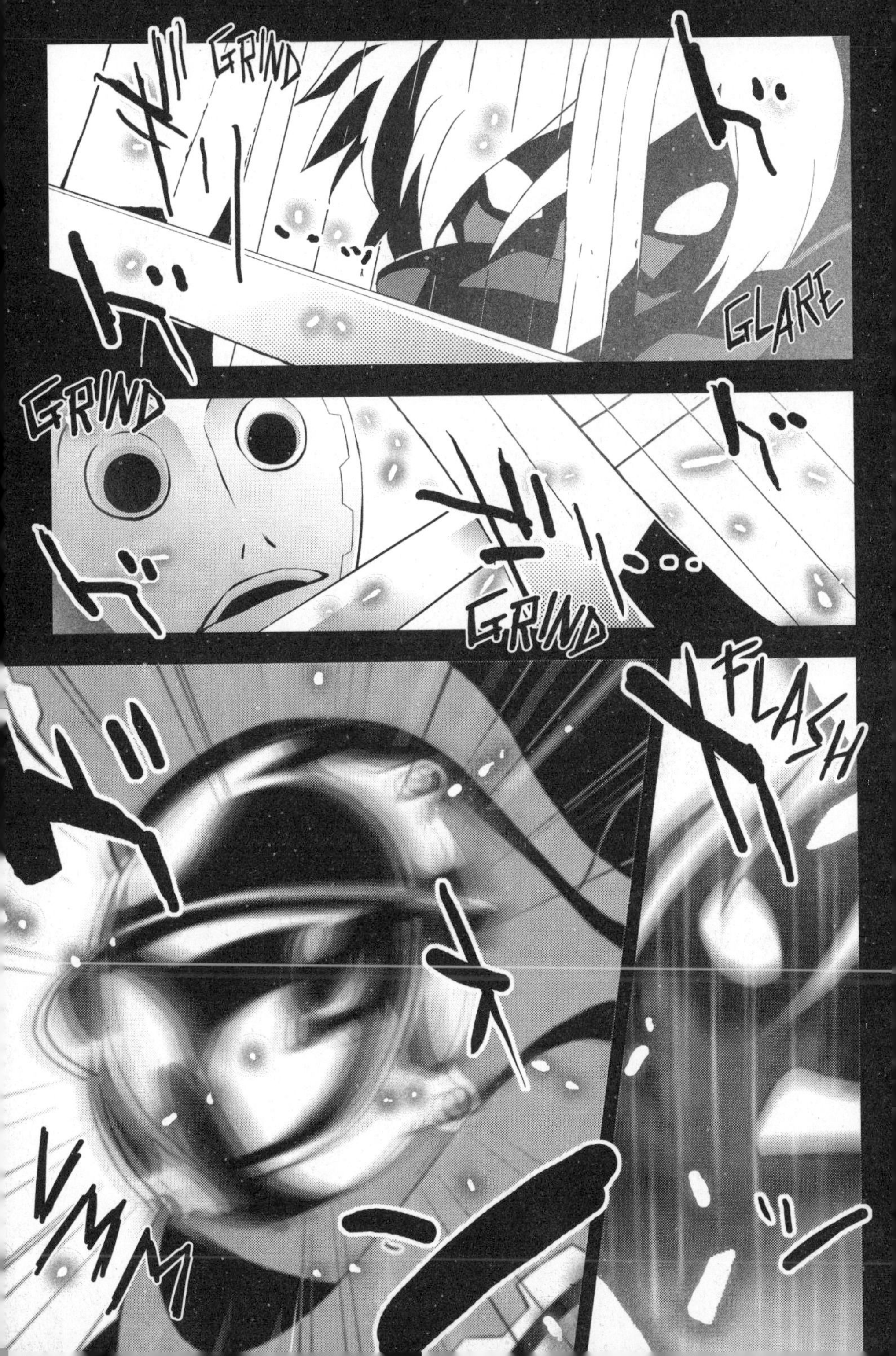
GRIND
GLARE
GRIND
GRIND
FLASH
VMM

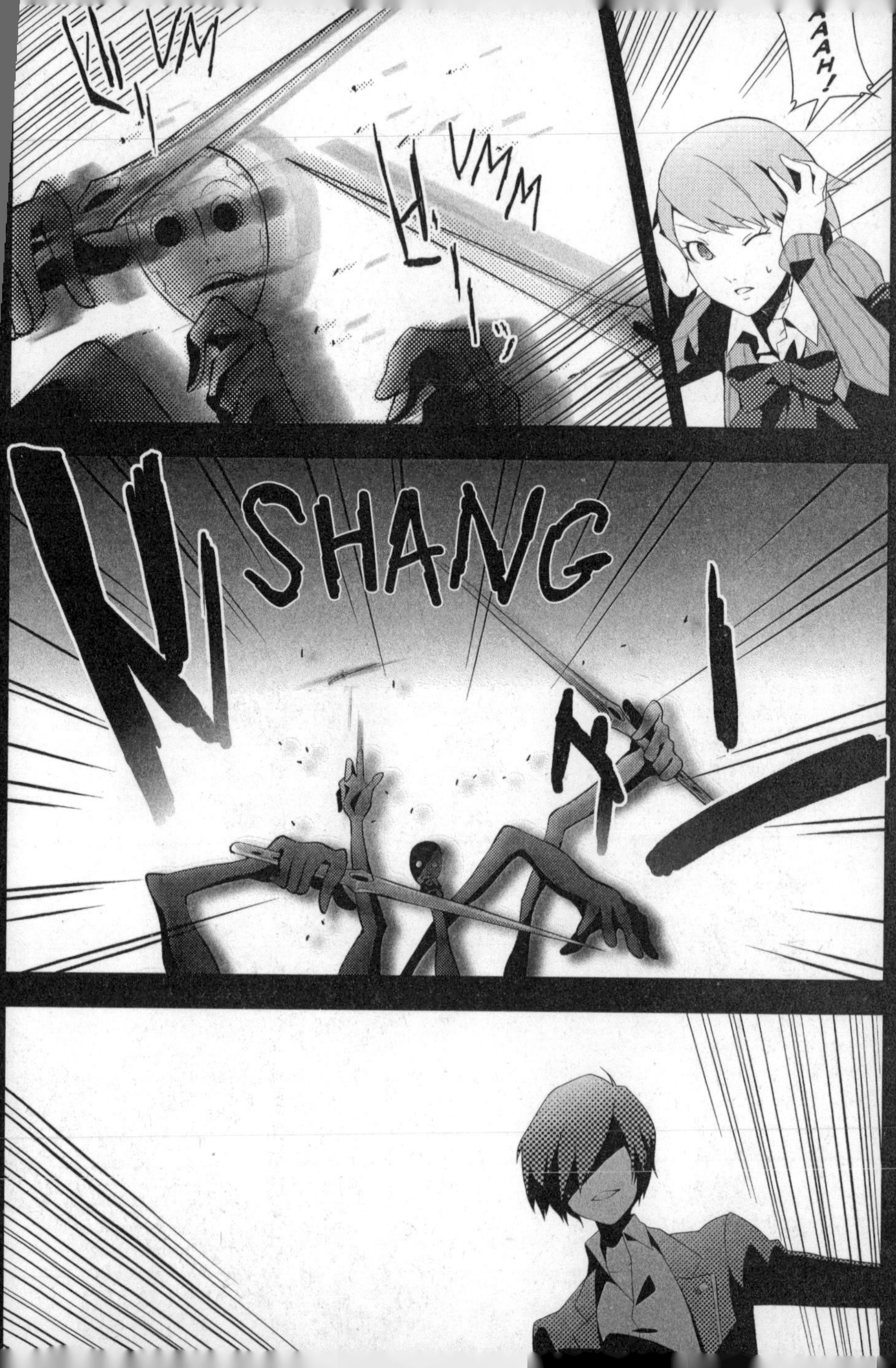
AAAH!
SHANG

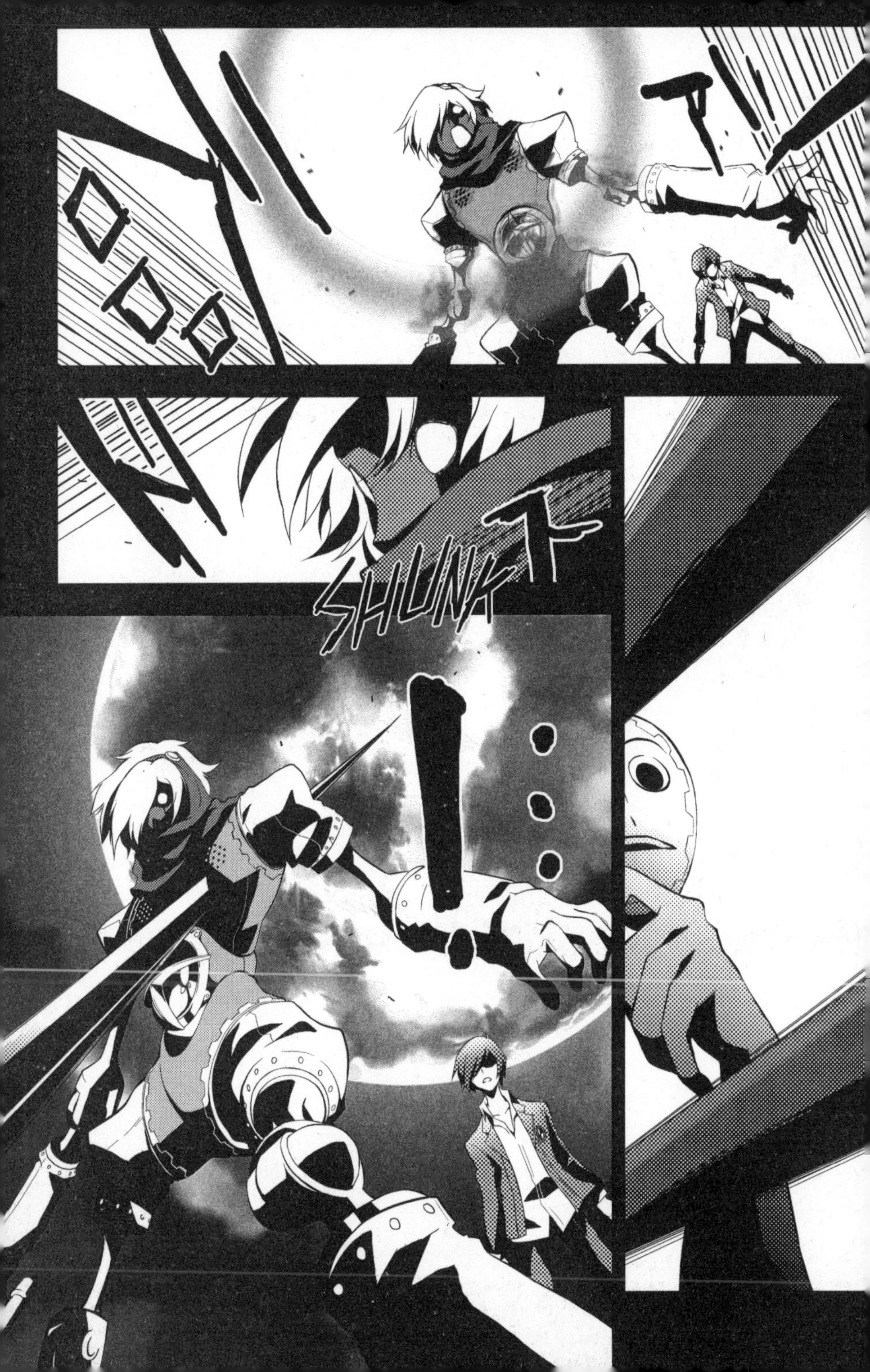
SHUNK

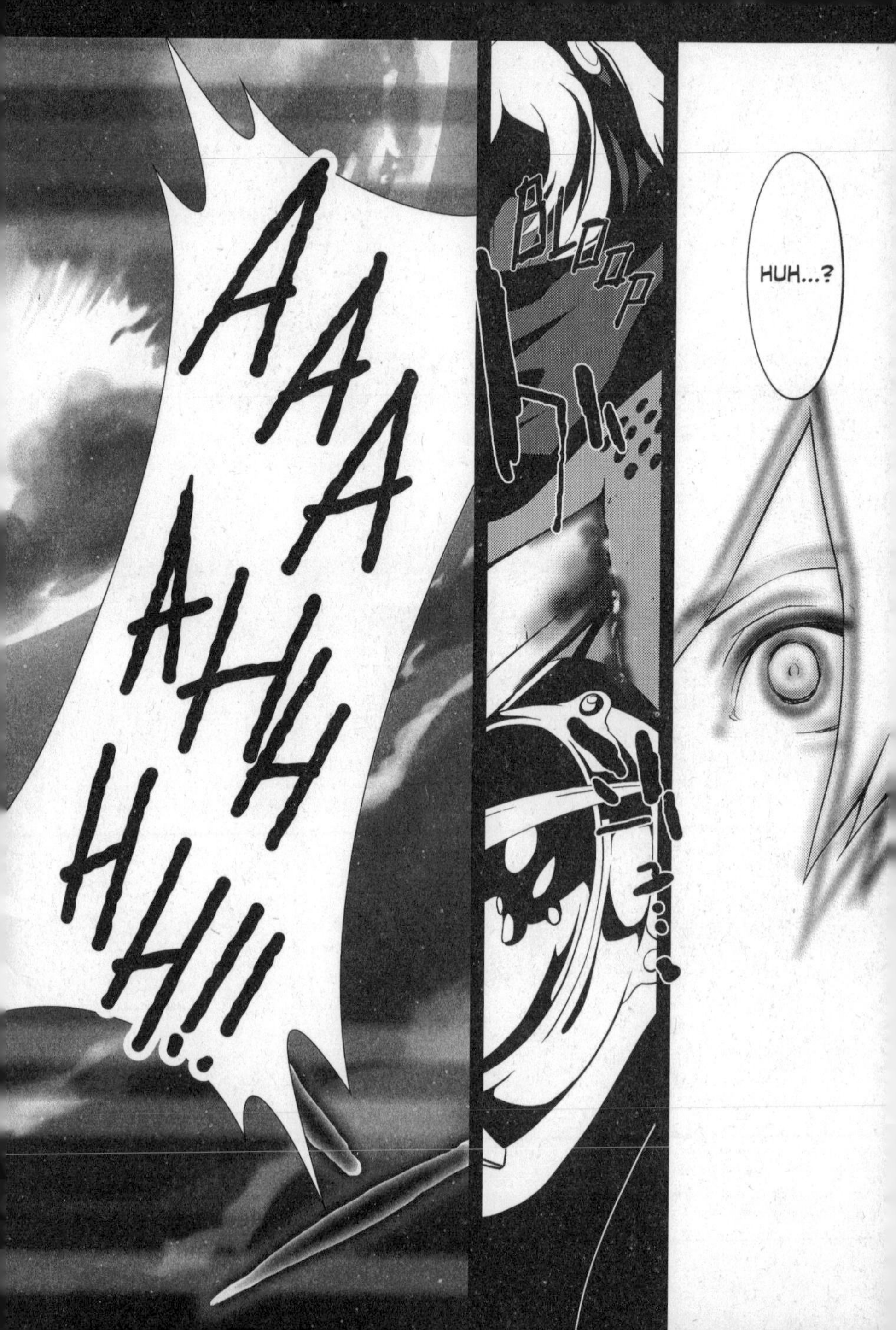
HUH...?
BLOOP
AAAAHHHH!!..

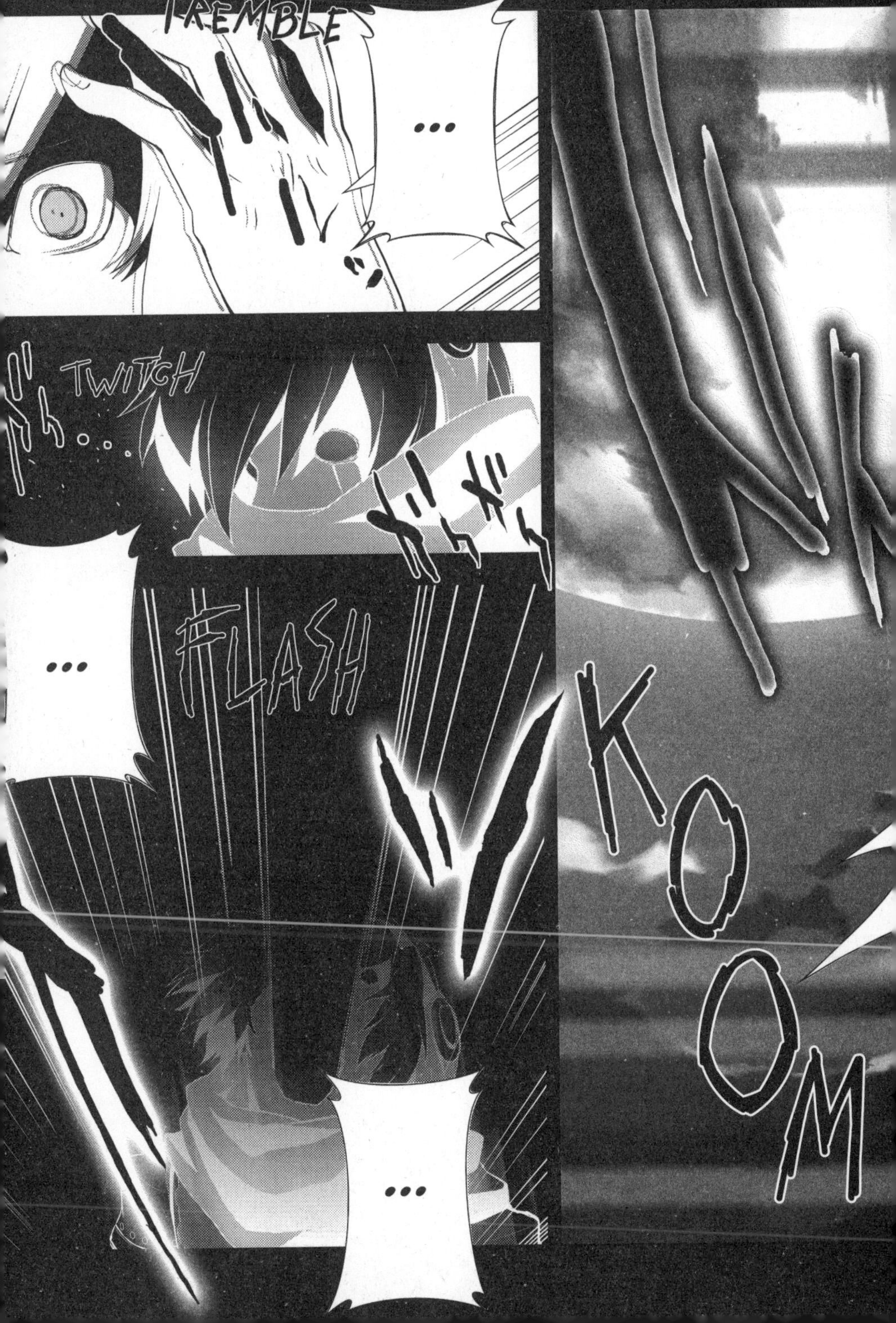

VKOOM
TREMBLE
...
TWITCH
...
FLASH
...
...

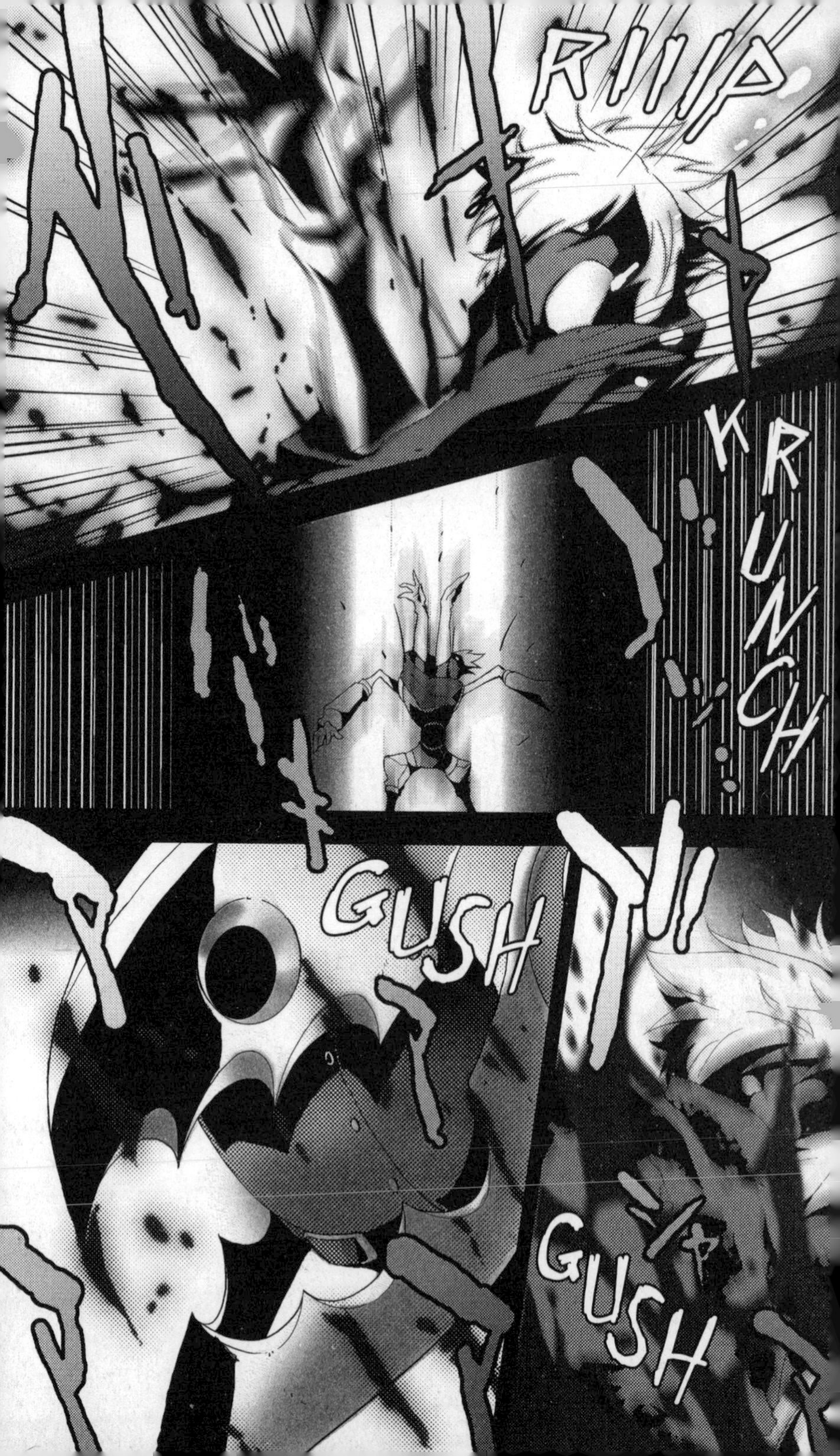
RIIIP
KRUNCH
GUSH
GUSH

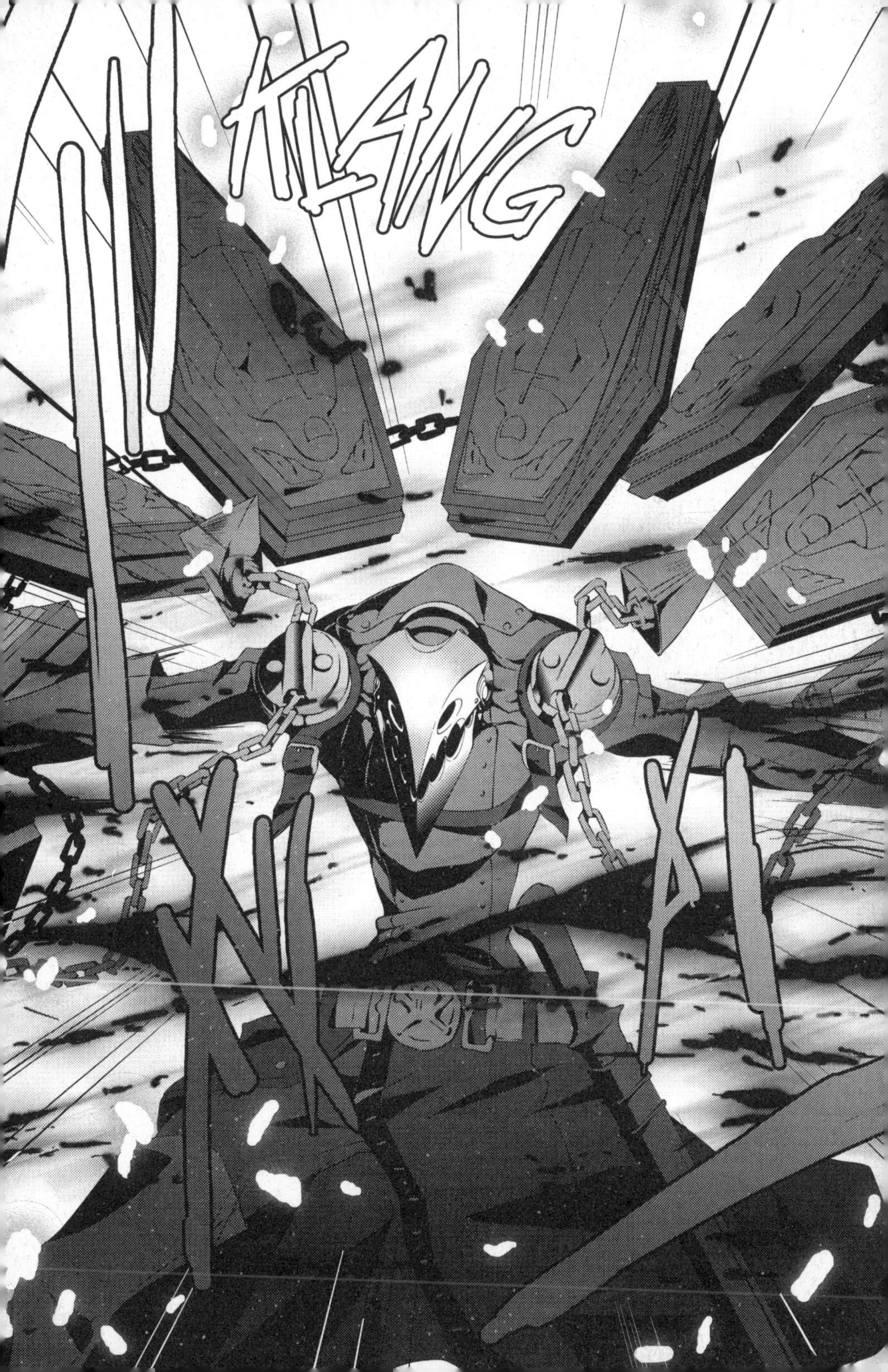
KLANG

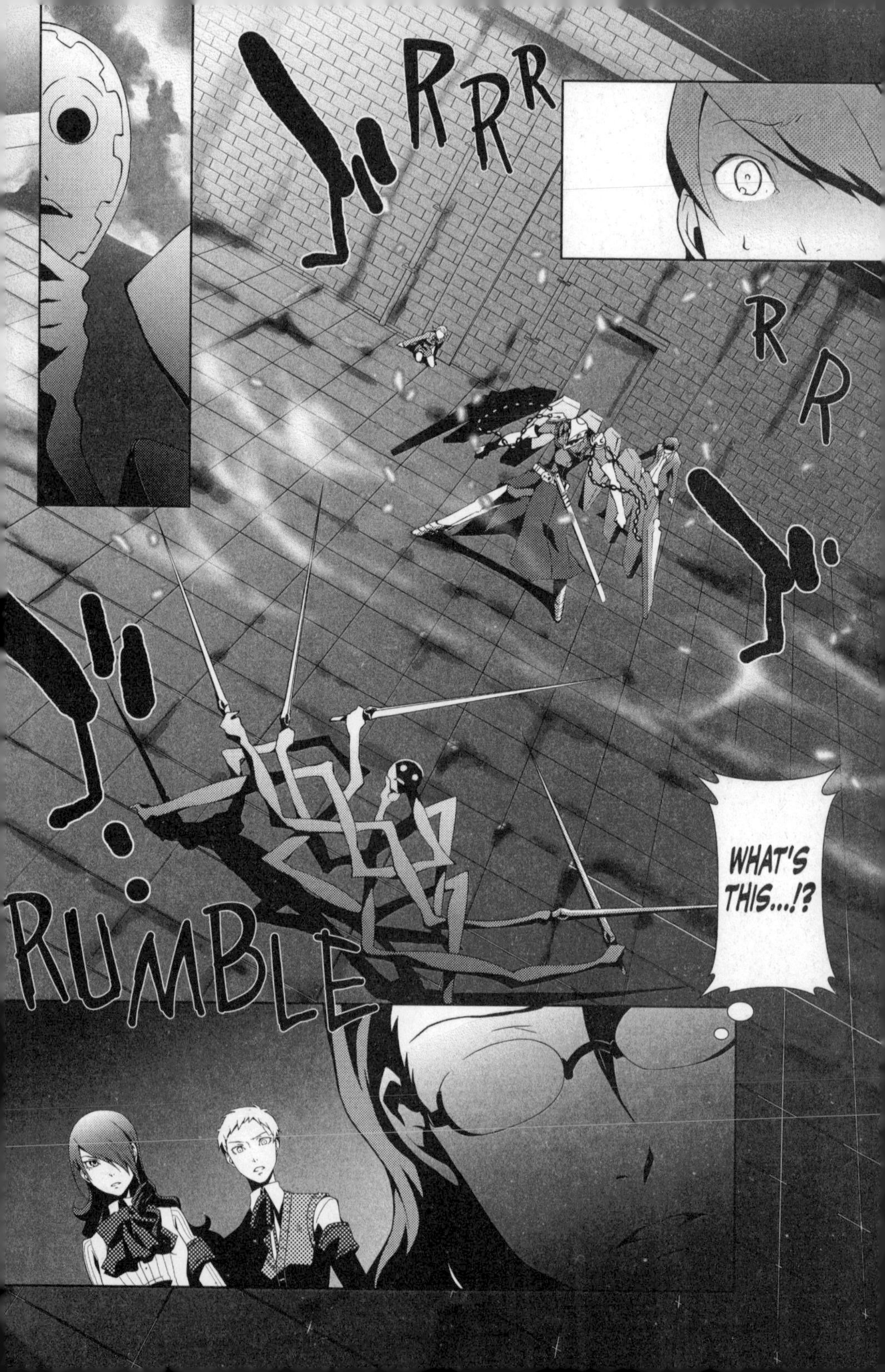
RRR
RR
RUMBLE
WHAT'S THIS...!?

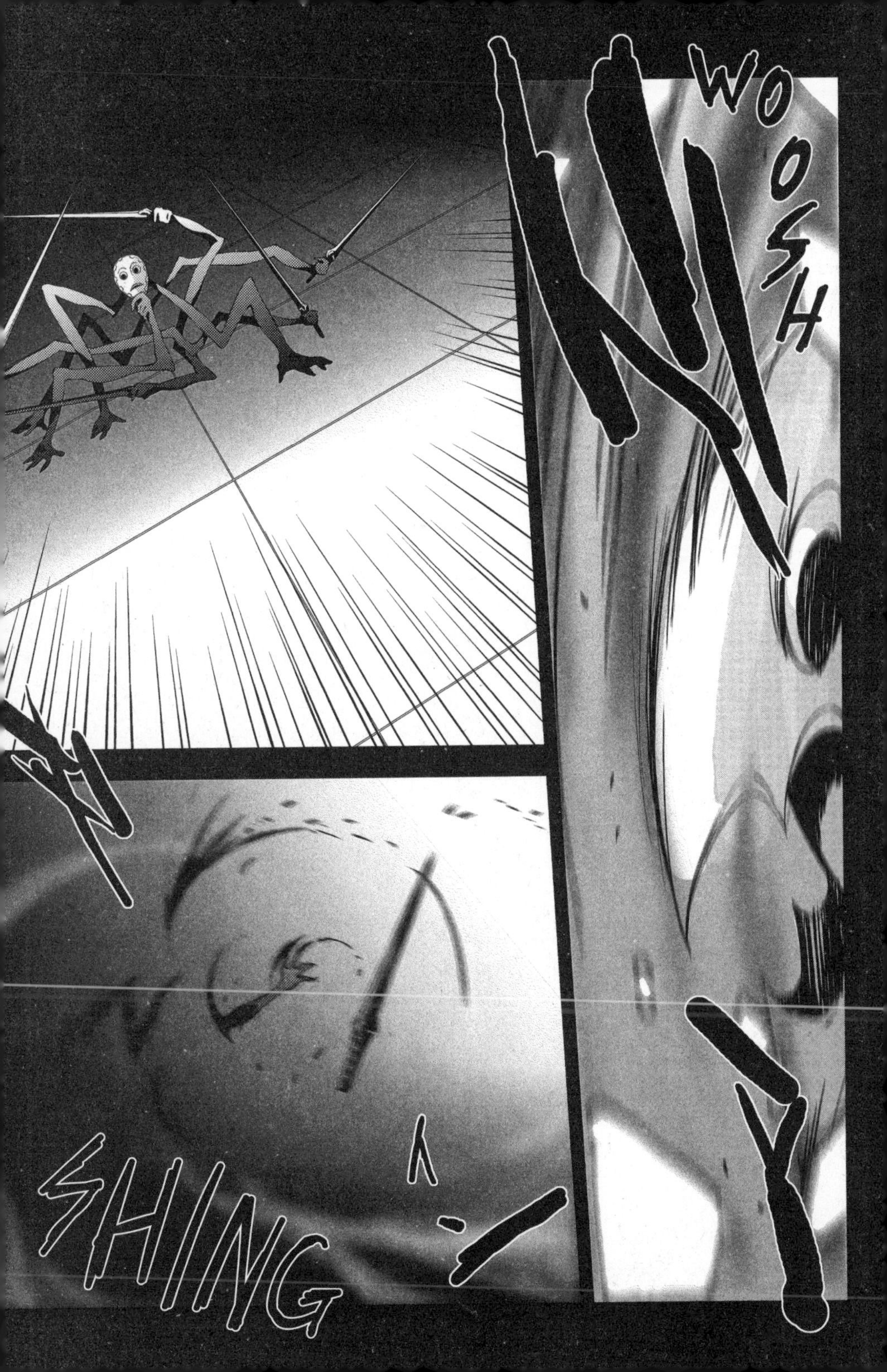
WOOSH
SHING

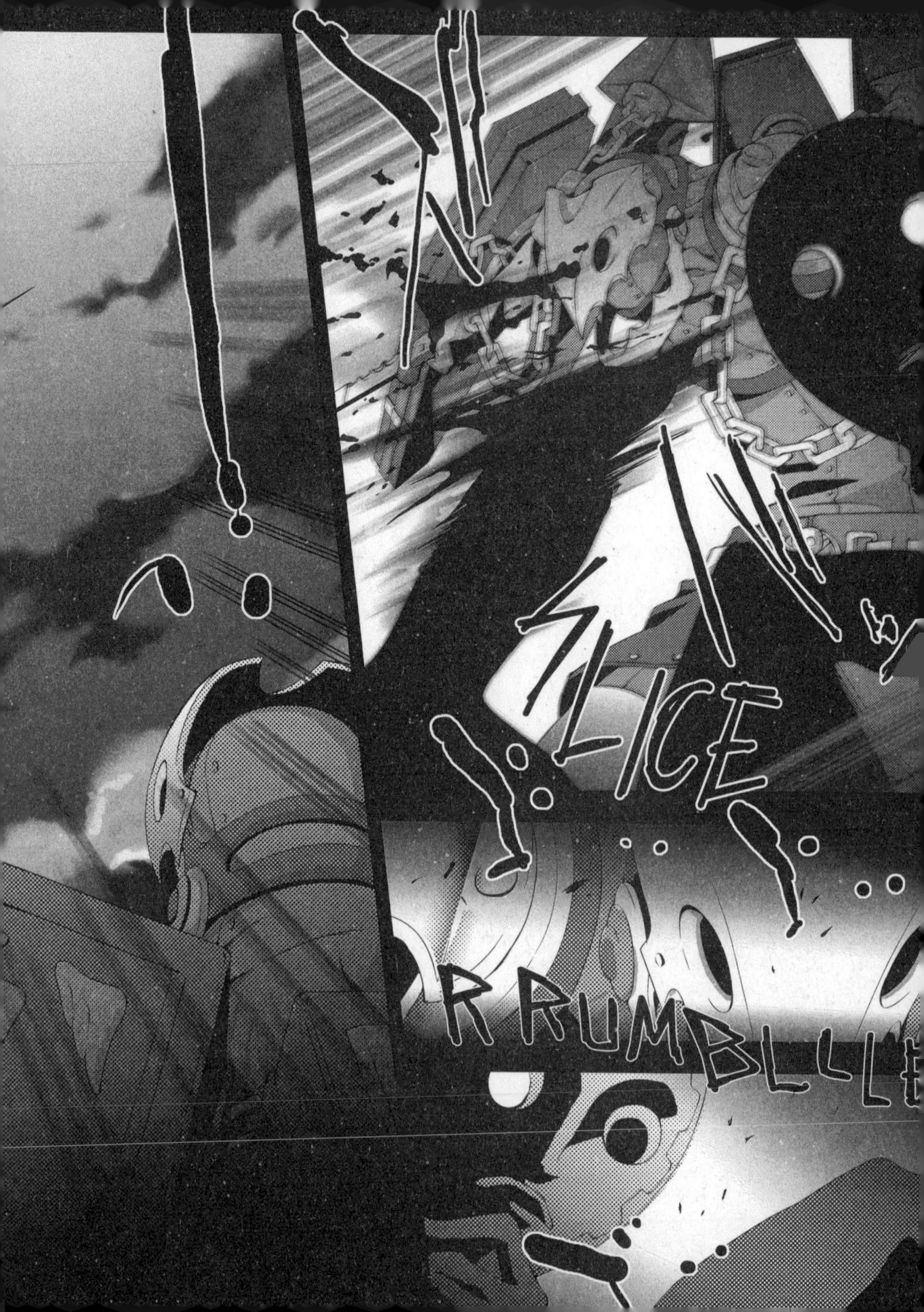
SLICE
RRUMBLLLE

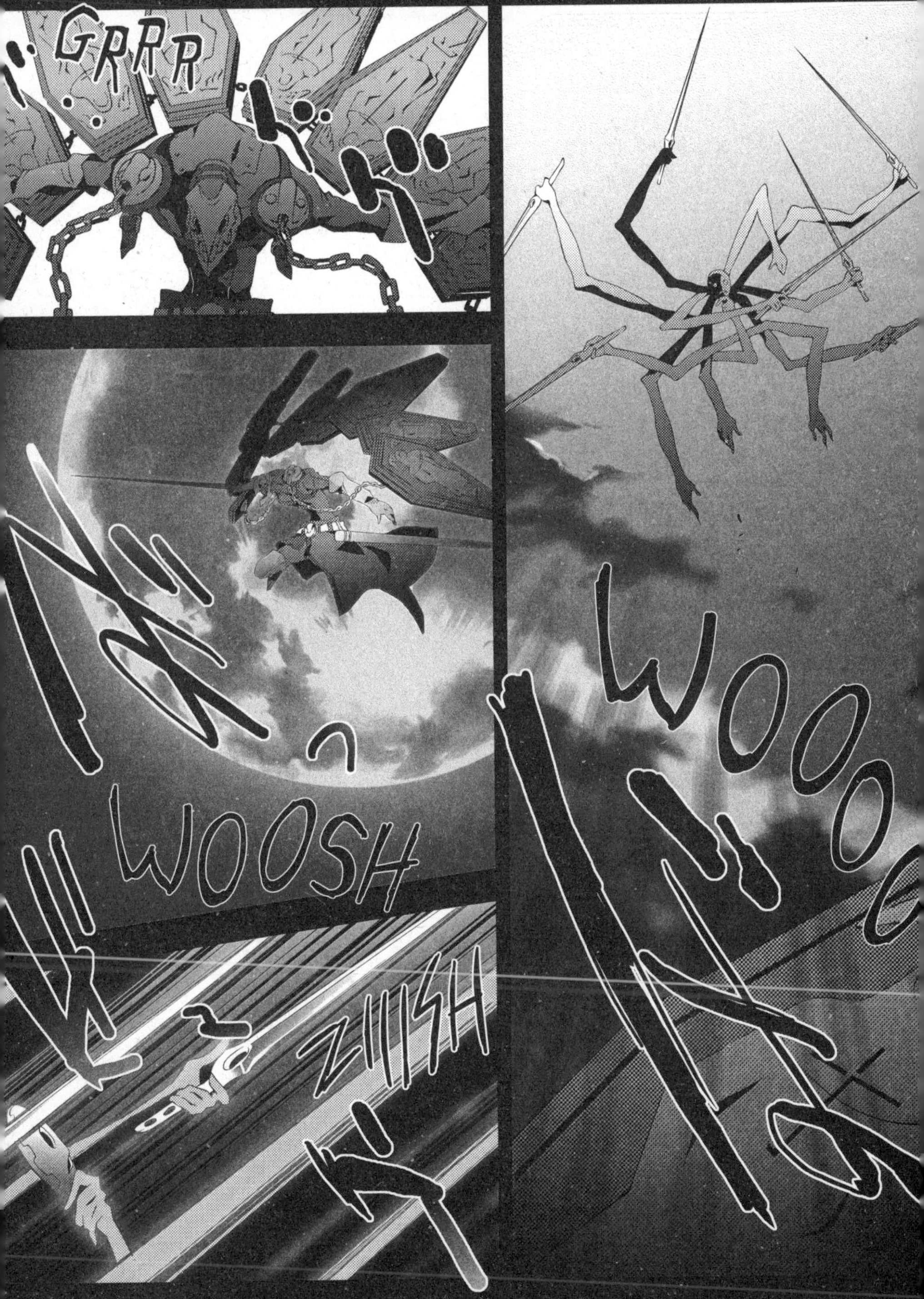
WOOO
GRRR
WOOSH
ZIIISH

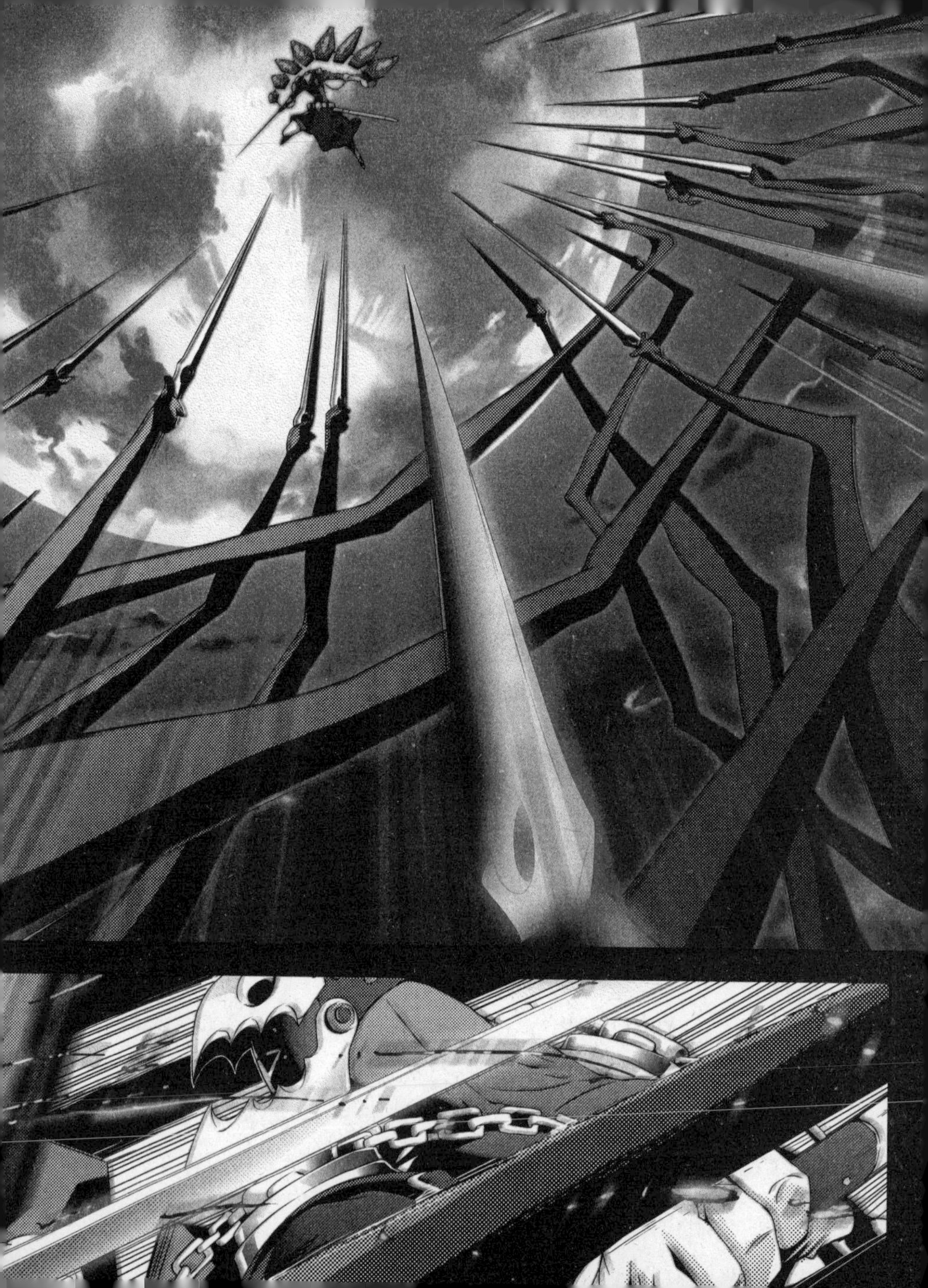

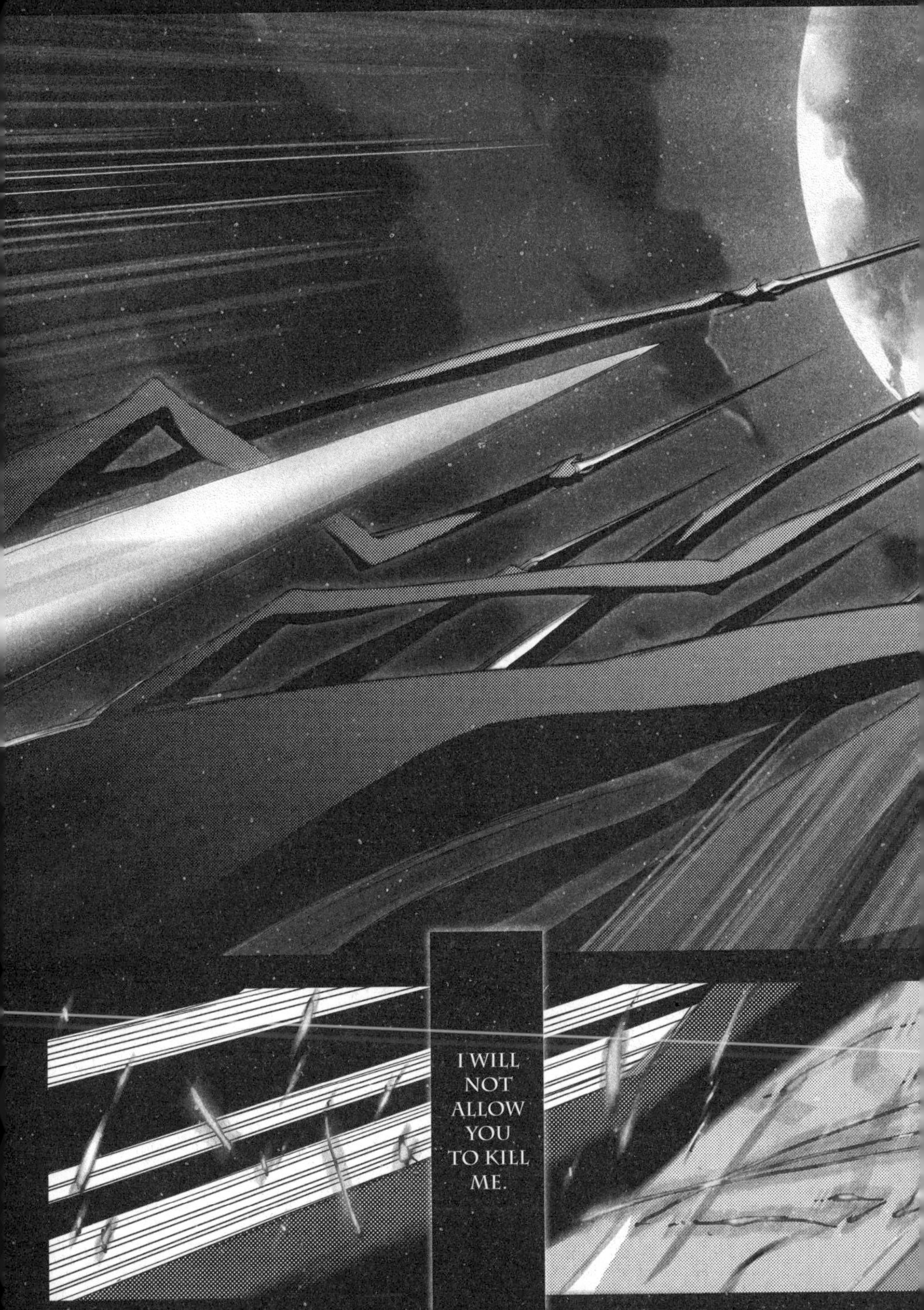
I WILL NOT ALLOW YOU TO KILL ME.

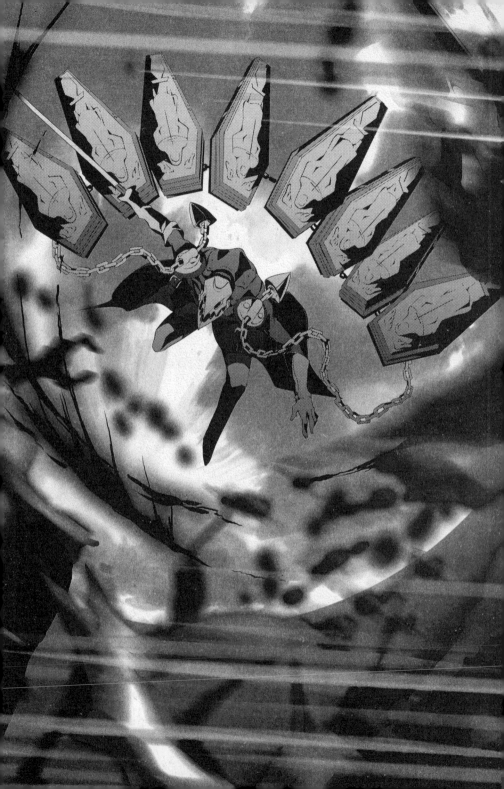

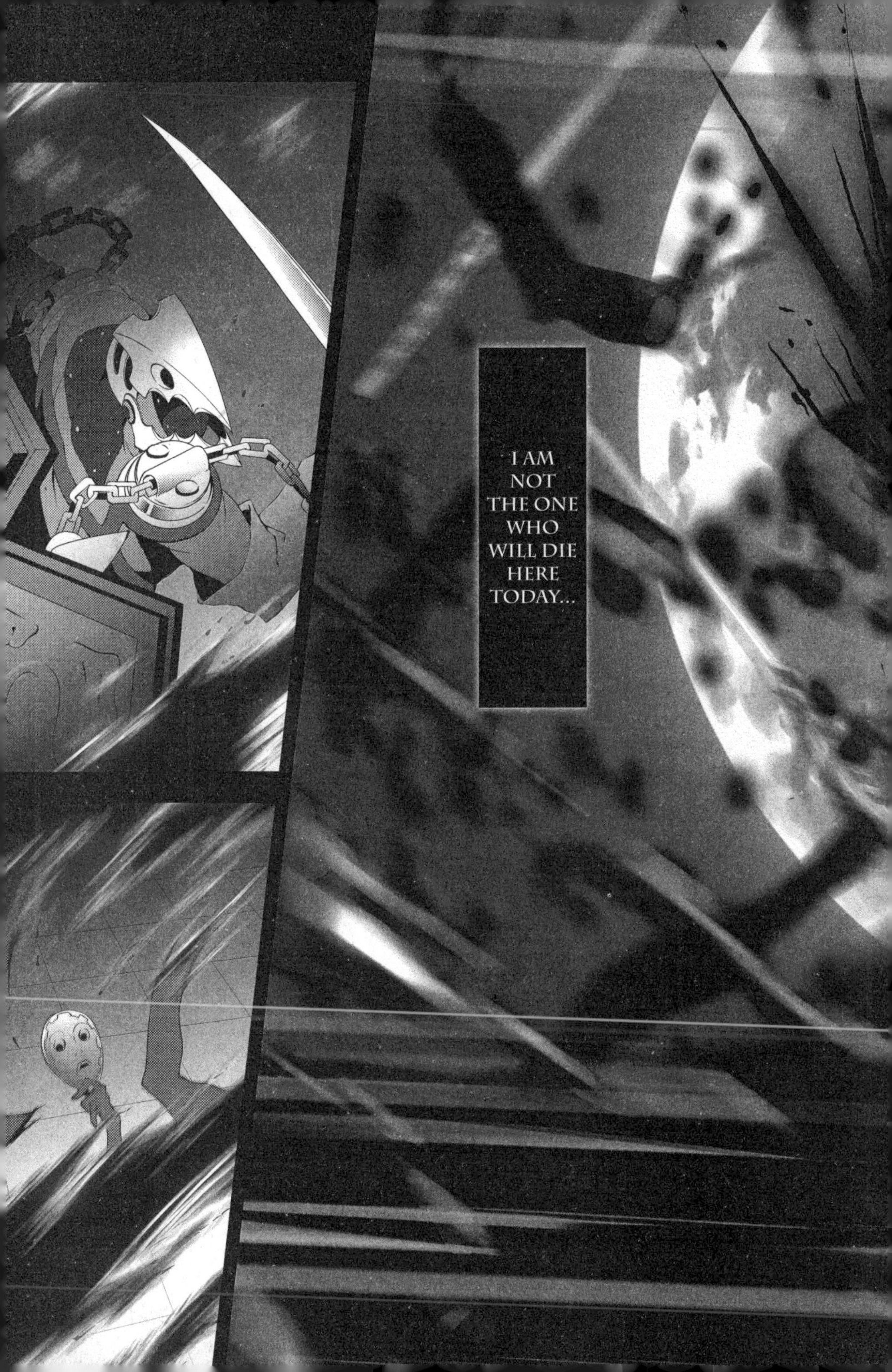
I AM NOT THE ONE WHO WILL DIE HERE TODAY...

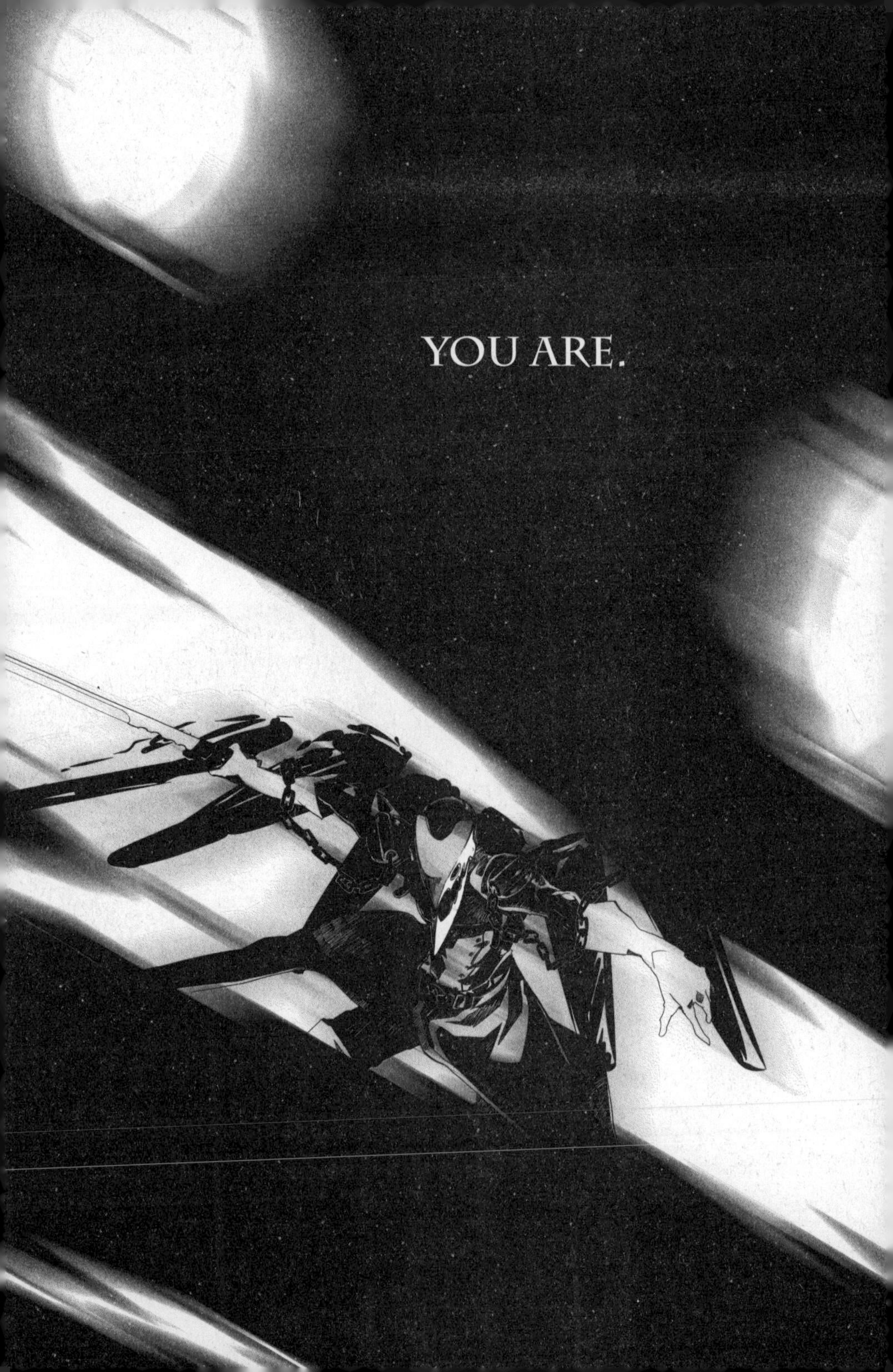
YOU ARE.

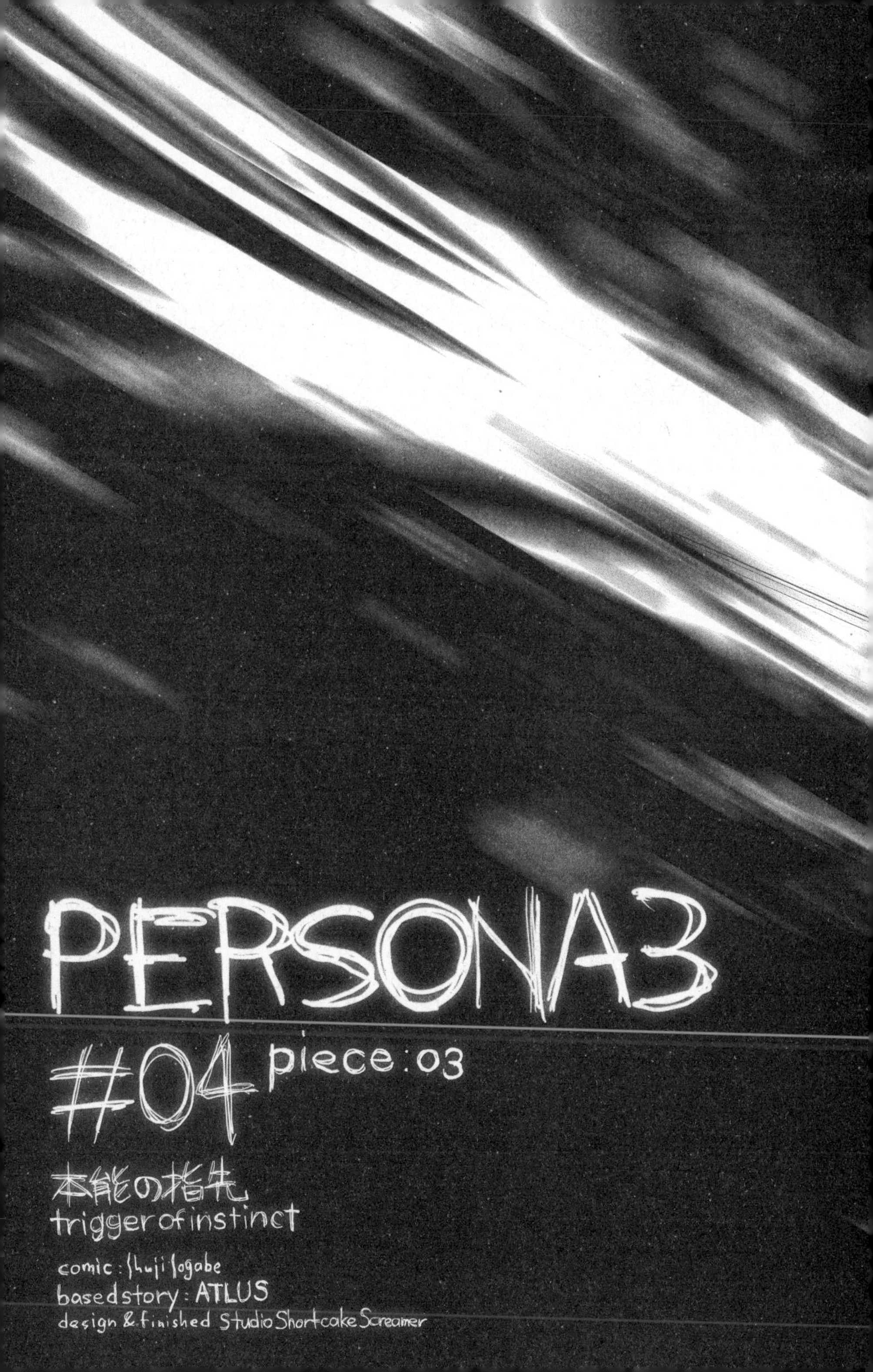

PERSONA3

#04 piece:03

本能の指先
trigger of instinct

comic : shuji sogabe
based story : ATLUS
design & finished Studio Shortcake Screamer

so ga be NOW
ソガベナウ 1

Art by Shuji Sogabe

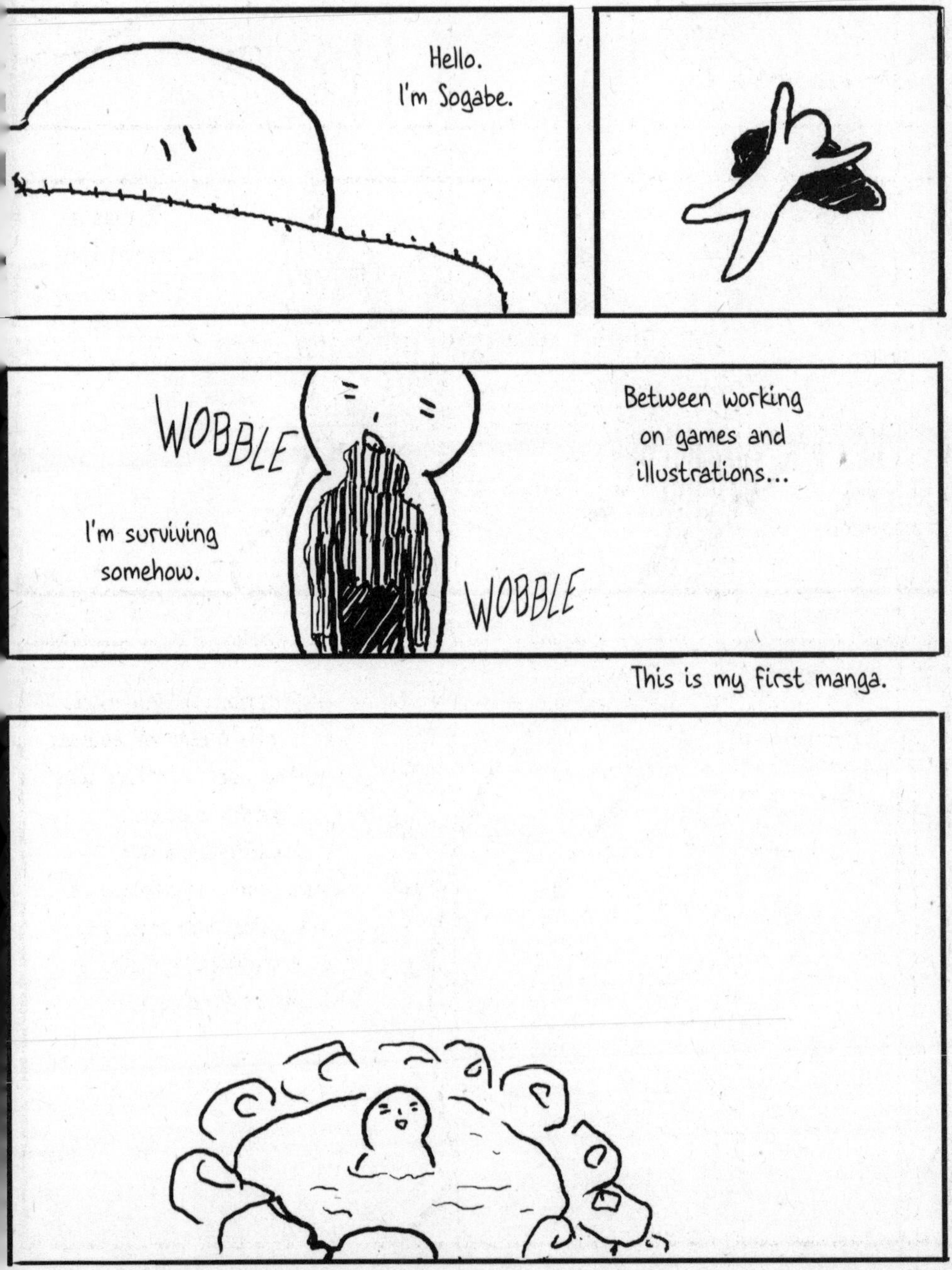
Hello.
I'm Sogabe.
Between working on games and illustrations...
WOBBLE
WOBBLE
I'm surviving somehow.
This is my first manga.

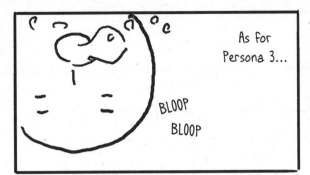

As for Persona 3...
BLOOP
BLOOP
It was a really fun game to play. (I cleared FES already too)
If you haven't played it yet, I highly recommend it!
The characters and music were both great, of course, but the user interface was really cool too. (which I think is uncommon in video games) The game mechanics and storyline are really interesting as well.
HEH
HEH
HEH
HEH

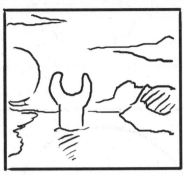

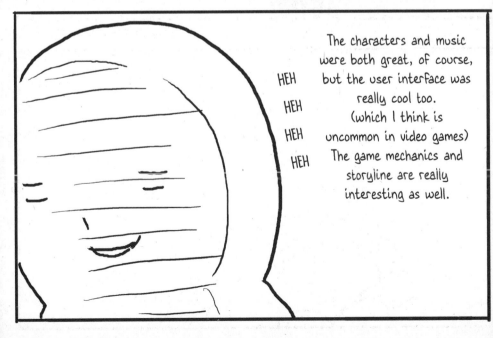

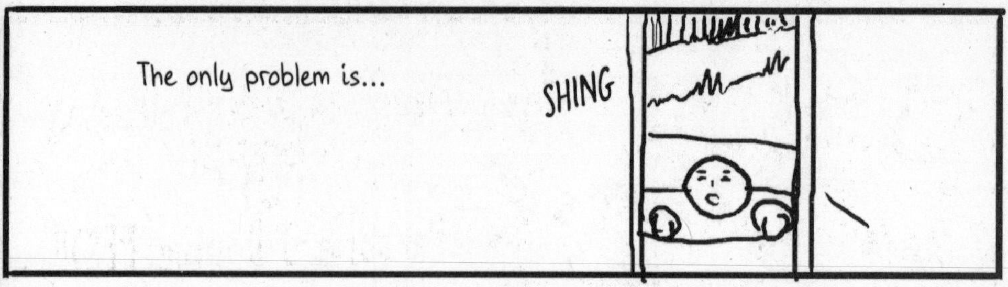
SHING
The only problem is...

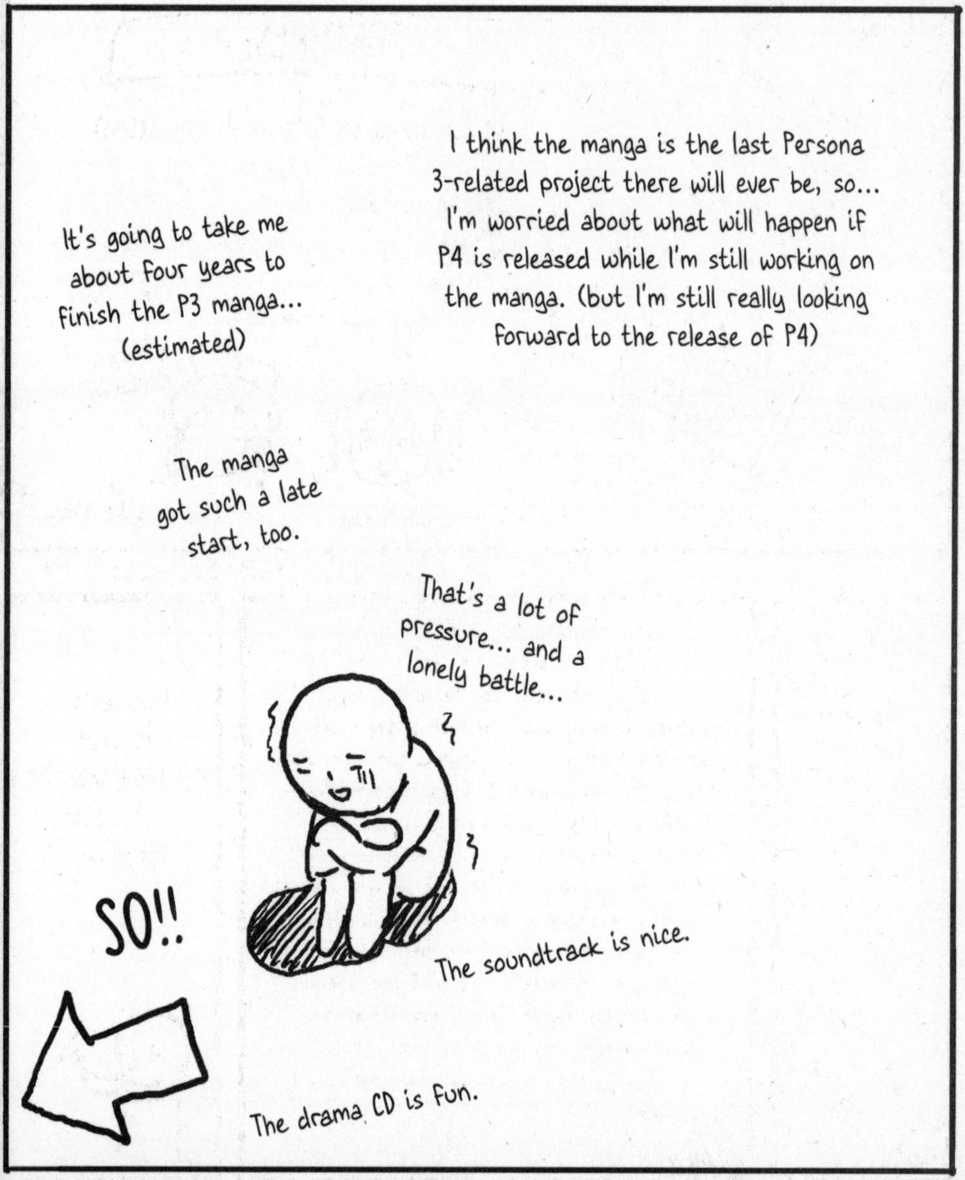
I think the manga is the last Persona 3-related project there will ever be, so... I'm worried about what will happen if P4 is released while I'm still working on the manga. (but I'm still really looking forward to the release of P4)
It's going to take me about four years to finish the P3 manga... (estimated)
The manga got such a late start, too.
That's a lot of pressure... and a lonely battle...
SO!!
The soundtrack is nice.
The drama CD is fun.

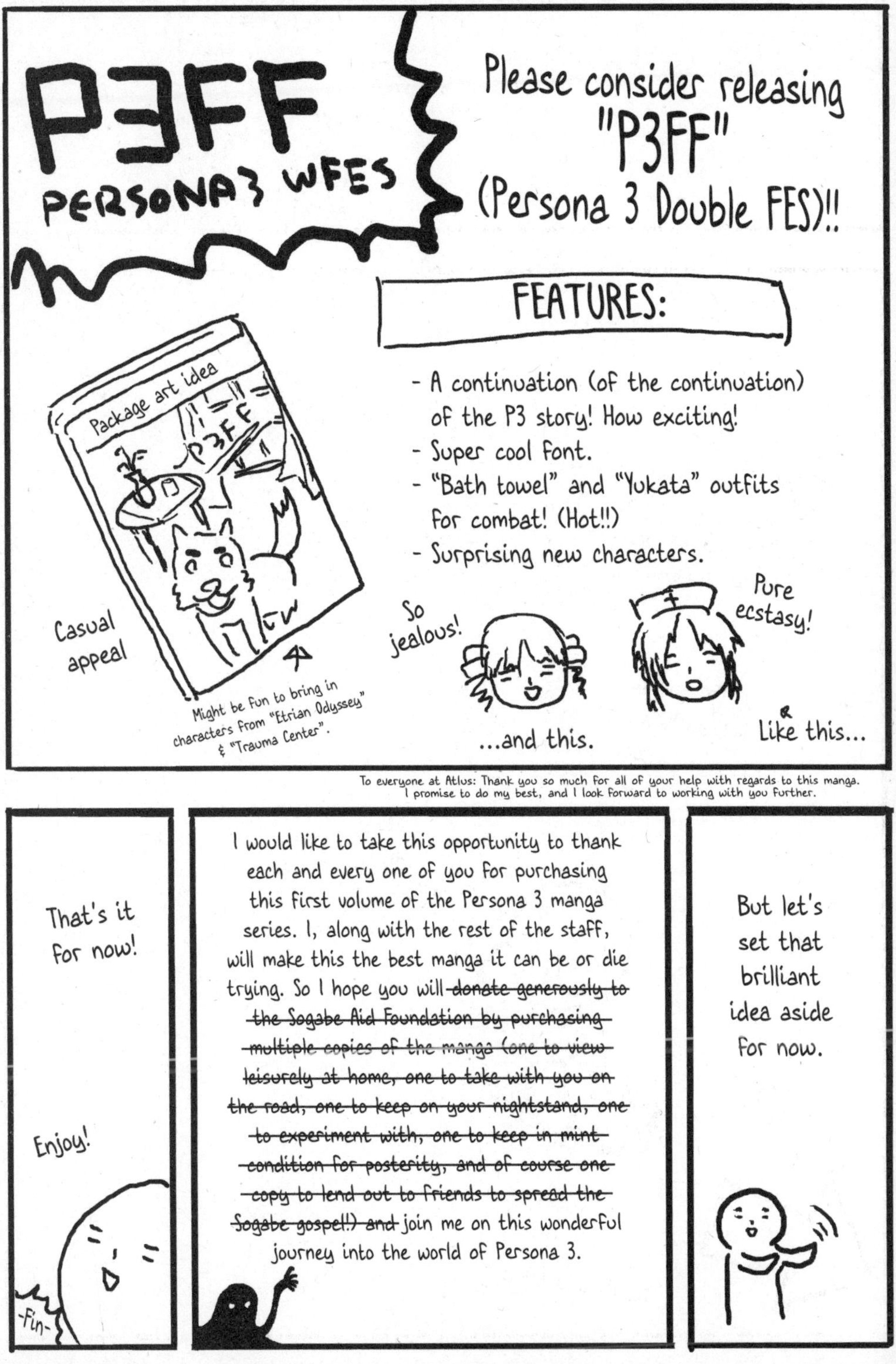

Please consider releasing "P3FF" (Persona 3 Double FES)!!
P3FF
PERSONA3 WFES
FEATURES:
- A continuation (of the continuation) of the P3 story! How exciting!
- Super cool font.
- "Bath towel" and "Yukata" outfits for combat! (Hot!!)
- Surprising new characters.
Pure ecstasy!
Like this...
So jealous!
...and this.
Package art idea
P3FF
Casual appeal
Might be fun to bring in characters from "Etrian Odyssey" & "Trauma Center".
To everyone at Atlus: Thank you so much for all of your help with regards to this manga. I promise to do my best, and I look forward to working with you further.
But let's set that brilliant idea aside for now.
I would like to take this opportunity to thank each and every one of you for purchasing this first volume of the Persona 3 manga series. I, along with the rest of the staff, will make this the best manga it can be or die trying. So I hope you will ~~donate generously to the Sogabe Aid Foundation by purchasing multiple copies of the manga (one to view leisurely at home, one to take with you on the road, one to keep on your nightstand, one to experiment with, one to keep in mint condition for posterity, and of course one copy to lend out to friends to spread the Sogabe gospel!) and~~ join me on this wonderful journey into the world of Persona 3.
That's it for now!
Enjoy!
-Fin-

Original Work by:
アトラス
ATLUS

Original Art Director:
副島成記 (ATLUS)
Shigenori SOEJIMA

Original Scenario Writer:
田中裕一郎 (ATLUS)
Yuichiro TANAKA

Manga/Story Composition:
曽我部修司
Shuji SOGABE

Production (Supervisor)/Layout/Animation:
Studio Shortcake Screamer
青木春菜 (#02)
Haruna AOKI

本間良太 (#04)
Ryota HONMA

Backgrounds/Coloring:
Studio Shortcake Screamer
菅野友美
Tomomi KANNO

野本季抄
Risa NOMOTO

高山瑞季
Mizuki TAKAYAMA

はなお
Hanao

Grayscale Painting:
Studio Shortcake Screamer
佐久間あさみ
Asami SAKUMA

3D Modeling and Layout:
Studio Shortcake Screamer
夏目彰浩
Akihiro NATSU

Special Thanks to:
彩塚ましろ
Mashiro AYATSUKA

望月穣爾
Jyoji MOCHIZUKI

森純一 (ATLUS)
Junichi MORI

ペルソナ3 オリジナルスタッフ
PERSONA3 ORIGINAL STAFF

Design:
スタジオショートケーキスクリーマー
Studio Shortcake Screamer

Translation:
タノヴァン フィリップ
TANOVAN Phillippe

Editing:
飯島直樹
Naoki IIJIMA

今井洸一
Kouichi IMAI

土井美知子
Michiko DOI

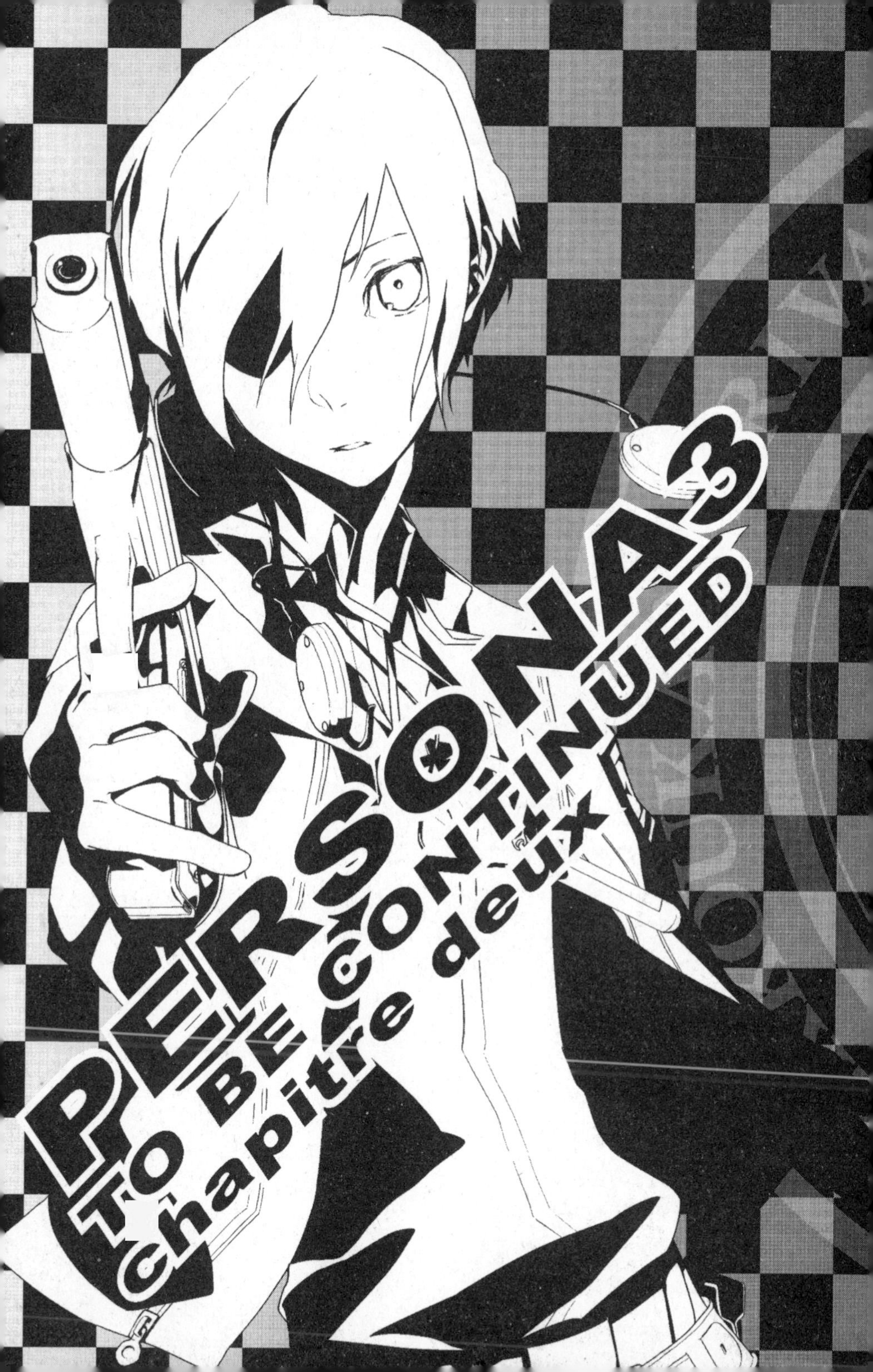
PERSONA3
TO BE CONTINUED
Chapitre deux

Persona3

Vol.1: Shuji SOGABE / ATLUS

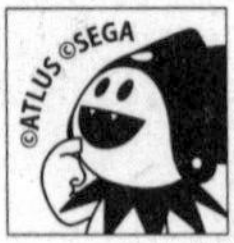
©ATLUS ©SEGA

ENGLISH EDITION
Translation: M. KIRIE HAYASHI
Lettering: MARSHALL DILLON

UDON STAFF
Chief of Operations: ERIK KO
Director of Publishing: MATT MOYLAN
VP of Business Development: CORY CASONI
Director of Marketing: MEGAN MAIDEN
Japanese Liaisons: STEVEN CUMMINGS
ANNA KAWASHIMA

ペルソナ３ 1
PERSONA 3 Volume 1

First published in 2007 by KADOKAWA CORPORATION, Tokyo.
English translation rights arranged with KADOKAWA CORPORATION, Tokyo.

English language version published by UDON Entertainment Inc.
118 Tower Hill Road, C1, PO Box 20008
Richmond Hill, Ontario, L4K 0K0 CANADA

www.UDONentertainment.com

Third Printing: April 2020
ISBN-13: 978-1-927925-85-0
ISBN-10: 1-927925-85-1

Printed in Canada